POWER JOURNALISM:
COMPUTER-ASSISTED
REPORTING

POWER JOURNALISM: COMPUTER-ASSISTED REPORTING

Lisa C. Miller
University of New Hampshire

Harcourt Brace College Publishers

Fort Worth Philadelphia San Diego New York Orlando Austin San Antonio
Toronto Montreal London Sydney Tokyo

Publisher	Earl McPeek
Executive Editor	Carol Wada
Product Manager	Ilse Wolfe West
Project Editor	Elaine Richards
Art Director	Garry Harman
Production Manager	Diane Gray
Electronic Publishing Coordinator	Cathy Spitzenberger

ISBN: 0-15-503976-8
Library of Congress Catalog Card Number: 97-73100

Address for orders:
Harcourt Brace College Publishers
6277 Sea Harbor Drive
Orlando, FL 32887-6777
1-800-782-4479

Address for editorial correspondence:
Harcourt Brace College Publishers
301 Commerce Street, Suite 3700
Fort Worth, TX 76102

Web site address:
http://www.hbcollege.com

Printed in the United States of America

7 8 9 0 1 2 3 4 5 6 067 9 8 7 6 5 4 3 2 1

PREFACE

Journalists begin by asking questions and chasing after the answers. They conduct interviews, search through their newspapers' archives, maybe visit a library or go to the scene of an event where they take notes about what they observe. They then sit down in front of their computers, put hands to keyboards, and write.

These days, though, journalists need to tap into the power of computers for more than just word processing. They must make computers work as reporting tools.

Power Journalism: Computer-Assisted Reporting will teach you how to do this. It demonstrates ways to find story ideas, reach sources, conduct interviews, and gather information using the Internet and other online resources; it also explains how you can use computer programs—spreadsheets and database managers—to analyze information, looking for trends, patterns, and surprises.

Armed with all of this data, you can conduct better interviews, tell more complete stories, and add color and context to what you write.

Computer-assisted reporting (CAR) doesn't replace the other techniques you already use; it gives you more tools for doing your job well. And it won't do stories for you; in fact, CAR is often only the beginning of your reporting work. After you've done your online research, after you've crunched all the numbers, you still have to go out and talk to and observe people. Their stories give meaning and life to the numbers and the facts. It's also important to treat information gathered through CAR the same way you would any information, verifying and attributing it when necessary, and to plan and craft stories carefully.

This book, then, emphasizes that learning CAR means building on what you already know about good journalism. You don't have to be a computer whiz to learn CAR. You have to be patient—some of this will take time to learn—and willing to try new things. And you should bring to CAR the skills and attributes every good reporter has: curiosity, the ability to ask good questions and get answers, and an understanding of what makes for a great story.

USING THIS BOOK

This book will show you why journalists use CAR as well as how. It's not a computer manual, nor does it offer directions for every software program available. It does explain the basic techniques for using different resources online and off, with examples of a few programs and easy-to-follow directions for using the resources. Learn how to use one program, and you'll have little trouble getting the same results with a different program.

Throughout this book you'll find tips for making the use of particular resources easier, comments from professional journalists about stories and research they've done using CAR, and ethical questions the new technology poses for journalists.

The first chapter provides an overview of CAR and the ways journalists use it. Chapters 2 through 8 discuss various online resources; Chapters 9 and 13 discuss the use of information that comes in different computerized formats. Chapters 10, 11, and 12 cover the use of spreadsheet and database management programs for analyzing information. Chapter 14 discusses how good writing and interviewing and CAR come together; Chapter 15 discusses legal and ethical issues raised by CAR; Chapter 16 suggests ways to continue learning new CAR skills.

You don't have to read these chapters in order, but note that Chapter 2 provides an overview of what's out in cyberspace for journalists, while Chapter 10 discusses what spreadsheet and database management programs can do and goes through some basic math journalists need to know.

Also included in the book are the following:

■ boxes posing ethics questions or offering tips on using computer resources
■ a list of URLs for World Wide Web sites
■ exercises for practicing CAR skills
■ the Society of Professional Journalists Code of Ethics
■ a glossary
■ suggestions for further reading about CAR, computers, and the Internet.

Databases discussed in Chapters 11 and 12 are available for downloading from the Harcourt Brace World Wide Web site at http://www.hbcollege.com.

This book is geared to students who already have basic journalism experience; extensive computer experience is definitely not required. If you already know a lot about online research and about analysis of databases, this book will show you how journalists use these reporting methods. If you have little or no online or database experience, this book will guide you, step by step, through cyberspace, spreadsheets, and database managers.

Although the main focus of the book is print journalism, you also can apply CAR techniques to broadcast journalism, magazine writing, or public relations.

ACKNOWLEDGMENTS

I would never have begun this book, let alone finished it, without the help and encouragement of many people. My colleagues at the University of New Hampshire have been very supportive. The English Department granted me a leave to work on the book and provided my first link to the Internet. Sue Hertz and Sandy Marsters were the first ones to suggest that I write about CAR. Sue urged me on all through the proposal, the waiting, and the drafting, as did Jane Harrigan, who also did everything she could to see that I had time and energy to work on the book. They gave me the courage to tackle this project and kept me from completely losing my sense of humor in the process. I also owe thanks to Andy Merton, who got me into journalism in the first place; he was my first newswriting professor and the one who sent me on my newspaper internship at the *Gloucester Daily Times*.

Without Don Murray, my mentor, reader, and friend, there would be no book. Don helped me put together the original proposal, believed in it when I didn't, helped me through rough patches along the way and has been rooting for me the whole time. His teaching and writing have inspired mine.

Diana Alie of the University of New Hampshire's Computing and Information Services was a great help, answering questions and reading parts of the book.

The University of New Hampshire's Center for the Humanities gave me a grant that aided in my research.

I owe a debt to my students, many of whom were absolutely aghast at the thought of anyone writing a whole book but who nonetheless told me they thought I could do it, who volunteered to read drafts or help out in any way they could, who asked again and again how the project was going, who read drafts and told me they were good, who keep pushing me to learn more.

Many family members and friends helped me through the creation of this book, asking gently now and again, "How is it coming?" My grandmother, sisters, brother-in-law, and aunt have always been wonderfully supportive, as has my brother, who read chapters of this book and turned out to be an excellent editor, and my uncle, who checked some online resources for me.

Especially, I want to thank my mother, who inspired my love of reading and writing, and who never gave up on me, even in times when I gave up on myself.

And this book is for Kell, who put up with my insecurities and my complaining and who cheered me on through difficult times and celebrated the good. Thanks for making the journey easier and more joyful.

Several people at the Poynter Institute for Media Studies were generous with their time and advice, including Chip Scanlan, Bob Steele, William Boyd, Kenneth Irby, Keith Woods, and Nora Paul, who reviewed the manuscript.

I thank my other reviewers: Paul Adams, California State University–Fresno; Joan Deppa, Syracuse University; Thomas Schwartz, Ohio State University; Thomas Shuford, University of Texas–Arlington; and Nancy Roberts, University of Minnesota–Twin Cities.

The journalists I contacted throughout my work on this project were unfailingly helpful and generous with time, advice, and examples. In particular I thank David Armstrong, who got me started, and Whit Andrews, Michael Berens, William Casey, and Elizabeth Marchak.

Finally, I want to thank my editor at Harcourt Brace, Carol Wada, who answered my many questions and helped make this book a reality.

TABLE OF CONTENTS

Chapter 1

SEARCHING, SORTING, AND STORYTELLING: WHAT COMPUTER-ASSISTED REPORTING IS ALL ABOUT

Reporter Michael Berens of the *Columbus* (Ohio) *Dispatch* began with this question: Were police car chases killing innocent people instead of stopping criminals? Interviewing people would help him get the answer—but only part of the answer. Reviewing 15,000 paper pages of federal, state, and local records would give him part of the answer, too. But to get the whole truth, he needed more. He needed a computer.

To report his stories, Berens analyzed 1.3 million federal computer records. When he compared that information to articles, available online, from more than 300 newspapers and magazines, he found chase-related deaths that weren't in the government records. He gathered reports on Columbus police and state highway patrol chases for the past three years, and he and others at the paper typed information from those into a computer. They created another computer database—a collection of data—using the cases of 100 people charged with felony fleeing in Columbus and statewide. Berens then was able to figure out what sentences, if any, those people were getting from Ohio judges.

Finally, he told readers what he had discovered:

Nationally, there will be 1,400 police chases today. One chase every minute. More than a dozen people will be injured. At least one will die.Each year, more people are killed in police chases than by officers' guns.

He wrote about a young woman and her 3-year-old daughter who were on their way to Bible class when a cruiser involved in a chase slammed into their car, killing them both. He wrote about a police officer killed when he collided with a motorist's car while speeding to join a chase, and about a 14-year-old boy who panicked when a cruiser began following his car and who drove into a utility pole.

The stories Berens told were compelling and important. And he wouldn't have been able to find some of his information without a computer. But his series, "Deadly Pursuit," also demonstrates that the best stories created with computer-assisted reporting have what every great news or feature story has: in-depth research, people who demonstrate the human side of issues, and strong writing.

COMPUTER-ASSISTED REPORTING DEFINED

Like Berens, reporters often begin with questions: When bus drivers are hired by our school system, does anybody check to see if they have criminal records? If you're sentenced to life in prison in this state, what are the odds that you'll end up back on the street instead? Does anything ever happen to doctors who have lots of malpractice complaints against them? How many people in this city name their dogs after themselves? (Nobody said all reporting had to be serious.)

After those questions come more: who, what, where, when, why and how. Your computer is a powerful, versatile tool for getting the answers.

Computer-assisted reporting (CAR) has two basic parts:

1. **Doing research using the Internet and other online services.**

   Cyberspace, where information is shared among computers around the globe, offers a wealth of information, serious and silly, useful and not. So . . . what do you need to know? How many schoolchildren across the country have access to the Internet? What the presidential candidates' schedules are for today? When an earthquake last hit your state? How much money special-interest groups gave to one of your state's Senate candidates? Whether anyone in your state built a better mousetrap this year? Where Elvis was last sighted? You can find answers to all of these questions online. (According to the Elvis Spotter's Page on the World Wide Web, one part of the Internet, somebody saw him in the stands at a New England Patriots–Kansas City Chiefs football game in October 1995, wearing a red sequined jumpsuit.)

   Reporters also find story ideas and people to interview, experts and everyday people, by searching online.

2. **Searching and/or analyzing a collection of information, a database, that comes in electronic form (online, on a floppy disk, on a CD-ROM, or on magnetic tape), or that you create yourself by typing data from paper records into a computer file.**

   Hundreds of databases are available for the asking. (Well, not always just for the asking. Some agencies balk at giving out databases in electronic form, and journalists across the country are fighting for access to them. More on this in Chapter 13.)

But if you get records in electronic form, you can put them into your computer, pull from them the information you need for your story, and use a computer program to help figure out what it means. For example, you can get data about crime in your city. Analyzing that, you might discover which neighborhoods are the most crime-ridden, whether certain crimes are on the increase, or whether repeat criminals are driving the crime rate up. The *Wisconsin State Journal* used this type of information to determine that violent crime was highly concentrated in a few neighborhoods in Madison, Wisconsin, and that one neighborhood had seen a 41 percent jump in violent crime in one year.

If you can get information in electronic form about misdemeanor and felony convictions in your state and a database of teachers and others working in your state's schools, you can compare them and see whether school systems are hiring people convicted of crimes. The *Birmingham* (Alabama) *News* found that in one particular year at least 68 teachers who had taught in the state had been convicted of crimes, including assault and battery.

Sometimes the information you want isn't available in computerized form. It's only on paper or scattered throughout different sets of documents. That means you've got to collect the information and create a computer database yourself. This can be very time-consuming, but it's often worth it. Such databases can give you the most specific, up-to-date information on a subject and help you separate the important from the unimportant. And the database you create for one story may be used for other stories in the future.

Reporter Michael Fabey of the *Fayetteville* (North Carolina) *Observer-Times* built a database with state information about complaints concerning pesticides. He found that the state Department of Agriculture's Pesticide Section had too few workers and too little money and time to do its job properly—and that meant people were being exposed to dangerous pesticides.

The Munster, Indiana, *Times* took results of a geography test given to more than 200 students in area school districts, then built a database to analyze the results. Readers were shocked to find out how little students knew about geography.

Computer-assisted reporting also entails using reference works such as directories, atlases, and encyclopedias that come on CD-ROM. Journalists on deadline can quickly search through these electronic resources to find people, places, or facts.

KEYS TO CAR

If all of this sounds daunting, take heart. Journalists all over the country have been starting from scratch and learning how to do this. You can too. You don't have to be a computer whiz to get started with CAR, and you don't have to know how to do everything at once, or perfectly. You do have to be curious, patient, and willing to try new things and make a few mistakes along the way.

GOOD JOURNALISM WITH COMPUTERS ADDED

CAR doesn't involve throwing out everything you already know about good journalism. You are still going to ask probing questions, find sources, check and double-check information, write interesting leads, and tell stories that pull readers along right to the last paragraph. But you're going to add some computer skills to your interviewing and notetaking and thinking skills, exploiting the things the computer does best.

"The computer is a tool for gathering information, just as the telephone is," says Stephen Buttry, staff writer for the *Omaha* (Nebraska) *World-Herald.* "The reporter who does all his reporting by telephone or by computer won't do a good job. But refusing or failing to learn how to use a computer is as silly as it would be to refuse or fail to learn how to use a phone."

Journalists are tapping into the computer's ability to store huge amounts of raw information and quickly sort through it. They are going online and connecting with computers around the world, gathering information and seeking out experts. They're using computer-assisted reporting for investigative projects that take months, like Berens' eight-month project, but they're also using the computer to add information to breaking stories and to gather information for feature stories as well as for hard news. Photojournalists are sharing information and displaying their photographs online.

No matter what the beat—education, environment, health, crime, government, sports—journalists are using computers to report on it.

Some of their stories change people's lives. Berens' three-day series, "Deadly Pursuit," sparked action nationwide. The National Highway Traffic Safety Administration began investigating why its files did not list all the deaths stemming from police chases. The country's top law enforcement organizations issued alerts about repairs that could make one brand of police cruisers safer. An Ohio senator drafted a bill requiring increased driver training and mandatory reporting of all police chases. The Columbus police department banned all chases unless the suspect was endangering someone's life. And plans were made to construct the city's first driver training track for police and firefighters.

In each of the past eight years, journalists using computer-assisted reporting have won Pulitzer Prizes. The Pulitzer Prizes World Wide Web site, produced for the *Columbia Journalism Review* by Columbia University's Center for New Media, offers information about 1996 winners:

■ The prize for public-service reporting was given to Melanie Sill, Pat Stith, and Joby Warrick of the *News & Observer,* Raleigh, North

Carolina, for a series covering the environmental, health, economic, and political impact of their state's growing hog industry. That series, called "Boss Hog," pointed out connections between people in the hog industry and state politicians. The computer-assisted reporting included analysis of campaign contributions and of records of long-distance calls from state officials. The reporters also obtained information from online resources.

- The prize for investigative reporting went to the staff of the *Orange County Register* of California for "Fertility Fraud," a series on misuse of eggs harvested from patients at the University of California–Irvine Center for Reproductive Health. Reporters used computer programs to analyze information about patients, used commercial databases to identify patients, and posted their stories on the Internet. Someone who saw the online postings helped them find one of the center's doctors who was under investigation.

(The Pulitzer Prizes site can be found at http://www.pulitzer.org. More on the World Wide Web, Chapter 8.)

CAR AT WORK: FOUR COMPUTER-POWERED INVESTIGATIONS

What stories call for computer-assisted reporting? Well, just about any kind. It's vital when you've got millions of records to analyze, or the information you want can be found only online (and the U.S. Census Bureau has begun putting some of its information only online), or you need an answer within the next few minutes.

Some journalists say they occasionally get a database and look through it to find ideas for stories. Others say it's better never to do that—always start with a story you want to do, then go after information, because otherwise you'll get bogged down searching for something that might not even be there.

It probably makes more sense for you to start with a story idea and questions you want to answer, then figure out whether the computer can help you get those answers. As you do your electronic research, you may get ideas for other questions and stories.

Consider some other stories reported in part with computers:

WERE CHILDREN IN STATE-LICENSED FOSTER CARE IN WASHINGTON STATE BEING PROPERLY PROTECTED?

When four babies died in a state-licensed foster home, reporter Duff Wilson of the *Seattle Times* was puzzled. The cause of death in each case was ruled sudden infant death syndrome (SIDS), but experts told Wilson that it was unlikely so many cases of SIDS would occur in one place.

Wilson collected information on that foster home, on the deaths of 44 children in foster care and 137 children in the care of the state Child Protective Services, and on license suspension or revocation actions against 64 foster homes in his state. He built three computer databases, obtained three more, and analyzed the information. He also used the Internet to seek out experts who could help him figure out the odds against four unrelated SIDS deaths occurring in one foster home. His story indicated that the state was slow to act on complaints of abuse and neglect of children in the state's homes. Within 18 hours of Wilson's first call to the state social services agency, the state suspended the license for the home where the four children had died, and by the next day, police had opened a criminal investigation into the children's deaths.

After the series ran, a state official ordered inspections of more than 3,000 foster homes statewide and suspended and revoked many licenses. Other official action to make foster homes safer followed.

DO UNSAFE ELEVATORS AND ESCALATORS ENDANGER PEOPLE IN MASSACHUSETTS EACH DAY?

When reporters at the *Boston Globe* got a tip saying a 3-year-old girl had been injured in an elevator accident, the reporters gathered information on 30,000 elevators and escalators scheduled for inspection each year in Massachusetts. It would have been difficult, if not impossible, to go through those 30,000 records by hand. But *Globe* reporters David Armstrong, Shelley Murphy, and Stephen Kurkjian used computer programs to analyze much of the information they gathered. They also reviewed hundreds of paper records and interviewed scores or people, including accident victims and elevator/escalator consultants. In a three-part series, titled "Risky Ride," they showed that although thousands of people rode the country's 600,000 elevators and 30,000 escalators every day, believing they were safe, many crippling accidents—even fatal ones—were occurring, and that some of the people and agencies who were supposed to be watching over the equipment weren't doing their jobs.

WERE CHICAGO RESIDENTS VOTING MORE THAN ONCE IN THE SAME ELECTION, AND WERE GHOSTS SHOWING UP TO VOTE, TOO?

Tom Brune and Deborah Nelson of the *Chicago Sun-Times* used computer analysis to investigate. By checking the names and birthdates in computer records of voters, they found 47,000 voters who were registered more than once and 1,400 dead people apparently registered to vote. They also found that many registered voters did not live in the wards where the Election Board records said they did, and that meant people could have been voting in elections they were not supposed to vote in. Records also showed a couple of votes cast by dead people—apparently the result of sloppiness in the keeping of the voter lists.

Their lead on one story said this:

The dead can still vote in Chicago—on paper at least—because their names remain on the active voter rolls for years.

The Sun-Times identified more than 1,000 names of registered voters on the current rolls who are dead, many for as long as four years.

And seven of them are listed among those who cast ballots in the November national election.

"No kidding," said a surprised Thomas Leach, spokesman for the Chicago Board of Election Commissioners.

After the stories ran, the commissioners promised to review the voter registration list and provide a clean list by the 1996 election.

WHAT BREED OF DOG IS TOPS IN NEW YORK STATE?

Gregory Racz of the *Buffalo News* decided to find out just what the records of dog licenses from Buffalo and from Erie and Niagra counties would reveal. His computer analysis showed readers that the most popular dog names included Max, Lady, Bear, and Sheba; that the most popular dog breeds were shepherd mix, mixed breed, Labrador mix, and Labrador retriever; and that some people do name their dogs after themselves. He found out which street in western New York was the most dog-friendly.

And he found out about Helen Stetz:

Call up the Town of Holland assessor's office and ask for the patron saint of lost dogs.

"Oh, that must be Mrs. Stetz," the assessor will say. "She takes in dogs."

A lot of dogs. At last count Helen Stetz was taking care of 22 dogs, many of whom were homeless, malnourished and fleeing abusive owners when Mrs. Stetz took them in. Mrs. Stetz houses so many dogs, the most in Erie County, in fact, that she had to secure a kennel license.

In each of these cases, the reporters used computers to help them report the stories. But they also used old-fashioned "shoe leather" reporting. They checked and double-checked the information they collected, and they interviewed people to get compelling anecdotes, to give sources a chance to explain the results of the reporters' investigations, and to show readers how the issues discussed in the stories affected real people. The computer was *one more tool* they used to do careful, accurate, and revealing reporting that would answer readers' questions.

GETTING STARTED: HARDWARE AND SOFTWARE

Your first CAR may involve online research, and for that you'll need a link to resources in cyberspace. Someone at school or at the newspaper you work for will get your computer hooked up, so this book won't spend much time on that.

Basically, you'll need a computer, one with a CD-ROM drive if possible, and some software. To get online, you'll use communications software to make your cyberspace connection. If you are working at a lab or in a classroom, you may have a direct link to a computer at your school that is on the Internet. You'll just start up the software and have your link.

Some newspapers and labs won't have that kind of direct link, and if you don't, or if you're working out of your home, you'll need a modem. This allows you to "telephone" another computer and make a connection to the Internet. (More on this in Chapter 2.) You can "call," or dial into, other online services besides the Internet, including commercial information services such as America Online or CompuServe, or into computer bulletin board systems that offer information and the opportunity to "talk" with others online (more on these in Chapters 2 and 3). Once you make your online connection, you'll have access to programs for electronic mail and other online resources.

To do the types of computer analysis that some of the reporters in the previous examples did, you'll need a spreadsheet software program and perhaps a database management program. A spreadsheet will help you keep track of information, add numbers, sort and order information, and analyze it. For instance, you might sort information in a dog license database to determine which part of your city has the most dogs or what the most popular breed of dog is.

You might get along with just a spreadsheet program for some projects, but eventually you'll probably need a database management program too. This type of program will do many of the same things, but it can handle more information than a spreadsheet, so you'll need one to analyze huge collections of data. And a database management program will let you take two separate databases—say, a database with the records of all people convicted of a felony in your state, and the database of all public school teachers and aides in your state—and compare them, to see if there are matches.

Once you become proficient with these programs, you might want to try some other software. Mapping programs can help you create maps to graphically explain the results of your computer analysis. Statistical programs can enable you to do sophisticated mathematical computations. You may also want to learn how to add your information to the Internet, which means working with a simple programming language used for posting information on the World Wide Web.

But you don't need to know all of this to begin computer-assisted reporting. This book will take you through the basics of the online world, electronic information, and spreadsheet and database programs. Once you're comfortable with these resources, you can move on to the others. You'll find lots of online help with learning how to do more advanced CAR. And computer-assisted reporting starts with something you already know a lot about—*asking questions.*

WHAT ELSE DO YOU NEED?

You'll need that question-asking ability, along with your healthy skepticism and your strong sense of ethics. When you go online to find information, you ask questions and search for answers. When you analyze a database on your computer, you ask the computer program to answer questions about that data. So keep asking.

Why do you need your healthy skepticism? Because that will help you sort out useful information from not useful, reliable information from unreliable. And of course skepticism may be what got you started on a story in the first place. When David Armstrong worked on the *Boston Globe* elevator/escalator series, he and other reporters found that the numbers they analyzed told a very different story than documents put together by the inspectors and committee overseeing inspection of that equipment.

You've got to be as vigilant with the information you get from computer-assisted work as you would be with information gathered in a more traditional way. As Stephen Miller, assistant to the technology editor at the *New York Times,* says, "Just because it's digital, doesn't mean it's true."

And your strong sense of ethics? The online world makes a lot of information available quickly, sometimes a little too quickly. You have to remind yourself of the power you have as a journalist to do good and to do harm, and keep thinking about the newsworthiness of information you uncover.

ETHICS AND THE NEW TECHNOLOGY

With computer-assisted research, you'll need to keep in mind all the ethical concerns you've always considered in reporting and writing stories. The new technology does, in fact, put a new slant on some old questions. For one thing, the computer makes it easier to get some information, thus giving journalists less time, or obscuring the reasons, to consider ethical consequences. And the computer allows journalists to create records that didn't exist before, such as a file showing all public school teachers and aides convicted of felonies. The information you discover is powerful, and that's exactly the reason you need to be cautious in using it.

As you go through this book, you'll see boxes posing questions and cautions about the computer techniques you're learning.

One thing it's important to remember, says Robert Steele, director of ethics programs at the Poynter Institute for Media Studies, is that ethical guidelines don't just tell journalists what they shouldn't do. "We should look at it (ethics) in terms of what we have a responsibility to do," Steele says. "For example, we have a responsibility to expose corruption in government."

In dealing with the new technology, he says, journalists should make sure that ethical questions get asked at the beginning of a reporting project, not just at the end. For you, the student, that means thinking through what you want to do and talking it over with your instructor or other reporters or a newspaper editor or adviser. At a newspaper, Steele says—and this means your student newspaper, too—it means having a protocol or set of guidelines in place *before* ethical questions arise. Newspapers develop protocols by looking at the principles of what journalists do, what Steele calls "the *why* aspect of journalism." That *why* aspect

includes journalists' service of a democracy and their commitment to give readers information they need.

Then newspapers need to decide on what their protocol will be, what
Steele calls the *how* part. This means figuring out who will make ethical decisions, when conversations about ethics will take place, and what sorts of guidelines the paper will follow.

Many news and journalism organizations, such as the Society of Professional
Journalists (SPJ), have their own codes of ethics. (See the SPJ code, Appendix
C.) Such guidelines apply to all types of reporting, computer-assisted or not.

CYBERTORTS—THE LEGALITIES OF CAR

As you read this, new laws probably are being created to deal with the online
world. But it's still fairly open territory, so journalists are proceeding with cau-
tion. Courts across the country will be dealing with various questions that at
least look different in the context of cyberspace, including issues surrounding
copyright law, libel, and access to information. Journalists are dealing with what
they always dealt with: data about people, places, and things. But in cyberspace
the information is easier to get and easier to disseminate. Laws meant to deal
with paper records are slowly being changed to deal with electronic ones, and
what is and is not private information is being contested. This book will look at
some of the legal ramifications of CAR.

ABRACADABRA IT'S NOT

As you begin your first CAR trip, repeat these words to yourself: *Computer-
assisted reporting isn't magic. Computer-assisted reporting isn't magic.* It
can take a lot of time and can be frustrating; it isn't always easy to find what
you want online or to make sure the information in a database is accurate. Sometimes even getting the data takes a lot of time. Officials at government agencies
are still figuring out what information they can or will give out in electronic
form, and many agencies don't have records in electronic form yet. If they do,
they may refuse to give it out; newspaper reporters have had to go to court
and file Freedom of Information Act requests and negotiate to get information.

INTERVIEWS AND OTHER "OLD-FASHIONED" REPORTING

Also remember that computer-assisted reporting is just the beginning of your
work. Having statistics and numbers and maps and expert opinion is wonderful,
but you know the numbers don't make a story. Once you've got them, you've
still got to go talk to people—not only to make sure your numbers are correct

and significant but also to show the people behind the numbers. The information you've gathered using your computer won't make your story sing by itself; your interviews, your quotes, your anecdotes, and your descriptions are also important.

Michael Berens did 150 interviews for his series on police chases. *Boston Globe* reporters interviewed accident victims, lawyers, elevator/escalator consultants, safety experts, and others for their series of elevator/escalator series. Duff Wilson of the *Seattle Times* interviewed state caseworkers and administrators, private child-care workers, doctors, and parents. And the *Buffalo News* dog license story wouldn't have been as interesting without the dog people.

So if the chance to talk with lots of people about lots of things is what you love about journalism, you'll find that computer-assisted reporting doesn't eliminate that. It just gives you more information to build your interviews around and more ways to find people to talk to.

The computer won't turn you into a great reporter or writer if you aren't already pretty good. It's just a tool. But it's an important one.

"Power is what it gives you," says David Armstrong of the *Boston Globe*. "You can have all this information in your computer, at your desk. And you aren't saying to readers, 'Here's a slice of the information,' or 'Here's some anecdotal information.' You're giving them the facts, *all* the facts. That's power."

OFF AND RUNNING

The best advice before you plunge into computer-assisted reporting is this: Don't be afraid to make mistakes at first and don't worry if it takes you awhile to get the hang of searching for things online, or using a spreadsheet or database management program. Everybody doing computer-assisted reporting once started out knowing nothing. You can learn this, by practicing it and by talking with others who've been at it longer than you.

Now it's time to start zooming around cyberspace, crunching numbers, uncovering great stories. Let's go.

Chapter 2

JOURNALISTS IN CYBERSPACE

cyberspace: 1. the realm of electronic communication. 2. VIRTUAL REALITY [1984, Amer.] CYBER + SPACE; coined by writer William Gibson in Neuromancer.

—RANDOM HOUSE WEBSTER'S COLLEGE DICTIONARY

Cyberspace. A consensual hallucination experienced daily by billions of legitimate operators...unthinkable complexity. Lines of light ranged in the nonspace of the mind, clusters and constellations of data.

—NEUROMANCER, A CYBERPUNK NOVEL BY WILLIAM GIBSON

"I wonder," he said to himself, "what's in a book while it's closed. Oh, I know it's full of letters printed on paper, but all the same, something must be happening, because as soon as I open it, there's a whole story with people I don't know yet and all kinds of adventures and deeds and battles. And sometimes there's storms at sea, or it takes you to strange cities and countries. All those things are somehow shut up in a book. Of course you have to read it to find out. But it's already there, that's the funny thing. I just wish I knew how it could be."

—THE NEVERENDING STORY BY MICHAEL ENDE

Electronic communication. Constellations of data. Storms at sea and strange cities and countries. Cyberspace is all of that. It's not a place you can touch, but it is real, and it's made up of information about millions of things. Imagine a library with rooms spreading out forever, filled with the marvelous and the mundane, books and reports, poems and statistics, maps and photographs, music and movies, and occupied by experts from all over the world, ready to answer questions. That's cyberspace.

It's not an orderly library; information is scattered everywhere, so sometimes it's hard to find what you want. It's not a complete library either; you won't always find what you're looking for, though new data are added every day. And it's not a quiet place. People in cyberspace whisper and yell and debate and discuss subjects ranging from solar energy to freedom of speech to which fast-food hamburger tastes best.

For journalists, cyberspace has become one more place to contact sources, carry out interviews, and gather information for stories. The Internet and other online resources make more people and more data available than ever before.

In fact, in a 1996 survey of newspapers and magazines, two-thirds of the 636 respondents said they or members of their staffs use online services weekly, while 85 percent said members of their staffs go online at least once a month. The survey, titled "Media in Cyberspace III," was conducted by Steven S. Ross, associate professor at the Columbia University Graduate School of Journalism, and Don Middleberg, chairman and chief executive officer of Middleberg & Associates, a public relations agency. In 1994, when Ross and Middleberg conducted their first such survey, only 44 percent of respondents said they or their staff members used online services at least once a month; in 1995, 71 percent reported that they did.

TRAVELING FAR AND WIDE

You can tap into cyberspace while sitting in front of your computer. Once you go online, connecting your computer to networks of computers around the world, you can "travel" to England or Australia or Japan with just a few keystrokes, gathering information as you go. Some of your fellow journalists should already have earned frequent flier miles, given all the cyberspace traveling they do. Many, including Stephen Miller, assistant to the technology editor at the *New York Times,* say looking for information online has become a part of their normal research routine.

"It's just another tool," says Miller of the online world. "It's like going to the newspaper's morgue or the library. Anywhere you can find the information you need, that's where you want to go."

So what do you need to know? Is anyone you recognize on the list of the ten most wanted fugitives in the United States? Which organizations gave money to your state senate candidates—and how much? What's the most dangerous railroad crossing in your area? In the Phish song "Lizards," are the words in the chorus "from the land of the big balloon" or "the big baboon"? Answers to all this and more can be found out there, somewhere in cyberspace.

READERS ONLINE

If you don't learn to find those answers online, you may miss information, story ideas, and sources that other reporters find. You also may miss information your readers are using. While there still are plenty of people around the world who aren't online, millions of people are. Many newspapers and magazines offer online versions, including the *Boston Globe, New York Times, Los Angeles Times, Wall Street Journal, Philadelphia Inquirer, San Jose Mercury News, Hartford Courant, Wired* magazine (the online version is called *HotWired*), *Time, People,* and *Atlantic Monthly.*

REPORTING IN CYBERSPACE: WHAT, WHY, AND HOW

Armed with mouse and manuals, journalists have braved the wilds of online world to do these things:

Contact people. Through electronic mail and online discussion groups and forums, journalists can reach sources they might not have known existed until they searched cyberspace. When a reporter at the *New York Times* was working on a story about couples with infertility problems, Stephen Miller, assistant to the *Times's* technology editor, sent a message to an online discussion group seeking people for the reporter to talk with. The reporter had already spoken with the experts, Miller said, but she needed to find folks who could tell her how they'd dealt with infertility. The reporter, he said, was overwhelmed with reponses from people who read Miller's query online and were willing to be interviewed.

Conduct interviews. When Stephen Buttry of the *Omaha* (Nebraska) *World-Herald* was reporting a story about Nebraskans on the World Wide Web, he conducted most interviews by electronic mail. When an earthquake hit Kobe, Japan, in 1995, communications were disrupted, but some Internet connections still worked, and reporters all over the world were able to get information by e-mail.

Share resources and ideas with other journalists. Every day journalists involved in online discussion groups—called mailing lists—ask for help, discuss new reporting resources, or offer solutions to other journalists' problems. For example, a reporter in New Mexico sent a message to one list asking for help with a story on a device that could be used to detect whether someone was carrying a concealed weapon. An editor at the *Baltimore Sun* sent e-mail to the list saying his paper had done a similar story and giving the name of the company that was developing the device and the name of the company's top executive.

A reporter at the *Palm Beach Post* sent a message to a mailing list telling other reporters of a resource he'd found. While working on a story about President Bill Clinton's drug policy, he went looking for statistics on drug use in America. He found a World Wide Web site put together by the University of Indiana's Prevention Resource Center that offered plenty of useful information, including a University of Michigan survey of drug use among eighth-, tenth- and twelfth-graders.

Gather information for stories and prepare for interviews. When Omaha reporter Buttry needed to know where the Union Pacific Railroad ranked among Nebraska's private employers, he went to his state government's online site and got the statistics he needed.

When Preston Forman of the *New Bedford* (Mass.) *Standard-Times* was writing about whether a town he covered was complying with the Americans with Disabilities Act, he needed to know exactly what the act said. He found the entire text on the Internet.

Mine for story ideas. Lots of resources on the Internet, serious and silly, can spark story ideas. Miller of the *New York Times* said that while surfing the Web, he often finds subjects for stories, such as a virtual art exhibit connected with the Vatican in Rome.

Reporter John Moran of the *Hartford Courant* wrote about a local men's right's group he discovered by monitoring online discussions mentioning Hartford or Connecticut.

Interact with and inform readers. Newspapers sometimes offer readers electronic mail addresses so they can comment on stories in the paper. And some newspapers showcase particular stories or information for readers on the Internet or elsewhere online. When the *San Jose Mercury News* ran a series called "Legislature for Sale," showing how big money influenced lawmaking in Sacramento, California, the paper also published locations in cyberspace where readers could get information about bills and legislators' voting records.

When the *Boston Globe* ran a series of stories titled "Choosing a Good Death," about hospice care for mortally ill people, the paper also published the stories online, along with information about hospice care and about breast cancer and video clips of one of the people featured in the stories. And the paper set up live online chats with the reporter who wrote the stories and with the manager of a hospice network, as well as online conversations about hospice that readers could participate in.

The online resources journalists use to report stories and reach readers vary in the types of data they offer, the ways they store information and the ways they work. In the next several chapters, you'll learn how to find information on these resources, view it, grab it and use it.

NOT THE INTERNET: ONLINE OPTIONS

The Internet gets the most press these days, but it's not the only online source of information. There are other options: commercial database vendors, bulletin board systems, and commercial information services such as CompuServe and America Online, which combine the offerings of bulletin boards and commercial databases and offer access to the Internet.

To get to many of these resources, you have to *dial in*—telephone the computer where the resources reside, using a modem and telephone line and a number to get into the system and connect your computer to the remote computer. (More on dialing in later in this chapter.) This is changing; you can now reach many bulletin boards and commercial services through the Internet (though you may be using a dial-in connection to get to the Internet too). But there are still some out there that you can't get to except by dialing in. There may be a charge to use these resources, or you may have to pay just the telephone charges if they're long distance.

ONLINE COMMERCIAL DATABASES

A database is simply a collection of information organized in some uniform way. Many such collections are available online through commercial database vendors that offer access to the public, including journalists.

Some government databases are offered this way online. Also available are databases of articles from newspapers and magazines, databases journalists use to find people or get background on them, and more. If you dial into these services, you can gather the data you need and download it into your computer. The information may be statistics, full-text articles from newspapers or magazines, bibliographies or abstracts, government documents, directories, transcripts, photographs, or graphics. Generally, you have to subscribe to these services, and the charges for them vary.

BULLETIN BOARD SYSTEMS

Bulletin board systems, or BBSs, also offer databases of various kinds. The difference between BBSs and commercial database services is that you can interact with other users of the BBSs. Some systems offer e-mail service, conferences where you can "talk" with other computer users in real time, and libraries with information and computer programs you can download to your own computer.

Some are large operations, such as FedWorld, which offers access to hundreds of government agencies; others are smaller ones, sometimes set up by a community or by one government agency. You may have to pay a fee to use a bulletin board, or you may just have to pay the telephone charges.

Some newspapers host their own bulletin boards. They allow readers to send e-mail messages to the paper and read files of information from the paper.

COMMERCIAL INFORMATION SERVICES

Nora Paul, library director at the Poynter Institute for Media Studies, calls commercial online services hybrids, because they combine the offerings of commercial database services and of bulletin boards. America Online and CompuServe are two online services journalists use. Users pay monthly fees to connect to the services and for a certain amount of online time; then (depending on a service's particular rate plan) they may pay an additional hourly charge for each hour beyond that or for use of some offerings on the services, such as commercial databases they are linked to.

These services offer e-mail, files you can download, and access to the Internet. You'll also find conferences or "forums" organized around various subjects. You may be able to get to a "chat room" where you can have real-time conversations with others who are online when you are.

On CompuServe, for example, journalists meet at the JForum, discussing a range of subjects from the best software to use for computer-assisted reporting to equipment available for handicapped photojournalists to frustration with news coverage of political candidates.

Archives of news stories and other information provided by news media can be found via these services too.

THE INTERNET

The Internet is a worldwide network of computers. While computer users usually have to pay for a connection to the Internet, lots of information out there is free for the looking at.

Through the Internet you can send and receive e-mail, subscribe to mailing lists on a wide range of topics, get involved in discussions on "newsgroups," and copy to your personal computer information from computers around the world. You'll find many resources: Gophers, newsgroups, mailing lists, Telnet, FTP, and the World Wide Web.

The Internet offers all kinds of databases, including archives of newspapers and other publications, people finders, and reference works. The fastest-growing part of the Internet is the World Wide Web.

THE WEB

Individuals, agencies, companies, and organizations post information on the World Wide Web every day, and journalists use that information for stories. You can search the Web for text and numbers, just as you can other Internet resources. But the Web also offers graphics, photographs, sound, and video.

What makes the Web particularly wild and wonderful is its links. Information on the Web is stored in a format called hypertext. (More on hypertext in Chapter 8.) This means that when you are reading a document on the Web you can, with just a click of your mouse, pull up a completely different but related document on a completely different computer halfway around the world. Say you are reading a document about the possibility of life on Mars. You click on a link in the text and suddenly you are looking at a new document covering Orson Welles and his radio broadcast of the science fiction drama *The War of the Worlds*, about Martians invading Earth, which panicked hundreds of listeners when it aired in 1938. Click again, and you can hear Welles reading the broadcast script, or pull up a document about his life, or go back to the original Mars file you were looking at. The Web makes millions of bits of information (not all of it useful, of course) available to you in seconds.

Many newspapers have staked out sites on the Web, putting up information and stories and photographs and even full-scale electronic versions of their print selves.

WHO AND WHAT CAN BE FOUND IN CYBERSPACE?

The Federal Aviation Administration is out in cyberspace, as are the federal Department of Housing and Urban Development, and the Library of Congress, and the Patent Office, and many more agencies federal, state, and local.

That's not to say that you can find everything about every agency out there. That would be wonderful, but it isn't going to happen. Governments are generally only going to put online the information they believe the public should have. Still, journalists have found useful data and have downloaded it so they could analyze it.

The big plus to doing this is that you can get the raw information and look for meaning in it, rather than accept what an agency tells you about a database.

ORGANIZATIONS

The Internet Society can be reached online, as can many organizations, including the Public Broadcasting System, Greenpeace, the American Red Cross, the American Kennel Club, and the National Rifle Association.

DIRECTORIES AND GUIDES

You can find directories of information online, including Galaxy, a directory of Internet resources catagorized by topic; guides to online magazines; the Electric Mystic's Guide, which lists Internet sites with a religious theme; and The Reporters Network directory of journalists, editors, and freelance writers.

JOURNALISTS

Many journalism organizations have a presence online, including the Society of Professional Journalists, the National Press Photographers Association, the National Institute for Computer-Assisted Reporting, Investigative Reporters and Editors, and the National Association of Black Journalists. The organizations offer information about computer-assisted reporting training, conferences, computer resources, and many other subjects.

Individual journalists have sites online too, with lists and links to point other journalists to useful and silly sites on the Web.

DEBATES

Say you want to figure out if a new treatment for epilepsy is any good or how people feel about needle exchange programs or what the hot political topic among voters is these days. Through online discussion groups—forums, newsgroups, and mailing lists—you can listen in on conversations among hundreds of people about these and thousands of other topics. If you can think up a subject, there's probably a mailing list, newsgroup, or forum that deals with it.

POLITICIANS

Where are the candidates today? What have they said recently about health care or Medicare or any other kind of care? You can find out online. And you can send the president of the United States e-mail at president@whitehouse.gov.

PHOTOGRAPHS

Photojournalists use the Internet as a forum for their work, as well as to "talk" with other photojournalists and gather information. Many online sites offer not just text but also photographs, so photojournalists have an opportunity to see what their colleagues are doing. At the National Press Photographers Association Web site, for example, you can link to the NPPA Digital Gallery and other photography sites; at the *Boston Globe* Web site, you can view photos by the newspaper's photographers. Time Warner's Pathfinder Web site features *Life* magazine photographs and links to other online photo archives.

OTHER PUBLICATIONS, OTHER STORIES

If you are doing a story on how your city deals with parking ticket scofflaws, or how your state deals with repeat offenders in drunken driving cases, you may want to look at stories that reporters at other papers have written about these subjects. Online, through the commercial services and through the Internet, you can find other publications and search online archives of stories.

The *Los Angeles Times,* for example, keeps stories from 1990 to the present archived online, and you can search for stories using keywords.

PEOPLE—SOURCES, OTHER STUDENTS, OTHER JOURNALISTS

Cyberspace is a great place to search for people. Using e-mail, discussion groups, online directories and other resources, you can get in touch with experts on a million subjects. You can find people to interview who care passionately about your subject. You can get tips on other people to talk to and other information sources to try. You can also track down background information on people you are writing about.

NERD TALK

Online is a great place to get information about all things online. You can find out about software and hardware; you can get information about research reporters and others are doing online; you can eavesdrop on debates about which type of computer is better; you can get statistics and information on the Internet and other online resources; you can learn about and contact people who use computers for fun or profit.

FUN STUFF

OK, you are supposed to be working. But part of the delight of going online is the weird stuff, the funny stuff, the surprises. You can hear what a cockroach sounds like when he rubs his feet together at the Yuckiest Site on the Internet; you can visit the Bureau of Missing Socks; you can check on how well your favorite college football team is playing; you can find lawyer jokes and journalist jokes and recipes and . . . well, start surfing around and see what you find.

YOU CAN'T ALWAYS GET WHAT YOU WANT

If you go online with little or no idea of what you're looking for, you'll find it difficult to get information (and it's very easy to get distracted, fall into the cyberspace rabbit hole, and get lost). There's so much out there, arranged in different ways, accessible with different computer commands and conventions. Luckily, there's lots of online help to lead you through the resources. And this book will introduce you to the basic ways many online resources organize and offer information, the ways you can search through these resources, and the ways you can use the information you find.

Keep this in mind: You can't always find what you need online. All the information in the world is *not* there. And online research does not eliminate the need to do more traditional kinds of reporting. It's just one more way to get at the truth of the stories you are trying to report and write.

WORKING ONLINE—WHEN YOUR COMPUTER DOESN'T ACT LIKE YOUR COMPUTER

Once you venture online, you'll probably find yourself having out-of-computer experiences.

You'll still be sitting in front of your personal computer, fingers on your familiar keyboard—but you may actually be working on a computer halfway around the world. Sometimes your computer will behave the way you expect it to, and sometimes it will follow commands you've never used when working offline. When you dial into a bulletin board system, for example, you'll make contact using a communications software program on your own computer. But once you've gotten access to the BBS, you'll really be working on the computer that hosts the BBS, using the software on that computer. So you'll have to use the computer commands that software and computer understand. Don't worry—you'll find online help for figuring out what those commands are.

You won't always be using software on another computer; how you are working in cyberspace will depend on the type of connection you make to the online services and the software programs you use.

GETTING CONNECTED

Your computer can be connected to the Internet and other online services in different ways. While you don't need to know all the ins and outs, it makes sense for you to understand a little about the different connections so you'll know what you're doing when you get online.

How is the connection made? You have to think about *hardware,* which is the cables and connectors that physically link one computer to another, and *software protocols.* Protocols are instructions that tell computers what methods to use in carrying out tasks, such as transferring files from one computer to another.

Your computer may be directly connected to the Internet or to a computer that is on the Internet with special hardware; you may also dial in to another computer to connect with the Internet, bulletin board services, commercial databases, and commercial information providers. And you can make these connections with either an IBM-compatible machine or a Macintosh.

If the computers in your classroom or lab are linked to one main computer on campus, that main computer is known as the host computer. Only that host is actually *on* the Internet, and it acts as a gateway to cyberspace for all the terminals or PCs in your lab or classroom. To make your connection, you use communications software installed on one of those terminals. You start up the program and make the link to the host computer. A dial-in connection requires a telephone line and a device called a modem. The modem translates signals a computer can understand, *digital* signals, into *analog* signals a telephone can understand. You tell the modem to dial the number of the computer you want to connect to—maybe that host computer on campus. A modem connected to the computer you "call" translates the telephone signals for that remote computer.

The communications software lets you tell your modem what telephone number to dial and helps you transfer files from another computer to your computer or vice versa. It also will keep a list of phone numbers, set up the right communications options for your computer, and, well, do what you need it to do to get connected.

AN EXAMPLE—ZTERM

Look at the way one program, called ZTerm, works. When you get ready to dial up, with your telephone line and modem connected properly, you open up Zterm (a program created by David P. Alverson). A communications document (see Figure 2-1) appears on your screen.

You type in a telephone number and tell your modem to make the connection. The other settings in the communication document tell the modem how best to make the connection and give the modem other information it needs. If you're having trouble with these settings, get a computer guru to help you; often the settings will be preset, so all you'll have to do is type in the telephone number. (You do not have to be a computer expert yourself to do this stuff. If you learn the right commands, your computer will take good care of you.)

SOFTWARE: COMPUTERS TALKING TO COMPUTERS

When you try to connect a computer in your lab to the host computer in another building or to a computer in another state or country, you may run into a problem. (Actually, you can run into lots of problems, including bad connections and buggy software. Call the computer guru.) Different types of computers don't always speak the same language and don't always operate in the same way.

To solve this problem, you may use *terminal emulation* software, which is part of your communications software program. This software tells the computer you've called that *your* computer is one basic type of computer called a *dumb terminal*. Such a computer has very little processing capacity and will accept whatever the other computer sends it.

The communications software you use must be a version that's compatible with the type of computer you work on, whether it's an IBM-compatible or a Macintosh. But once you connect to the host, you don't have to worry about what computer you're using. As far as that host computer is concerned, your powerful computer is no longer an IBM-compatible or a Macintosh. It's a box with a little computer power that needs a major assist.

FIGURE 2–1

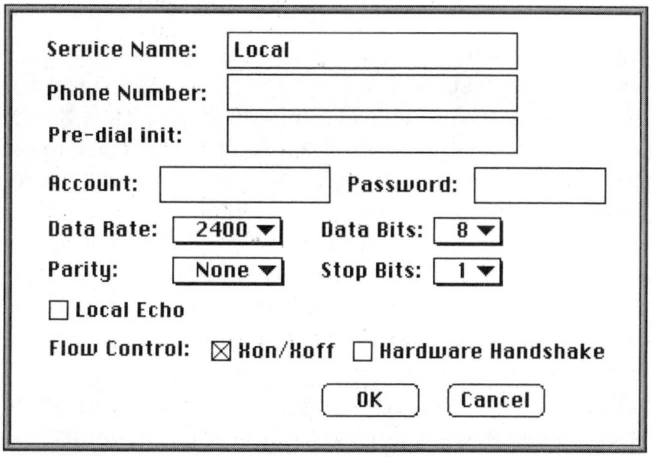

```
┌──────────────────────────────────────────────────────┐
│  ┌────────────────────────────────────────────────┐  │
│  │                                                │  │
│  │  Service Name:  ┌──────────────────────────┐   │  │
│  │                 │ Local                    │   │  │
│  │                 └──────────────────────────┘   │  │
│  │  Phone Number:  ┌──────────────────────────┐   │  │
│  │                 └──────────────────────────┘   │  │
│  │  Pre-dial init: ┌──────────────────────────┐   │  │
│  │                 └──────────────────────────┘   │  │
│  │                                                │  │
│  │  Account: ┌──────────┐  Password: ┌────────┐   │  │
│  │           └──────────┘            └────────┘   │  │
│  │  Data Rate: ┌ 2400 ▼┐  Data Bits: ┌ 8 ▼┐       │  │
│  │  Parity:    ┌ None ▼┐  Stop Bits: ┌ 1 ▼┐       │  │
│  │  ☐ Local Echo                                  │  │
│  │  Flow Control:  ☒ Xon/Xoff ☐ Hardware Handshake│  │
│  │                   ┌──────┐   ┌────────┐        │  │
│  │                   │  OK  │   │ Cancel │        │  │
│  │                   └──────┘   └────────┘        │  │
│  └────────────────────────────────────────────────┘  │
└──────────────────────────────────────────────────────┘
```

A communications document created in the program ZTerm. You type in the telephone number of the online resource you want to dial into.

A Shell Account: No Heavy Lifting

Suppose you are working on a PC in your lab, using terminal emulation software. Your computer is connected to the host computer on campus that is actually on the Internet. You have an account on that computer, often called a *shell account.* You fire up your link by starting the communications software and telling your program to connect to the host computer.

That host computer now thinks you have a dumb terminal. Dumb terminals can't run their own software; they work with what the host computer uses. The host computer does most of the work, but the commands you type in have to be ones that the host computer's software understands.

Online help can prompt you and explain commands. And usually the host computer will offer all the software you need to search and navigate the World Wide Web, wander around in Gopherspace (more on this in Chapter 4), or transfer files from a computer in Finland to your computer.

Your computer works in a similar way when you dial into a bulletin board service or a commercial database. You also use the software running on that bulletin board host or on the database vendor's host computer.

When you connect to America Online or another commercial service, you'll be using software installed on your own computer. The company provides software that allows you to use all the offerings on the service. So the commands you give your computer will be the commands that service and software accept, and it won't matter what type of computer you are using. Again, there will be online help to get you through, and the software provided by CompuServe or America Online comes in versions for Macintoshes and PCs and operates with icons and menus.

GETTING THE BIG PICTURES—A DIFFERENT WAY TO CONNECT

With terminal emulation software and a shell account, the connection you make to the Internet allows you to search through text stored in cyberspace, including the stuff on the World Wide Web. But you cannot view the graphics and color and photographs that make the Web such a jazzy place to visit, and you can't choose your own software programs for using different Internet resources. To do that, you need different software and protocols.

This software is installed on your computer, and you control it. The protocols you need are called SLIP (serial line internet protocol) or PPP (point to point protocol). With these you use other software, called TCP/IP (transmission control protocol and internet protocol). The TCP part controls how information is sent between computers connected to the Internet; the IP part deals with the electronic addresses for each of the computers attached to the Internet.

Don't worry about understanding exactly how these protocols work. (If you are truly interested in the technical aspect of all of this, many books out there will tell you exactly what each protocol does). Just know that they allow you to make different kinds of connections to the Internet.

With an SLIP/PPP account, you still link up to the Internet through a host computer, as you would with a shell account. But instead of doing all the work for your "dumb" computer, the host now simply acts as a connection point between you and the Internet—it thinks you are working with a "smart" computer that can do most of the heavy lifting itself. And you can make this type of connection directly or by dialing in.

With a shell account, you work with character-based software programs, navigating with typed commands. With an SLIP/PPP account, you can use graphical programs to browse the Web and use other Internet resources. These programs operate through keystrokes too, but there are also menus and icons you use your mouse to pull down or click on.

You'll make your connection with a graphical program compatible with the type of computer you're working on. Once you're connected, you can work with online resources in the same ways no matter what type of computer you've got.

JOINING IN

There's no master map showing how to get from one site to another in cyberspace. The best way to learn your way around is to plunge in and start searching for information. Don't be nervous; you can't break anything, and you won't get so lost that you can't get home again.

Begin with an idea you want to investigate. Think about what sorts of information you'll need and which sources you'll want to interview. Can you find any of those facts or folks in cyberspace? Who? What? Where? When? Why? How? Read on; the answers lie just ahead.

Chapter 3

BBS, AOL, AND OTHER LETTERS OF THE ONLINE ALPHABET

Were California communities breaking a state law requiring equality in school spending?

Were taxpayers in New York getting their money's worth?

Were police enforcing Louisiana's gambling laws?

Did the federal government lie to the public about a creature called Bat Boy?

Journalists went online to find answers to the first three questions.

Reporters at the *Fresno* (Calif.) *Bee* got school spending figures from an electronic bulletin board. They found out that districts were not complying with the law.

Syracuse Herald-Journal reporters in New York used commercial database services to gather information on campaign contributions and background on people and companies doing business with the state legislature. Their series of stories, "Secrets of the Chamber," showed, among other things, that members of the legislature had padded its payroll with political workers and that legislators were taking tax breaks that saved them thousands of dollars each year—tax breaks that only legislators could use.

And as part of their investigation, reporters at the *Times-Picayune* in New Orleans used a commercial information provider, America Online, to search newspaper archives for data on individuals and corporations. They found that the police charged with overseeing gambling were often overwhelmed by the many rules they were supposed to enforce and were sometimes stymied by government officials.

Bat Boy? You can search the archives of the *Weekly World News* to find out about that one. (You can find these archives, complete with photographs, on America Online.)

You've used various resources in the past when reporting stories: books, periodicals, and microfilm at your library; telephone books and dictionaries and encyclopedias and street directories; in-person interviews; and clips from issues stored by your local newspaper.

Now, like the reporters at the *Bee,* the *Herald-Journal* and the *Times-Picayune,* you can add bulletin board systems, commercial databases and commercial information providers to your reporter's toolbox.

BULLETIN BOARD SYSTEMS

Before government agencies started flocking to the World Wide Web, many made databases available on electronic bulletin board systems, or BBSs. Even as the Web's popularity grows, Bruce Maxwell, author of *How to Access the Government's Bulletin Boards—1996,* says BBSs remain an excellent source of information from and about federal, state, and local agencies. Sometimes, he says, the BBSs offer information that's not on the Internet, and many people find them easier to use than the Internet. For journalists without Internet access, BBSs can be vital resources.

These are a few examples of BBSs and the information they offer:

- The Massachusetts Department of Environmental Protection maintains a BBS that offers information about waste site cleanup, water pollution control, various state regulations, and other environmental BBSs.
- FedWorld is a much-used BBS, since it acts as a gateway to more than a hundred other federal agencies' online sites. It also offers White House documents, brochures, and handouts from the Securities and Exchange Commission, documents from the National Highway Traffic Safety Administration, and more.
- The NIH Information Center offers files from the National Institutes of Health. The offerings include information about Agent Orange, cancer treatment, Lyme disease and other subjects; an index of diseases being investigated at NIH; press releases; and a list of federal health information centers and clearing houses.
- Maui Online offers information for anyone interested in a virtual tour of Hawaii, including articles by local writers.

LOOK, MA, NO THUMBTACKS

How does a BBS work? Consider the low-tech company bulletin board, complete with cork and thumbtacks. It hangs in a place where lots of people have access to it. You can take information that's posted there and run it through a copying machine. You can tack up messages for groups or individuals and pick up messages people have left for you.

With an electronic bulletin board you also can post messages to a group and retrieve messages for yourself; you can browse through libraries of files and often can download or copy information from them to your own computer. You may also be able to upload information from your computer to the bulletin board. The bulletin board that holds the information you need can be in the next room or the next state or another country. You can still get to it.

On many bulletin boards, you can participate in conferences or forums, also called special interest groups or SIGs. With these, you can post messages about specific topics and get answers and reaction from other bulletin board users. SIG topics range from sports to human rights to cooking to ecology to writing.

Many BBSs also allow you to send electronic mail to other users of that particular BBS or even to users of other BBSs linked to that one. Some bulletin boards even offer interactive chat—you can talk, in real time, with other users.

FINDING BBSS

Various resources list bulletin boards. Bruce Maxwell's book is an excellent one. There are also magazines devoted to bulletin board systems, including *Boardwatch,* which features BBSs in a certain category each month. Asking other journalists for tips is a good way to find out about useful bulletin board systems, and so is searching the World Wide Web. (More on the Web in Chapter 8.)

MAKING A CONNECTION

When you connect to a BBS, you are linking your computer to another computer that is running bulletin board software. Your communications software will tell that other computer that yours is a "dumb" terminal, and you will use the BBS software on the remote computer to carry out most of the tasks you attempt; the communications software on your computer or your host will help you download or upload files.

Though you may be unfamiliar with the BBS's software, there are usually online prompts and help so you can navigate fairly easily.

Many bulletin board systems can be reached by "dialing in" using a telephone, modem, and communications software. (See Getting Connected, page 21.) Even though BBSs often have several modems, you may get a busy signal if many users are connected to the BBS, and you might not get an answer if the BBS isn't running 24 hours a day.

You can reach some BBSs through the Internet, using a resource called Telnet. You'll learn more about this in Chapter 6.

To dial into a BBS, you open up a document using your communications software and plug in the BBS telephone number, then tell your computer to make the call.

Once the connection is made, you might see only a blank screen on your computer monitor. Hit your return button a few times, until some sort of message, usually a welcome or information about the BBS, shows up. The first message you get if you dial into the Massachusetts Department of Environmental

BBS Etiquette

Online, you are trekking from one computer to another without any regard for country boundaries, oceans, rivers, longitude, or latitude, so you need to keep time zones in mind. It may be after regular business hours where you work but 10 a.m. where the BBS exists.

Some bulletin boards ask that you download information only during hours when the system does not see heavy use. You should comply with such a request. If you don't, you're likely to get kicked off the system for good. And it's easy for a BBS operator to decide not to make information available to the general public if users cause problems.

You'll find that some bulletin boards accept only so many users at a time. You may also get only a certain amount of time to work. If you aren't on deadline, you might consider going to the bulletin board after hours—but again, after hours for wherever the bulletin board happens to be.

In John Hedtke's book, *Using Computer Bulletin Boards,* the author suggests that you not try a BBS number in the middle of the night or before 10 a.m. if you haven't dialed that number before, because you might wake someone up. BBSs can go out of business quickly, he says, leaving the number, no longer connected to a BBS, circulating among computer users for months afterward.

Protection BBS tells you the full name of the BBS and offers a telephone number you can call if you are having problems with the BBS. It also asks you to type in your first name; another screen later asks for your last name, address, and other information.

Most BBSs require you to log onto their computers by typing in your name or some passwords, the way you may do to get access to your university or college computer account, or by typing in information about yourself and where you are from. This registration doesn't mean you have to pay for access to the BBS; those who run the system just want to know who is using it.

It's usually best to use your real name when logging on or registering. Many boards, especially government boards, will require you to anyway. And if you use a lot of bulletin boards, it can be confusing to keep up with your aliases.

As part of the logging-on process, you may be asked to choose a secret password. Write it down somewhere! As you zip merrily from one online resource to another, it's hard to remember which password goes with what.

Some BBSs are free; with others, you pay a monthly fee or an hourly amount. Some offer free use for a brief period, so you can try out the BBS. With some BBSs you must register and pay to use any of the resources.

WHAT'S ON THE BBS MENU?

After you've logged on to a BBS, you'll usually see a Main Menu listing the services or information categories available on the BBS, like the one from the Massachusetts environmental board (see Figure 3-1). To get access to different types of information, such as bulletins, a newsletter, or files to download, you have to type in the letter that appears on the menu next to the listing of your choice. For example, you'd type in "D" and hit the return key if you wanted to check out the files in the Program Area.

Menus and keystrokes are the tools you use to navigate and obtain information from BBSs. BBSs don't all run the same software, so they don't all look the same, or use the same keystroke commands, or even ask the same questions when you are logging on. But all of them work with menus and keystrokes. Usually you'll see your keystroke choices right on the menu or at the bottom of the computer screen. And as with the Massachusetts board, there is usually a command you can use to get onscreen help (in this case, you get it by typing in "?"). That help will explain what keyboard commands you can use and what they do.

If you choose "D" from this menu, you'll see another menu (see Figure 3-2). This one is a menu of DEP programs, which are subject areas with files you can look at. You can then choose one of those, say Water Pollution Control, and get a menu of files concerning that subject. On a BBS, you are working through hierarchies, which are categories of information from the broadest (the list of all the BBS offerings) to the narrowest (one text file dealing with one subject).

FIGURE 3–1

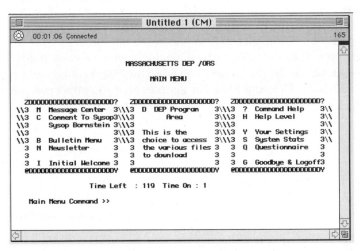

The main menu for the bulletin board system of the Massachusetts Department of Environmental Protection. You can reach this BBS by dialing in with a modem.

FIGURE 3–2

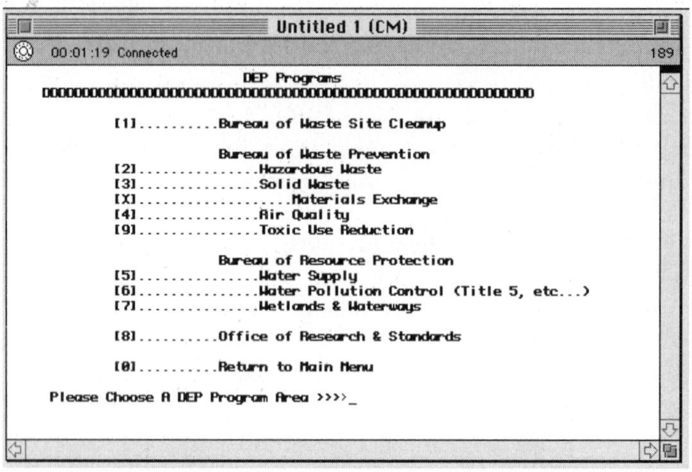

```
┌─────────────────────────────────────────────────────────┐
│■□         Untitled 1 (CM)                              ▣│
│ ✪  00:01:19 Connected                               189 │
│                    DEP Programs                        ⇧│
│ ▯▯▯▯▯▯▯▯▯▯▯▯▯▯▯▯▯▯▯▯▯▯▯▯▯▯▯▯▯▯▯▯▯▯▯▯▯▯▯▯▯▯▯▯▯▯▯▯▯▯▯▯▯▯▯▯ │
│       [1]..........Bureau of Waste Site Cleanup         │
│                                                         │
│                  Bureau of Waste Prevention             │
│       [2]...............Hazardous Waste                 │
│       [3]...............Solid Waste                     │
│       [X]...................Materials Exchange          │
│       [4]...............Air Quality                     │
│       [9]...............Toxic Use Reduction             │
│                                                         │
│                  Bureau of Resource Protection          │
│       [5]...............Water Supply                    │
│       [6]...............Water Pollution Control (Title 5, etc...) │
│       [7]...............Wetlands & Waterways            │
│                                                         │
│       [8]..........Office of Research & Standards       │
│                                                         │
│       [0]..........Return to Main Menu                  │
│                                                         │
│   Please Choose A DEP Program Area >>>>_                │
│                                                        ⇩│
│◁                                                     ⇨▣│
└─────────────────────────────────────────────────────────┘
```

A menu of information stored on The Massachusetts Department of Environmental Protection BBS. This menu lists various DEP programs. Choosing any one of these will bring up information connected with that particular program.

BRING THAT HERE—DOWNLOADING FILES

Journalists often make use of information on BBSs by downloading it, copying it into their own computers. You do this the way you do everything else on a BBS, with menus and keys.

Figure 3-3 shows a menu of some files of information available on the Massachusetts board. Each file has a number beside it. Then comes the name of the file, the size of the file in bytes (this will give you some idea of how long the file might take to download), and the date the file was uploaded to the BBS (this may give you some idea of how recent the information in the file is). The right-hand side of this menu offers a summary of what each file holds.

Look closely at the file names. You'll see they have suffixes or extensions, such as ZIP, ASC, TXT, and EXE. The suffixes give you important information about the files.

GOOD THINGS IN SMALL PACKAGES

When you go after files of information online, you'll discover that, to save computer space and to make the transfer of information from one computer to another go quickly, some files of data have been compressed using special software. You can download compressed and uncompressed files. But to use compressed files, you need a program that will decompress them. Without such a program, you won't be able to open up a compressed file, or, if you do get it open, all you'll see will be gibberish.

FIGURE 3–3

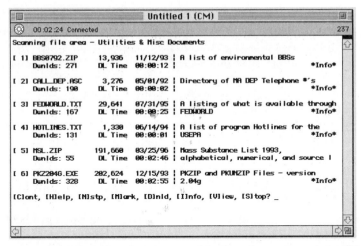

A list of files available on the bulletin board system of the Massachusetts Department of Environmental Protection. This list includes information about the name or subject of the files, the size of the files, and the dates the files were uploaded to the BBS.

Bytes

The amount of space that information takes up on a computer hard drive, or on a floppy disk, is measured in units called bytes. Each byte is made of of eight bits; it takes eight bits, or one byte, to describe one letter or number.

John Hedtke, in his book *Using Computer Bulletin Boards*, says you can get an estimate of how long it will take to download a file if you divide the number of bytes the file takes up by the speed of your modem. Modem speed is measured in bits per second (bps).

The suffixes on the file names will tell you which decompression program you need. A common suffix is ZIP; this means the file has been compressed with a popular IBM-compatible program called PKZIP and can be decompressed with a program called PKUNZIP. Popular programs for Macintosh users include versions of a program called StuffIt. The extension TXT means the file is regular text; you won't need to decompress it.

If you are working in a laboratory or classroom, you'll probably have access to various decompression programs. And you'll need them again if you try to get information using the Internet's FTP, or file transfer protocol. (See FTP, Chapter 6.)

TOTE THAT BARGE, GET THAT FILE

Downloading files is fairly simple. Suppose you looked at the menu in Figure 3-3 and decided you wanted to download the first item, which is a list of environmental BBSs. You'd look at the menu choices: [C]ont , [H]elp, [N]stp, [M]ark, [D]nld, [I]nfo,[V]iew, [S]top? These choices tell you that you can view individual files, continue looking for more files or stop what you are doing. And there's a download command—but what does Mark mean? If you choose Help, you'll be told that Mark will designate a file for downloading. So you'll type in "M" and hit the return, tell the computer to mark file No. 1, which is the file for the list of BBSs, then type in "D" and hit the return.

HOW DO YOU WANT THAT INFORMATION SENT?

When you download files from a BBS, you also have to choose a protocol, which is a set of instructions for transferring information. The BBS you're working on will tell you which protocols it supports. You also have to know which ones your own computer or computer system supports, because you can't transfer information unless both computers are using the same instructions. Your instructor, newspaper adviser, computer guru, or communications software will let you know which protocols you can use.

For example, if you use the communications software program ZTerm on a Macintosh computer, there's a menu titled Settings. If you pull down that menu, you can choose the Transfer option (for transferring files). Then you get a dialogue box like the one in Figure 3-4, which offers options for protocols.

FIGURE 3–4

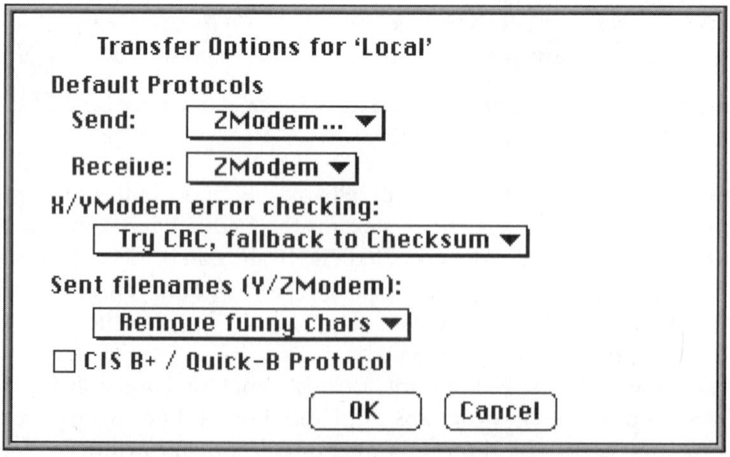

A screen showing file transfer protocols available with the communications program ZTerm.

The protocols have names such as XModem, Ymodem, and Zmodem. Sometimes you'll have to specify which protocol you want to use right after you've logged onto a BBS, before you've even looked at the files available. Otherwise, you'll be asked when you tell the BBS to start downloading the file.

You tell the BBS computer what protocol to use, and you tell your own computer, through your communications program, to use the same one. You may also have to tell your computer, via your communications program, to receive the file from the BBS. Then you wait until the downloading is completed and you've received a copy of the file.

GET THE MESSAGE?

Many BBSs also offer access to online discussion groups, sometimes called conferences, forums, or special interest groups. You can read messages posted by other users or post messages yourself.

The CapAccess BBS, for example, provides all sorts of federal government information under various headings, including Media Center, Education Center, and Science and Technology Center. In each of these areas, there are forums where people post messages and debate various points. One thread of discussion in the media forum in 1997 had to do with the pros and cons of civic journalism. To get to that forum, start with the CapAccess main menu and keep selecting menu items having to do with forums until you reach the Media Forum. You will eventually reach a menu (like the one in Figure 3-5) listing messages that have been posted to that forum. Onscreen help shows you how to contribute or post a message to the forum, how to read messages, how to get help and information about other options, and how to quit the forum.

FIGURE 3–5

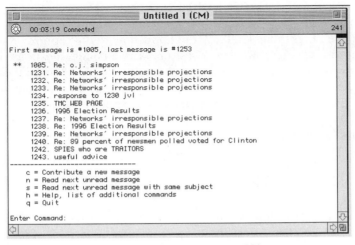

A list of messages posted to the Media Forum on the CapAccess BBS.

A Question of Ethics

Journalists sometimes post messages asking for help from other users of a BBS. There's nothing wrong with doing this—it can be a good way of reaching sources and getting information. But when you post a message about someone or some organization, you are raising the possibility that something is going on with that person or organization that is worth investigating by a newspaper. That may raise questions about the person or organization in the minds of other BBS users.

Again, that doesn't mean you shouldn't do it. But even a brief post can affect a person's reputation. Suppose you make a telephone call to an administrator at a hospital asking for some information about a certain doctor. When you do that, you alert that administrator to your investigation, possibly raising questions in that administrator's mind about the doctor, even though you are only asking a question. And if the administrator sounds concerned, you can explain in greater detail what you are doing. You won't have that same interaction when you post something on a BBS. Consider these issues when you are deciding to post and when you are composing your message.

Also remember that a posted message might alert the person or organization you are reporting on. You might not want to post a message right at the start of your investigation—it might make sense to wait until later in your work.

CAPTURING INFORMATION

There's one other thing you'll want to know how to do: capture or log what happens during your online work session. With a communications program like Zterm, there is usually an option (with Zterm you'll find it under the Settings menu) that lets you "capture to file"—save in a text file on your computer—all the text that rolls across your computer screen while you are online. You'll be able to look at all the menus and information you pulled up and determine what's useful and what's not.

COMMERCIAL DATABASE VENDORS

A second type of online resource valued by journalists is the commercial database service. Commercial databases, which are collections of information,

---

CAR in action

Preston Forman mined an electronic bulletin board and struck gold.

Forman, a reporter for the *New Bedford Standard-Times,* uses the Massachusetts Department of Environmental Protection board and another run by the Massachusetts Department of Revenue. Forman checks the boards every couple of months to see what new information has been posted.

Forman was seeking data on school spending. Again and again, sources in the towns he covered had told him that the schools were "swallowing up" so much money that general government, including police, fire, libraries, and other community services, was suffering, says Forman. He wanted to write a story about this, but all he had to go on was anecdotal evidence, and he didn't think that was proof enough.

But on the Department of Revenue bulletin board service, he found information about towns' spending from 1986 to 1994. He downloaded the numbers, analyzed them in a spreadsheet program, and found that his sources had been right. What he discovered led his story:

> Schools, traditionally the bulk of any community's budget, have been swallowing a larger percentage of municipal budgets the past two years, a trend that developed even before the landmark 1993 Education Reform law, a Standard-Times study has found.
>
> And while schools are the beneficiary of more dollars, general government—everything from libraries to police and fire—is increasingly scurrying for scarcer dough.

Reporter Preston Forman interviewed finance officials in several communities to get their takes on the situation. In one town, for example, he discovered that in years past about 60 percent of the spending had been for general government funding and about 40 percent for education; by 1994 these numbers had been reversed. And some officials felt this was resulting in a lessening of the quality and quantity of community services.

"It was the type of story where as a reporter you sometimes believe what people say, after a while, if it's repeated enough times," says Forman. With the information from the BBS, he had hard evidence to prove that all those people were right.

---

come in many flavors, and some of them are expensive to use. But they still offer some information you can't get anywhere else for free. So if your school or newspaper has access to any of these, learn to use them.

Biographical information, businesses' financial data, and articles published by newspapers and magazines can be found in commercial databases. Often you'll have to dial into these databases, though some are showing up on the Web. The ones journalists use include these:

- Lexis/Nexis, operated by the Mead Corporation. Lexis is a law database, with the text of law cases and decisions made concerning bankruptcy, property, and other issues. Nexis is a compilation of full-text articles from newspapers and magazines, which journalists use to see what else has been written about a subject. (Remember, Michael Berens of the *Columbus* (Ohio) *Dispatch* used this service to compare the official records of police-chase-related deaths with accident reports in newspapers and magazines and discovered many discrepancies.)
- DIALOG, run by Knight-Ridder Information, Inc. This service maintains more than 400 databases, including the complete text of more than 2,500 journals, magazines, and newsletters; the complete text of more than 60 newspapers; and financial information on millions of U.S. companies.
- DBT Online, a Database Technologies, Inc., service. This resource provides information about individuals, including their past and present addresses and the addresses of neighbors and relatives.

FINDING THE DATA

Other journalists may be your best source for information about useful databases. Nora Paul, library director at The Poynter Institute for Media Studies, offers excellent information about databases in "Computer Assisted Research: A Guide to Tapping Online Information," which you can find on the World Wide Web at http://www4.nando.net/prof/poynter/chome.html. There are directories such as the *Gale Directory of Databases.* Some commercial databases are available through commercial information service providers such as America Online and CompuServe. They differ in how they look onscreen, what information they offer, and exactly how you search for the information you want. If you know how to do a keyword search, you'll be able to find useful stuff.

A FEW WORDS ABOUT SEARCHING

There is so much information online that if it weren't categorized somehow, you'd have to spend every waking minute surfing from one computer site to another looking for what you wanted. Imagine walking into your library and trying to find a book you want without the books being shelved in any order and with no card catalog.

The online world, including the Internet, is a little like that library. Without some ways to catalog things and to find what you want, you'd never get out of cyberspace with anything useful.

One way online information is organized is through menus, like the menu you get when you log onto a BBS. There are menu-based resources on the Internet too.

Often, when you link to a commercial database, you get an onscreen menu, as you would with a BBS. You begin your online work, then, by choosing a menu item, and another menu item, and maybe another menu item. Then, you need to do a keyword search.

KEYWORDS

Often, these menu categories are broad. To find what you really want in a commercial database—or other online resource—you need to do a search using keywords.

Keywords describe the subject you are interested in; a search for keywords will find the files in which they appear. To be successful at choosing keywords, you need to think both about *focus* and about *connections* between subjects.

For example, if you are using the Nexis database and looking for stories about crime on America's college campuses, you might first try a search for "crime." With that keyword, you're going to get back so many possibilities that you'll be overwhelmed; that category is too broad. A two-word search, say of "campus crime" may be better; narrowing the search even more, to "campus crime" and "New England," will produce more specific results. This is where thinking about focus comes in.

Considering connections is important if you don't find anything useful using particular keywords. If you are looking for information on elephants, for example, you might also want to search under "zoos." If you want information about computer hackers, you might also try "computer security" or "privacy," since hackers threaten both.

LET'S GET LOGICAL

To be successful in searching, you also need to think about logic, or the way the computer is doing the search.

One of the basic ways is through the use of Boolean logic. This logic, which tells the computer something about the relationship between the words you are using in your search, is named after a nineteenth-century mathematician named George Boole. Boolean logic uses words or phrases, called "operators," to tell the computer how you want it to relate your keywords. The operator *and* tells the computer to search for all the words you are connecting with it. If you tell the computer to search for "campus *and* crime," it searches for files or documents with both of those words in it. If you tell the computer to search for "campus *or* crime," using the Boolean operator *or,* it will find documents or files with either word or with both—a much broader search in this case. Finally, you can use the Boolean operator *not* to exclude some things in the search. You might do a search for "campus crime *not* city," for example, if you were only interested in what was going on in rural areas.

Often, if you aren't given the chance to actually choose a Boolean operator, you'll find that the search you are doing is using *and* anyway.

You'll use Boolean operators when searching the Internet, and you'll use them with database and spreadsheet programs. So don't file this away and forget about it—you'll need it again. (For more on Boolean logic, see Chapter 7, pages 116-17, and Chapter 8, pages 143-44.)

CAR in action

It was supposed to be bigger than the Indianapolis Speedway.

At least that's what officials in a New Jersey township were told when they met with executives from a company that wanted the officials' help and support with a project. The company, which the township officials had never heard of before, wanted to build a speedway in the area, and the executives promised the project would bring in lots of jobs.

Reporters at the *Press of Atlantic City* weren't convinced and set out to discover if the proposal was on the up and up.

Ray Robinson, who helped with research for the story, says the company wanted to set up a private-public partnership with the township, and local officials hadn't done much checking into the company.

So reporters used Lexis and DIALOG to look into the company's background. "We were able to find out that there wasn't really much to this company except the incorporation papers," says Robinson; the company didn't have the resources executives had told officials it had. The speedway project "just melted away."

Robinson says the paper often used such online databases to check into the background and financial health of companies. The database services, he says, provide detailed reports on companies, including information on investors and credit histories.

ONE-STOP SHOPPING: COMMERCIAL INFORMATION SERVICES

With a few keystrokes, you can reach cyberspace sites that offer lots of different resources from one starting point, including searchable databases and online discussion groups and files you can download. These commercial information services, including Prodigy, CompuServe and America Online, also offer e-mail and connections to the Internet.

The services aren't free; you pay a monthly charge to connect and extra hourly charges for all the time past a certain amount that you spend online using the service. There are also additional charges to use some of the services and databases you can reach through these information providers. But they are good places to get information and find sources.

You get to these information services by dialing in, just as you might connect to a bulletin board service or commercial database.

CompuServe and AOL offer similar services, and this book can't cover every one of them. But there are a few you might find particularly helpful as you work on stories. Take a look at CompuServe's Phone*File and Journalism Forum and at AOL's Newsstand and Reference Desk.

COMPUSERVE

The first screen you'll see will when you dial into Compuserve will be the one in Figure 3-6. The center screen, with the icons labeled News, Computers, Education, Internet, and so on, is the service's main menu. To get to one of the named areas of CompuServe, click your mouse on one of those icons.

A pull-down menu bar at the top of the screen allows you to open menus filled with commands. A tool bar offers icons that represent commands for getting around in CompuServe, so you can use these instead of the menus.

CompuServe also assigns "Go" words to different services and areas, so you can quickly move from one place to another. If you click on the traffic light icon, you'll get a box where you can type in the Go word. You might type in the Go word "JFORUM" to get the the CompuServe Journalism Forum, or click on the News icon to bring up a menu of offerings that include News Source USA and Newspaper Archives. If you click on the traffic light and type in "PHONEFILE," you'll get access to a resource for tracking down people all over the country.

OPERATOR, GIVE ME THE NUMBER, PLEASE

James Bond lives in California. Clark Kent and Lois Lane live in Massachusetts, though not in the same towns. Bruce Wayne has apparently moved his mansion from Gotham City to Texas. And Homer Simpson can be found in Florida.

FIGURE 3–6

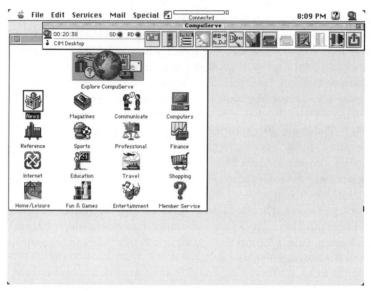

The main CompuServe screen, with icons representing various areas and services you can tap into with this commercial information service.

OK—these people probably aren't renowned spies or the alter egos of Superman or Batman—and they're definitely not cartoon characters. They are real people living in real places, and you can find them and hundreds of others with Phone*File. This is a people finder, a database of more than 80 million U.S. households. If you have a surname, and know the geographic or metropolitan area you want to search, you can find all the people who are listed in telephone directories with that surname in that state. If you have a first name, you can narrow your search even more. You can search for a surname on a particular street. The information you get will include the person's address and telephone number.

If you have only an address, you can also use Phone*File to find the name of the person who lives there. And if you have only a telephone number, you can match the number to a person too. You work through menus to set search parameters and conduct a search. (And yes, Phone*File costs money).

After you get into Phone*File, you'll get to choose how you are going to search. If you pick "by state," you're asked to type in a two-letter abbreviation for the state. Then you'll be asked to specify the surname you want to search for, the first name if you know it, and the street if you know it. So if you choose *TX* and *Wayne, Bruce,* you'll find out there's only one listed in Texas—and you'll have his address and phone number.

Other searches may yield more than one result; you'll get a list of all of the results. This is one quick, inexpensive way to track somebody down. It isn't the only one, but it's one more resource you can try.

Go JFORUM

CompuServe has a number of message board areas, or special interest groups, arranged around various subjects. Its Journalism Forum, or JFORUM, is frequented by many journalists.

The forums on CompuServe offer places where you can read messages posted by other members of the forum (and of course, you can post replies or your own messages or questions); libraries with files you can download; and chat rooms where you can converse with other people logged on at the same time you are. JFORUM offers message board areas and libraries covering a wide range of topics, including various journalism organizations and Jobs/Stringers, Internet & J-Tools, Comment/Controversy, Radio/TV, BizNews, The Soapbox (where you can sound off about what the media cover or don't cover and how), Ethics, Future Media, Sports Writing, and Journalism Law. When you Go JFORUM, you get a menu with icons for the different areas in the forum.

On a given day in the JFORUM's discussion areas, you might find debate raging over whether the media give enough coverage to politicians outside of the Democrat-Republican mainstream, or whether a newspaper should charge people for running obituaries, or what software is useful for computer-assisted reporting. You can read the messages, join in the debate, or send a message on a new subject. If you're looking for advice on how to handle a story or find a good source, there are lots of journalists in this cyberspace place to help you.

If you browse through the JFORUM libraries, you'll get a menu like the one in Figure 3-7. Double-click on a category, and you'll get another menu listing

FIGURE 3–7

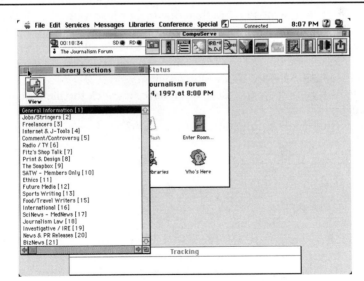

A list of library sections, by topic, offered on CompuServe's Journalism Forum. You can download copies of documents stored in these library sections.

FIGURE 3–8

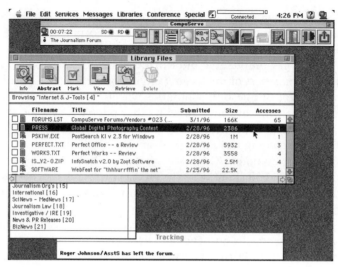

A directory of files stored in the Internet & J-Tools library on CompuServe's Journalism Forum.

files, with the file name, title, date the file was submitted to the forum, the size of the file, and the number of times the file has been accessed. (See Figure 3-8.)

You can see at the top of the library menu buttons labeled Mark, View, and Retrieve. If you want to view a file, highlight it by clicking on it, then click on View; if you want to download a file, highlight it and hit Retrieve. If you think you may want to download more than one file, or just want to wait until later to download it, highlight it and hit Mark. Later, go to the Library pull-down menu and choose Retrieve Marked, and the download will begin.

The files will be copied to your computer's hard drive, and you'll be able to open them using a word processing program.

Some files will be compressed; you'll have to check the file extensions, as you would with files on a BBS.

You'll find information about software and hardware, ethical and legal issues, and tips on story sources and ideas in these online libraries.

AMERICA ONLINE

America Online operates in ways similar to CompuServe, with buttons you can click on, pull-down menus, and keywords. When you start up your AOL connection, you get a main menu with various choices (see Figure 3-9). The choices include Today's News, The Newsstand, Clubs & Interests, Sports, and the Reference Desk.

FIGURE 3–9

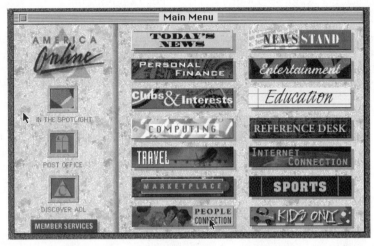

The main America Online screen with buttons to click on so you can gain access to different areas and services of AOL.

Choose The Newsstand, and you'll get a list of magazines, television programs and newspapers such as *Investor Business Daily, ABC News InFocus, Newsweek Interactive* and the wild *Weekly World News,* where you can find headlines such as "Was Bat Boy Starved By The FBI?" and "Wax Dummy Found in Elvis' Coffin!" The Newsstand also offers links to newspapers on the World Wide Web.

QUICK FACTS

The Reference Desk—which you can reach by clicking the Reference Desk icon on the AOL main menu—offers searchable resources including *Compton's Encyclopedia,* the *Columbia Concise Encyclopedia,* the *Dictionary of Cultural Literacy, Merriam-Webster's Collegiate Dictionary* and *Medical Dictionary,* and *Que's Computer and Internet Dictionary.* You can also search for listings of bulletin board services. When you're in a hurry and need just a definition or a few facts, these resources can provide them.

Click on the icon for the *Dictionary of Cultural Literacy* (second edition, edited by E. D. Hirsch Jr., Joseph F. Kett, and James Trefil) and you'll get a screen where you can type in the word or phrase you're wondering about. The search will produce a list of online dictionary entries; you can choose the one you want. Looking for the word "raven," for example, produces five listings:

"The Raven," wolf in sheep's clothing, wolves in sheep's clothing, motif, and Edgar Allan Poe. Choose "motif," and this definition pops up:

> *In literature, art or music, a recurring set of words, shapes, colors, or notes. In the poem "THE RAVEN," by Edgar Allan POE, for example, the word nevermore is a motif appearing at the end of each STANZA. Likewise, the first four notes of the Fifth Symphony of Ludwig van Beethoven are a motif that is developed and reshaped throughout the work.*

If you've got all these resources in paper form (or on CD) sitting on your desk, by all means use them. If you don't, AOL's Reference Desk is a handy way to check a reference or definition when you're trying to find a fact or phrase for a story. You might even find some surprises while you're investigating. Did you ever connect ravens with Beethoven?

CAR in action

Did drivers of Twin City buses have good reason to be afraid they'd be victims of crime?

Dan Browning of the *St. Paul* (Minn.) *Pioneer Press* used computer-assisted reporting to find out. According to Investigative Reporters and Editors' *100 Computer-Assisted Stories,* he got 40,000 police incident reports, which he analyzed using a database management program (more on database managers in Chapters 10 and 12), and he used several commercial databases, including CompuServe's Magazine Database Plus, to look for stories in other publications about crime on buses. He found a *Los Angeles Times* story about bus crime that mentioned the only government study of crimes on buses. Browning was able to get the study and interview the researcher, who was at the University of California at Los Angeles.

Browning also did more traditional reporting: He reviewed minutes from meetings of the bus drivers' safety committee and interviewed bus riders, bus drivers, crime victims, gang members, and others.

Browning reported that violent crime on buses was increasing and that the victims of these crimes were often the poor, the elderly, and minorities. He showed which bus routes were the most dangerous and at which times of day, documenting many assaults on passengers and drivers and telling readers about innovative programs to fight crime that communities in other states were using.

AND CYBERSPACE GOES ON AND ON

These commercial information services are the beginning, not the end, of the online world. They also offer access to the Internet, with its e-mail and Gophers and World Wide Web sites.

In cyberspace, you'll want to use whichever resource will work best and provide the most reliable data for the story you are working on. You may find that you end up working on the Internet more than you do with BBSs, or that you really like the way America Online works but aren't so excited about the Internet's Gophers.

But don't divide information into categories according to how it is delivered, says Bill Dedman, former director of computer-assisted reporting for the Associated Press. At a May 1996 computer-assisted reporting conference in New Hampshire, Dedman said reporters should think about types of content, about what good information is in cyberspace, and how it can be used in reporting great stories.

If you know how to use all types of online resources, you'll be prepared no matter where you have to go to get that good information. The next *where* you're going to learn about is the Internet; the next *how* is e-mail.

Chapter 4

SPECIAL DELIVERIES: FINDING PEOPLE AND STORIES WITH ELECTRONIC MAIL

You're writing a story about a train crash that happened late last night, and you need an expert to explain how someone could sabotage a railroad crossing.

You're working on a story about how violence on TV affects children, and you've already talked with doctors and experts on child development. Now you need to find parents and kids to interview.

Send some e-mail.

Electronic mail, or e-mail, is the most used resource on the Internet. If you have someone's electronic mail address, you can send that person messages and pictures and even computer programs through cyberspace, and he or she can send messages to you. You can also send e-mail to people who aren't actually on the Internet, such as people who use a commercial service like America Online.

One of the things you can do with e-mail, of course, is reach other students or professional journalists. When you run into a problem with an assignment or story or just need to let off some steam, it can help to e-mail someone else who understands. Journalists collaborate on stories this way too; it's a fast, simple way to send story ideas, reporting techniques, information, and stories back and forth.

You can use e-mail for reporting in several ways:

- Sending a message to anyone in the world with an electronic address, and getting a message back, or conducting an interview by sending questions to and receiving answers from someone.
- Subscribing to an electronic mailing list so that you can see what people are saying about a particular subject, and so you can ask questions and reach sources who subscribe to the same list.
- Locating experts in subjects from aardvarks to zebras, at universities and other institutions, so you can gather information or verify what other sources have told you.

Before you start sending messages into cyberspace, though, you need to understand the way the Internet lets you contact and exchange information with computers—and people working on those computers—far, far away.

CLIENTS AND SERVERS

All the Internet tools that journalists use work through programs called clients and servers. Clients are programs that perform certain tasks; for example, you tell your computer that you want to use Telnet to log onto a computer in London, and the Telnet client program makes the connection to that computer, letting you log on and use the resources there.

When you are working with terminal emulation software, with your computer acting as a "dumb terminal," you'll have a shell account and be able to run only the client programs that your host system makes available. If you have an SLIP/PPP account, you can run on your own computer whatever client programs you want to.

Server programs do not run on your host computer or your own computer; they run on the remote computers that have the information you want. Client programs request information from the server programs, and the server programs make that information available.

Say you want to use a Gopher—a collection of information displayed as a series of menus—and that Gopher is on another computer in another country (more on Gophers in Chapter 7). You start up the Gopher client program and type into your computer the electronic address of the remote Gopher, and the program takes you there. Each time you select an item from the Gopher's menu, your Gopher client goes and gets the information you asked for. The client program interprets the commands you type into your computer and the keys you hit. The Gopher server program provides the resources that your client program requests.

In essence, this setup is what makes the Internet work. Because the client and server programs don't have to be on the same computer, you can connect with, get information from, and work on other computers all over the world.

The commands and procedure for using the various client programs differ. But it's not hard to learn the basic commands for each, and the programs offer built-in online help in case you get stuck. The best way to learn is to plunge in and try out some of the Internet tools journalists use everyday, including client programs for e-mail.

GETTING THE MESSAGE

Because mail programs don't all operate in exactly the same way, there's no one set of instructions that shows you how to use every program. This book will show you examples of ways to use Pine, a character-based program developed by the University of Washington, and QUALCOMM's Eudora, a graphical program with pull-down menus. Your host computer may offer a different program, such as Elm or Mush.

You can learn the commands for a particular program easily enough—especially with the online help—and if you get used to one program and then have to switch to another, you'll know what you want to ask the new program to do. Regardless of which e-mail program you use, what's most important is that you understand what you can do with e-mail.

WHO LIVES WHERE ON THE INTERNET

Electronic addresses do not look like regular addresses because cyberspace doesn't operate like regular space. When Publishers Clearinghouse Sweepstakes heads to your house to tell you that you've won the big jackpot, the sweepstakes van driver needs to know the street and street number, the city, and the state you live in. The driver might also call to get a description of your house and find out if that pink flamingo mailbox is yours.

But in cyberspace you have to use an electronic address that explains which computer the message should go to and which person's electronic mailbox it should settle into when it gets there.

The average e-mail address looks something like this:

```
lcm@zippo.unh.edu
```

The first part of the address, lcm, is the user identification—the name of the account this person has on the computer she or he uses to connect to the Internet. Often this phrase, name, or collection of letters and/or numbers is the person's "logon," which the person uses to log onto a host computer.

After the user ID comes the @ or "at" sign, signaling that the next thing coming is the user's computer address.

When you write an address on an envelope you're going to send via snail mail, you start with the most specific information you have and work down to the most general: the person's name, the street name and number, the city, the state, and maybe the country.

With electronic addresses, you're also moving from most specific to most general. Look at the address above. First after the @ sign comes the name of the computer that this person logs onto and where his or her electronic mailbox is—in this case, "zippo." Then comes the name of the institution or organization, in this case: "unh," or the University of New Hampshire, where that computer is located. The last part, "edu," tells what type of organization UNH is, in this case an educational institution. (Zippo is not the real name of any computer at UNH, so don't try sending a message there.)

The part of the e-mail address that comes after the @ sign is called the domain; the parts of the domain that are separated by periods are called subdomains.

You will sometimes see addresses that have more or fewer than three subdomains. A subdomain might be added to make the address more informative; for example, in addition to telling you this computer is at UNH, there might be a subdomain such as "cis" to say that it's a computer in the Computing and Information Services department.

Some addresses have only two domains. This can mean that the organization you are sending the mail to is very small and has only one computer on the Internet, making a specific computer name unnecessary; or it can mean that the organization is very large, with many computers, so that all the mail goes to one computer that sorts it, using a list of user IDs and computer names for that network, and sends it on to the correct computers and electronic mailboxes.

One exception you'll see to this type of addressing is with people who use CompuServe. CompuServe addresses consist of numbers, separated by commas. To use these addresses with your mail program, over the Internet, you have to replace the comma with a period.

UPPER CASE OR LOWER CASE?

Some computer systems don't care whether you type addresses using upper-case or lower-case letters, but some do. Case usually doesn't matter in the domain part of the address, but sometimes the first part of the address is case sensitive. If you get a message and the e-mail address on it uses upper-case letters in the first part of the address, you should do the same when you reply. If you don't know whether there are upper-case letters in the address, a good rule of thumb is to stick with lower-case letters.

WHAT'S THE NAME OF YOUR SUBDOMAIN?

Various subdomain names in electronic mail addresses designate the type of institution the address is for. They include these:

    com—a commercial enterprise
    edu—an educational institution
    gov—a governmental agency
    int—an international organization
    mil—military
    net—a computer networking organization
    org—a nonprofit organization

TRACKING DOWN E-MAIL ADDRESSES

There are a number of ways to find people's electronic mail addresses so you can contact them. One is to use a client/server program called Finger. Not every network on the Internet runs it, and some computer systems won't allow people outside their systems to get Finger information.

If you just type the word "finger" at the system prompt once you're logged onto your host computer, you'll get a list of all the people logged onto the same computer as you at the same time as you. That's a start, but it's not very helpful for finding people outside your own system.

To use Finger outside your system, you need some information about the person you are trying to find: the name of the computer host where the person has his or her account, and either a user ID, last name, or first name. You type in what you know, with the finger command. If you are looking for someone named Charles Chip, with a user ID of cchip, you might use any of these:

```
finger cchip@cookie.com

finger charles@cookie.com

finger chip@cookie.com
```

You do not need to know all three of these pieces of information to find someone—any one piece, along with the computer name, will do.

The information you get may include the person's user ID, the person's full name, the date of the last time that person logged into the system using that ID, whether the person has read his or her e-mail, the person's telephone number and office number, and any other information the person has decided to make public, such as office hours.

The message you get will look something like this:

```
Login name: cchip            In real life: Charles Chip
Last login: Mon Mar 12 2:45
```

If the computer can't find the person you are looking for, you'll get a message that looks like this:

```
login: cchip                 In real life:???
```

The computer couldn't locate the name or user ID at the computer address you gave. This doesn't mean the person doesn't exist; it may mean you don't have the right information about the user or the computer he or she might work on.

You can also use Finger to see who is logged in on that host. Use the finger command with @ sign and the name of the host:

```
finger@zippo.unh.edu
```

You can also get some specialized information about things, rather than people, using Finger—not always useful information, but it's fun. You might try these:

`finger quake@geophys.washington.edu`

(for information about recent earthquakes in Washington and Oregon, including time, location and magnitude, and computer addresses you can use to get data about earthquakes in other parts of the country)

`finger nasanews@space.mit.edu`

(for the latest bulletins from NASA's news service)

`finger pepsi@cunix.cc.columbia.edu`

(to find out if there's still cream soda in a drink machine—as well as what other drinks are available and when the machine was last filled—at Columbia University.

There—you can amaze your fellow reporters with your arcane knowledge.

E-MAIL: READING, REPLYING, SAVING, SORTING

Once you've got an account (a shell account or an SLIP/PPP account) on an Internet host or with a commercial service you'll be assigned a user ID or logon, and a secret password so that nobody else can get into your account. You'll use these to hook up to your host. Once there, you can read your mail. While your computer is probably not on 24 hours a day, electronic mail is coming in all the time and being stored on the host computer. Once you start up the mail program, all your mail shows up as messages in your e-mail box. Using a program such as Pine, you can read mail, reply to messages, send new messages, and save interesting or useful mail so you can easily find it later.

E-mail Tip

The easiest way to get someone's e-mail address is to call the person and ask for it. Yes, it's old-fashioned, but it works.

There are online directories too; you'll learn more about those when you read about the World Wide Web in Chapter 8.

Let's look at the way the Pine program works. You can use this type of program with a shell account.

PINE POSSIBILITIES

When you start up Pine, you get a message screen like the one in Figure 4-1, with a menu of choices for things to do. From the menu you can choose to get online *Help* with the program; *Compose* a message; look at an *Index* of all the e-mail messages you've recently received; look at a list of the *Folders* of e-mail messages you've saved; add some electronic addresses to your *Address Book;* change the *Setup* of Pine; and *Quit* the program. At the bottom of your screen are other commands you can use while working with this menu. All the time that you work in your mail program, you'll see possible commands at the bottom of the screen. The commands change, depending on what you are trying to accomplish. When you add an address to your address book, for example, the commands at the bottom of the screen (the only commands you can use for this task) will be different from the commands you'll see there when you are composing an e-mail message.

FIGURE 4–1

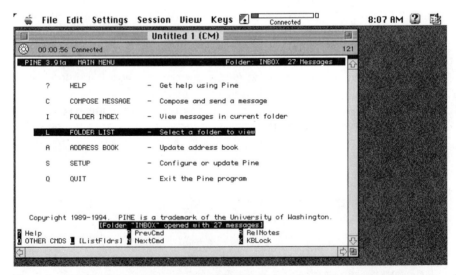

The main screen for the e-mail program Pine. This menu lists various options, including viewing an index of messages (L) and composing a message (C). At the bottom of the screen are other commands you can use while working with this menu.

AND SPEAKING OF SENDING A MESSAGE ...

If you type **C** for compose, you'll get a screen set up to take your message. (See Figure 4-2.) At the top of the screen, you'll see a place to type in the electronic address of the person you are sending a message to.

Type the address into the address field, where it says **To:** The next field, **Cc,** is for the e-mail addresses of any additional people you want this same message to go to. The next field, **Attchmnt,** can be used to attach another file to this message, so that file gets sent along too. You might have a report or other document, a spreadsheet, or even some software, that you want to send as well—you'd put the name for this file here. Finally, you get to the subject field. Here, you want to put a word or phrase that indicates what your message will be about.

Then you move to the message field and type in your message. When you've finished, you hit Control and **X,** as shown at the bottom of the screen, and your message will be sent zipping through cyberspace to the right person's mailbox.

When the message gets to that person, your e-mail address will be at the top of it, along with the date and time you send it, and the subject line. Still, if the recipient of the message doesn't know you well or might not recognize your e-mail address, you should sign your message before you send it. Some

FIGURE 4–2

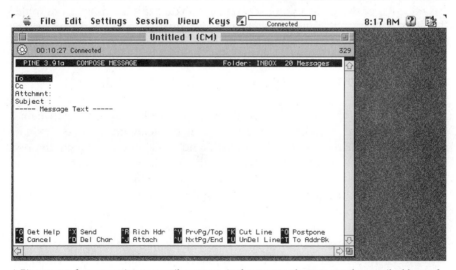

A Pine screen for composing an e-mail message. At the top are places to put the e-mail address of the person you are sending the message to; the e-mail addresses of others who should also see the message (Cc); the file name of a text document or other file you are sending along with the e-mail; and the subject of the message.

people create and save elaborate signature files with their names, addresses, telephone numbers, and with quotations they like, or with pictures they create using keyboard characters they can type in. Each time they send an e-mail, this file is automatically attached to the end of the message. You don't have to do this; you can simply sign your messages.

MORE ABOUT MAIL

When you receive an e-mail message, you can read it and/or save it, print it out, forward it to someone else, reply to it, or delete it. The commands for doing each of these will show up on the screen at the bottom. With Pine, if you are saving the message, it will automatically go into a folder called Saved Messages unless you tell the computer to save it somewhere else. It may make sense for you to create folders for messages on different subjects. For instance, if you cover the health beat and are getting messages about various health and medical subjects, you may want to create folders for, say, HMOs, cancer treatment, child-hood diseases, and AIDS. That way, when you're looking for information on one subject, you won't have to go through all the messages to find it.

To create a folder, choose a message you want to save and hit **S.** You'll see a message on the bottom of your screen asking you what folder you want it saved into. Type a name for your new folder and hit the return key.

The program will tell you no such folder exists and ask if you want to create it. Type **Y** for yes; the new folder will be created and the message saved into it. To see a list of the folders you use, type in **L.** You can then move from folder to folder reading and saving and deleting messages.

SO MANY ADDRESSES, SO LITTLE TIME

Another useful feature of Pine is the Address Book. You can keep e-mail addresses you use often here, listed by a name or nickname, such as Kevin or JJ. When you type the nickname into the **To** field of a message screen, the person's entire e-mail address will be placed in the field. This saves you from having to remember many addresses and from having to type in long ones.

The reply feature of the e-mail program can also save you time. If you read a message and want to reply immediately, you tell the program by typing **R** while you are still looking at the message. It will ask you if you want to include the original message in your reply. Then it will display a new message screen, complete with e-mail address already in place. You might want to include the original message if it has been awhile since the person sent it and he or she might not remember exactly what he or she asked or said.

You can also reply within the original message. For example, if you get a message from a fellow newspaper editor asking three or four questions about how you decide what letters to the editors get printed in your newspaper, you might choose the Reply option. Then, within the message that editor sent, you can type your replies under each question.

EUDORA

If you have a SLIP/PPP Internet connection, you can use a graphical program such as Eudora, rather than a character-based one.

In other chapters of the book, you'll see examples of how to use other Internet resources using character-based programs like Pine; in Chapter 8, on the World Wide Web, you'll see a graphical option to those programs. If you understand how the resources work and how journalists use them, you'll be able to work with whichever type of program is available to you.

To start up with Eudora, you log on with your password, as you do with Pine. You'll have to wait a few moments while your e-mail is downloaded from the host computer. Then you'll get a screen like the one in Figure 4-3, displaying a list of your e-mail messages with the name of the person who sent the message, the time and date, the size of the message in bytes, and the subject line.

There are no onscreen commands at the bottom of your screen as there are with Pine. Instead, you use pull-down menus (which also show you some keyboard commands you can use) and your mouse. To read a message, for example, just double-click on the subject line.

To compose a message, go to the Message menu and choose *New.* You'll be presented with a message screen like the one in Figure 4-4. Your e-mail

FIGURE 4-3

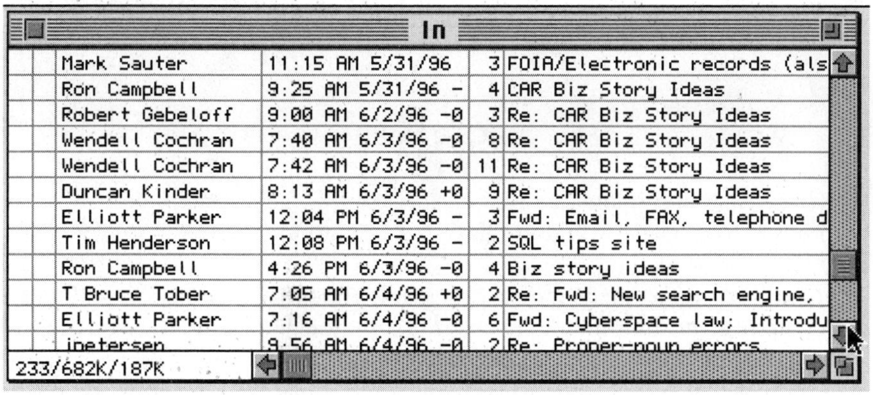

	In			
Mark Sauter	11:15 AM 5/31/96	3	FOIA/Electronic records (als
Ron Campbell	9:25 AM 5/31/96 -	4	CAR Biz Story Ideas
Robert Gebeloff	9:00 AM 6/2/96 -0	3	Re: CAR Biz Story Ideas
Wendell Cochran	7:40 AM 6/3/96 -0	8	Re: CAR Biz Story Ideas
Wendell Cochran	7:42 AM 6/3/96 -0	11	Re: CAR Biz Story Ideas
Duncan Kinder	8:13 AM 6/3/96 +0	9	Re: CAR Biz Story Ideas
Elliott Parker	12:04 PM 6/3/96 -	3	Fwd: Email, FAX, telephone d
Tim Henderson	12:08 PM 6/3/96 -	2	SQL tips site
Ron Campbell	4:26 PM 6/3/96 -0	4	Biz story ideas
T Bruce Tober	7:05 AM 6/4/96 +0	2	Re: Fwd: New search engine,
Elliott Parker	7:16 AM 6/4/96 -0	6	Fwd: Cyberspace law; Introdu
inetersen	9:56 AM 6/4/96 -0	2	Re: Proper-noun errors

233/682K/187K

A list of e-mail messages displayed with the Eudora e-mail program.

SOURCE: ©1997 QUALCOMM Incorporated. All rights reserved. Eudora Pro™ is a trademark of QUALCOMM Incorporated.

FIGURE 4–4

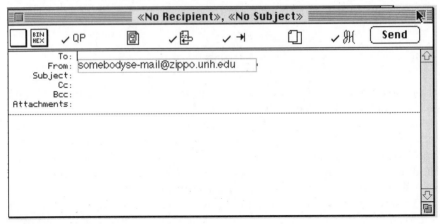

A Eudora screen for composing an e-mail message.

address will appear at the top in the **From** line. As with Pine, you'll see places to type in the address of the person you're writing to **(To)**, addresses of others you also want the message to go to **(Cc and Bcc)**, names of other files to attach to the message **(Attachments)**, and a **Subject** line. You type your message in the blank field below this header.

When you are done, click on the *Send* button at the top right of your screen to send the message immediately. You can also wait until you have a bunch of messages ready to go, then send them all at once.

The Message menu also offers you options for replying to a message, forwarding one, and deleting one.

NICKNAMES

Pine has the Address Book; Eudora has nicknames. The principle is the same; both offer shortcuts so you don't have to remember or type in a long address each time you send a message.

In Eudora, go to the Window menu and choose *Nicknames.* You'll get a screen with a *New* button in it; click on that button and you'll be asked to type in the nickname. Then go back to the first screen, where you can type in the e-mail address that goes with the nickname. (See Figure 4-5.) The next time you want to send a message to one of the folks you've nicknamed, just type the nickname into the **To** field. When Eudora sends your message, it will add the entire e-mail address to that field.

FIGURE 4–5

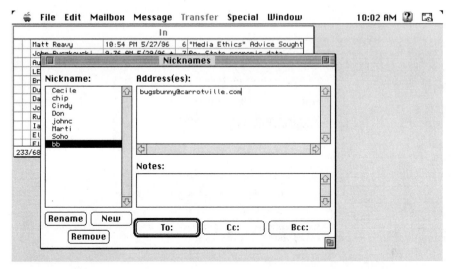

A Eudora Nicknames file.

SOURCE: ©1997 QUALCOMM Incorporated. All rights reserved. Eudora Pro™ is a trademark of QUALCOMM Incorporated.

MORE THAN ONE MAILBOX

With Pine you could save messages in various folders. In Eudora, you can create different mailboxes to hold messages, and save those mailboxes in different folders. So you might have a folder for computer-assisted reporting, in which you have mailboxes for software, hardware, sports stories, and business stories, for example. It's a way to file messages so you can find what you want more easily.

Go to the Window menu and choose *Mailboxes.* You'll get a screen with a button labeled *New.* Click on that and you'll get a box where you can type in a name for the mailbox; you'll also see a button to use for creating a new folder instead of a mailbox. (See Figure 4-6.) When you've typed the name, click on *OK.* You'll be returned to the first mailbox screen, and the name of your new mailbox (or folder) will appear there. You'll also see buttons you can use to move mailboxes or folders around or rename items.

SEARCHING FOR THE RIGHT ANSWER

As the many messages you receive start to pile up in your electronic mailbox, it gets harder to quickly find the one you want. Eudora offers help: You can

FIGURE 4–6

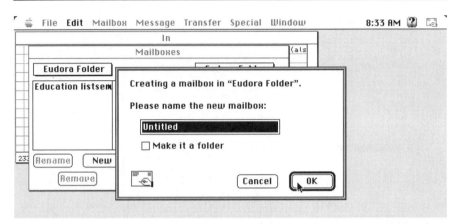

The onscreen prompt you'll see when you create a mailbox or folder in Eudora. You can use mailboxes and folders to sort and store your e-mail messages.

SOURCE: *©1997 QUALCOMM Incorporated. All rights reserved. Eudora Pro™ is a trademark of QUALCOMM Incorporated.*

search through the full text of all your stored mail messages to find ones matching keywords you select. Just go to the Edit menu and choose *Find.* You'll get a window where you can type in a word or words you want Eudora to search for. Hit your return button and Eudora will find messages including those words and display them.

No matter which program you use, you can send e-mail anywhere in the world to anyone who has an electronic mailbox. But what if you need to find a

Warning!

Sometimes your e-mail messages won't go through. This can happen because there's a glitch in the network or a person's e-mail address has changed. It can also happen because you typed the address incorrectly. The computer can't send a message to the address you meant to type in, only to the one you actually typed in. If you keep getting a message returned, make sure the address is OK and try sending it again.

If you don't get a reply to an e-mail message within a day or two, it might be because the person you e-mailed doesn't check his or her e-mail regularly or is on vacation. A problem with a host computer, computer connection, or e-mail program can also interrupt e-mail service. Try again.

certain someone, or several experts on a particular subject? You can track those people down using e-mail and two online resources, ProfNet and mailing lists.

PROFNET—WHEN YOU NEED AN EXPERT

ProfNet, the online Professors Network, sends journalists' questions to public information officers at colleges, universities, medical centers, national laboratories, nonprofit organizations, corporations, and government agencies around the world. According to the users guide put together by ProfNet systems operator Dan Forbush, 2,700 public information officers at 1,400 institutions (including 720 colleges and universities) were involved in the network as of February 1997; through these officers journalists can reach thousands of people around the world. A journalist doing research on a subject can send a query to ProfNet seeking experts in the subject. ProfNet finds them, and there's no charge for journalists to use the service.

Student journalists can use ProfNet too, says Forbush—but only if they are working on stories for their student newspapers or other publications. They cannot use the service for work on class projects.

You send an e-mail message, a query, to the ProfNet e-mail address, profnet@vyne.com. Your message should state which news organization you are with, what your project or story is about, what kind of expertise you need, and how quickly you need the help.

You might not get help immediately; ProfNet distributes collections of queries twice each day, so it can take a day or so to get a reply. But you will get results fairly quickly, and this is an easy way to find people who know what they're talking about and to get away from "the usual suspects" you might be used to interviewing.

Of course, there's no guarantee that you are always going to get useful replies. Sometimes you'll get more help than you imagined you could; sometimes you might not find experts who are exactly on the mark. But it's worth taking a few minutes to compose a query and send it off.

ProfNet even offers a way to deal with queries that might compromise your story if a competing news organization learned about them. You can call ProfNet and work with the staff to develop a way to "cloak" your query, says Forbush in his users guide. (The guide is available online at http://time.vyne.com/profnet/profsearchguide.html. No, this isn't an e-mail address. See the World Wide Web, Chapter 8.) There's also a form at the Web site that you can fill in and send, rather than having to compose a query with your e-mail program.

What institutions is your query going to? According to the guide, they include Stanford University, the Massachusetts Institute of Technology, and the University of Chicago; medical centers including those at Vanderbilt University and the University of Utah; schools of business and public policy including Harvard's John F. Kennedy School of Government; federal organizations including the National Science Foundation and the Smithsonian Institution; corporate research labs including IBM's Thomas J. Watson Rsearch Center; and scientific and educational organizations including the American Astronomical Society and the National Association of Independent Colleges and Universities.

(ProfNet also offers, at http://time.vyne.com/profnet/ped/eg.acgi on the World Wide Web, an Experts Database with biographical and contact information for more than 2,000 experts, at colleges and universities, who specialize in all sorts of subjects. You can search the database using keywords.)

MAILING LISTS—HOT DEBATES, HELP, AND JUNK MAIL

If you love getting mail, even the junk, mailing lists—also called listservs—are for you. Mailing lists are online discussion groups organized around a particular subject. You subscribe by sending an e-mail message to the computer that runs the discussion group. After that, you receive all messages that other subscribers post to the newsgroup, in your e-mail mailbox, and you can do with them just what you do with e-mail: save, delete, read, print out, and reply. You can send a reply to the e-mail box of the particular person who posted a message, or you can post a message to the mailing list so all subscribers receive it.

By "listening in" on discussions in a particular mailing list, you can get ideas for stories or find sources to interview. And you can post questions of your own and gather information for stories.

SUBSCRIBING

All mailing lists have official electronic addresses. Lists also have administrators who are charged with keeping mail address records updated. Some lists are "moderated," meaning that all messages go to a someone who decides which messages get posted on the list and which don't. Other lists are maintained by a computer program. You send a message to the address, and it is processed by the program. You have to send message in a special format for that to work (more on this shortly). While most lists are public, some are private and require you to get the permission of the list's administrator to subscribe.

One of the most common mailing list programs is Listserv; generally the computer running the program is known as the listserv, for list server, and often Internet users call the lists themselves listservs, or discussion lists.

Other programs you'll encounter include ListProcessor (you'll see an address that begins with *listproc*) and Majordomo (an address that begins with *majordomo*). The commands for all three are similar. When you subscribe to one, you'll receive a welcome message explaining the commands for that list or explaining how to get a message detailing the commands.

The messages will look like any other e-mail message you might receive.

CAR in action

Stephen Buttry, staff writer for the *Omaha World-Herald*, uses ProfNet and listservs often for finding sources and interviewing. For stories on health care markets and on the Union Pacific Railroad, one of his state's biggest employers, Buttry sent queries to ProfNet seeking experts and located several sources for each story. He often uses the listserv run by Investigative Reporters and Editors, called IRE-L, and the National Institute for Computer-Assisted Reporting listserv, NICAR-L, to get ideas and sources from colleagues. When the *World-Herald's* military reporter was working on a story about electronic reconnaissance planes, he had trouble getting Air Force spokespeople to talk freely. So Buttry posted a request for help on IRE-L and got names of other sources the reporter ended up using for the story.

Buttry ran into trouble when he tried to get information about a privately owned cement company, so he again sought help on IRE-L. A journalist wrote back with several suggestions and told Buttry that the state of Kansas requires more information than other states (including Nebraska) in its corporate reports. The company was headquartered in Kansas, so Buttry was able to get data about total liabilities and net worth of the company—information he hadn't been able to get before.

USING MAILING LISTS

Pay attention to this part, because if you don't, you're likely to get flamed, which means someone will write an angry message to you for not knowing what you're doing.

You subscribe to a mailing list and send a message to the mailing list in the same way—by sending an e-mail message. But the address for subscribing is different from the address for posting a message to other list subscribers.

For example, to subscribe to the Student Electronic Newspaper Mailing List, you'll send an e-mail message to this address:

`listserv@vm.temple.edu`

But if you want to send a message to all other subscribers on the list, you send your message to this address:

`STUEPAP@vm.temple.edu`

To subscribe to listservs, you send the message to the correct address—the listserv address—and in the message area type this:

`Subscribe STUEPAP your name`

You should use your real name, not your user ID; the listserv will pick up your electronic mailing address, complete with ID, from the header of the message you send. So your message will look like this one, with your name in it:

`Subscribe STUEPAP Lisa Miller`

. You must type the messages correctly. Remember, Listserv is a program, not a person, so it can handle only the messages it's programmed to deal with.

To unsubscribe, send a message to the same address you used to subscribe, with "unsubscribe" and the name of the list in the message area.

NETIQUETTE

When you are sending e-mail, keep a few rules of netiquette in mind:

- DON'T SEND A MESSAGE IN ALL CAPS. This indicates that you are screaming at whomever you send the message to. The people who get your message can't see your face or hear the tone of your voice. The only way they can tell your mood is by looking at the way you've typed and phrased your message. If you are sending a joke or are gently making fun, be sure someone reading your message would understand that.
- If you are a reporter working on a story, identify yourself that way when you post to the newsgroup or mailing list, or send a private e-mail message. Otherwise, you are deceiving by omission.
- Be concise. Some people are paying for the time it takes to read their mail, so make your messages clear and as brief as possible.

A Mailing List Tip

People who subscribe to mailing lists often get many messages each day, and they may go through the list of subject lines and delete messages that don't look interesting or important without reading the messages. So what you type into the subject line of your message is important. Don't be too general; try to think of a phrase that is specific and interesting. If you are looking for help, use the word "help" in your subject so people will know you need them.

■ When you reply to other people's messages, it probably makes sense to include parts of their messages in yours, so they will understand what you are writing about. If they don't get back to their mail right away, they might have forgotten the message you're replying to.

YOUR MAILBOX RUNNETH OVER

When you start out on the Internet, it's tempting to subscribe to lots of mailing lists just to see what's out there. And there's nothing wrong with this except if you leave your computer on Friday afternoon and don't check your e-mail until Monday morning, you'll find you've got hundreds of messages to wade through. There are ways to avoid this. You can unsubscribe to a mailing list easily, by sending a message:

```
unsubscribe STUEPAP
```

You can often stop mail temporarily:

```
set STUEPAP nomail
```

Then you can start things up again:

```
set STUEPAP mail
```

Smileys

Because it's difficult to convey tone of voice via e-mail, some people use a shorthand language—"faces" called smileys—to let the recipients of their messages know their mood or their intended tone. You have to turn your head sideways to see the smileys.

Here are a few from the *Unofficial Smileys Dictionary,* part of the *Electronic Frontier Foundation's (Extended) Guide to the Internet* by Adam Gaffin:

:)	Writer grinning.
;-)	Writer winking.
:-(	Writer frowning.
:-O	Writer surprised.
:-I	Writer showing indifference.
>:->	Writer making devilish remark.

With many mailing lists, you can get digests or collections of messages, rather than receiving each message individually; the welcome message you receive when you subscribe will detail how. You can decide what works best for you, and you will find out quickly which mailing lists are the most useful.

CAR in action

Why were there so few women executives in the California computer industry?

Ilana DeBare, staff writer for the *Sacramento Bee,* decided to find out. For her series of stories, "Women in the Computing Industry," she used various Internet resources. She posted messages on several listservs, including one for expectant mothers, and sent a query to ProfNet to find experts who'd studied computers in the workplace. She also used discussion groups on America Online and Compuserve.

She says these resources gave her "an ability to cast a wide net very quickly, in a much broader geographical range and demographic range than I would normally reach—posting a query on a nationwide discussion group of romance writers, for instance! It was a quick way to get a whole lot of responses."

DeBare also employed some "old-fashioned" reporting methods, conducting in-person interviews, calling government agencies for employment and education information, and even spending some time at a video arcade. And she didn't connect with sources contacted online solely through e-mail. She says that when she interviews someone by e-mail, she misses "voice cues that give me some sort of feeling for who they are."

"It is also much easier to miss having your questions answered when you're doing e-mail," adds DeBare. "What I mean is, you type something, and they type back some long monologue that isn't really to the point, but you can't step in spontaneously and say, 'No, no, what I meant was . . .' or 'wow, tell me more about that little episode' the way you would in a voice conversation."

She also says interview subjects are less spontaneous by e-mail. "You miss the emotion, the colloquialisms and human speech patterns, the stumbles or emphases."

Another reason DeBare conducted research for her series offline was that she recognized that the e-mail responses she got to her online queries came from people who had strong opinions about her subject and from people who had access to computers and knew how to use them—not necessarily a group that represented a cross-section of society at large.

SPECIAL INTERESTS

Whatever subject you can think of, there's a mailing list for it. The many journalism lists include those run by the National Institute for Computer-Assisted Reporting, Investigative Reporters and Editors, the Society of Professional Journalists, and the National Press Photographers Association. On a given day you might find a reporter on the NICAR list asking other journalists where he can find census data or information on a certain corporation.

On the NPPA list, you might see a debate about whether it's ethical to take photographs of someone in suffering rather than helping them. There's also a computer-assisted reporting list called CARR-L, where you can get tips on online resources, and that student media list called STUMEDIA (see Listserv box). One recent topic of discussion involved how much reporters should change quotes, if a person they interview speaks in poor or ungrammatical English. Reponses ranged from "Never, ever change quotes!" to "I almost always fix grammar in quotes, so the quotes will be clear to the reader."

There are also mailing lists dealing with hundreds of subjects besides journalism. If you were doing a story on Parkinson's disease or on eating disorders, you might subscribe to lists where those subjects are discussed to gather information and contact sources. Other lists discuss business, computers, education, the environment, medicine, law, politics and more. And there are light-hearted ones, such as BEACHES-L, where you'll find comments on the best beaches around and the level of sunscreen protection you might need wherever you go.

FINDING LISTSERVS

One way to find listservs is to get on one of the journalism lists and ask. But you can also send an e-mail message or search in various ways on the Internet to find lists.

CAR in action

A reporter in Lithuania posted a message to the CARR-L list saying that the first McDonald's restaurant was opening in his country and that he needed to find information online about the company and any lawsuits that might have been filed against it.

A journalist in the United States suggested a World Wide Web site he might try, the EDGAR site run by the Securities and Exchange Commission. That site includes all sorts of financial information about public companies.

Some journalism mailing lists:

CARR-L, a list for discussing computer-assisted research and reporting
`listserv@ulkyvm.louisville.edu`

STUMEDIA, the Student Media List, for high school and college students
`listserv@uabdpo.dpo.uab.edu`

STUEPAP, the Student Electronic Newspaper Mailing List, to discuss
publishing student newspapers online
`listserv@vm.temple.edu`

COPYEDITING-L, a list for copy editors
`listproc@cornell.edu`

IRE-L, a list of Investigative Reporters and Editors
`listproc@lists.missouri.edu`

NICAR-L, a list of the National Institute for Computer-Assisted Reporting
`listproc@lists.missouri.edu`

FOI-L, a list for persons interested in freedom of information issues,
the First Amendment and the public's right to know. It is a project of
the National Freedom of Information Coalition, located at Syracuse
University and managed by Barbara Fought.
`listserv@listserv.syr.edu`

NPPA-L, discussion group for the National Press Photographers
Association.
`listserv@cmuvm.csv.cmich.edu`

SPJ-L, a list for the Society of Professional Journalists
`listserv@psuvm.psu.edu`

To get a list of lists, send a message to any listserv with this message:

```
list global
```

But beware—this will be a long list, so you may not want to hang onto it
very long after you've looked at it. You can narrow your search by entering a
keyword:

```
list global/sports
```

You can go to an anonymous FTP site to search for lists of lists. (See FTP, Chapter 6.) And there are sites on the World Wide Web where you can search databases to find lists on a particular topic, such as the Liszt site (http://www.liszt.com) and the tile.net site (http://www.tile.net). You can also search these sites for Usenet newsgroups (newsgroups, Chapter 5), and you can search tile.net for FTP sites (FTP, Chapter 6).

INTERVIEWING BY E-MAIL

If you locate a source through a mailing list or ProfNet, there's nothing wrong with conducting interviews by e-mail, just as there's nothing wrong with conducting interviews by telephone. But if you're not sitting face to face with your interviewee, you'll miss some things. You can't see the person's expressions, body language, and mannerisms, and you won't get any clues from his or her surroundings. With e-mail, you'll also miss tone of voice and the way a person speaks.

For these reasons, e-mail interviews may not always be the best way to go. You'll have to decide whether you can get all the information you need via e-mail. A mix of e-mail and in-person interviews may be called for. Writing a profile about a person without doing a face-to-face interview will be difficult, and you may not get much of a story.

For some stories, of course, e-mail interviews are appropriate. Stephen Buttry of the *Omaha World-Herald* conducted most of his interviews by e-mail when working on a story about Nebraskans on the World Wide Web. But he also called some of his sources to actually talk to them. E-mail, he says, was an excellent resource for finding people for the story, but when he called a third-grade teacher at a small school whose class had created its own Web page, he could "catch her excitement about using the computer with her kids." That excitement, he says, can't come through as well over e-mail.

Also, keep in mind that the people you can reach through mailing lists or straight e-mail aren't all the people who might be interested in or affected by the topic you are talking about. You are reaching people who have and use computers and an Internet or online connection—and that's not everyone; you are reaching people who have enough interest in your topic to have subscribed to a discussion group about it—and that's not everybody. If you send out an e-mail questionnaire, you'll probably find that the people most likely to reply with it are those who have strong opinions on the subject—and that's not everybody. Ilana DeBare of the *Sacramento Bee* says that because of these limitations, she combined "old-fashioned" reporting with the online work she did for her series about women in computing. (See CAR in Action, page 64.)

VIRTUAL QUOTES

Should you tell readers when quotes come from an e-mail interview? If it's pertinent to the story, if readers need to know this to understand the context of the quotes or to understand where the story comes from, then the answer is yes.

You certainly are likely to get more reasoned responses with e-mail than with an in-person or telephone interview, since the person responding can sit and think about his or her words, type them, and look at them and revise before sending them to you.

Stephen Miller, assistant to the technology editor at the *New York Times,* says, "As with most questions like this, the answer depends on the circumstances. With any new technology, it is usually a policy in the beginning to indicate how the information was obtained. Newspapers used to indicate if an interview was done by telephone. You rarely see that anymore. We rarely say that an interview was done by e-mail anymore.

"I think that you should only say that the interview was done via email when it's pertinent to the story. For example, I did a story about the reaction on the internet to the Oklahoma City bombing. It was important to the story to say when an interview was done via e-mail because the point of the story was reaction in cyberspace. I did, in fact, a number of telephone interviews, and I mentioned that in the story because it was also pertinent."

As for quotes in e-mail being different from quotes gotten during a telephone or in-person interview, Miller says he doesn't think this matters.

"If you've done your research, and have your own facts straight, no amount of preparation by the subject will alter those facts. 'Mr. Mayor, we have information that a major campaign contributor got a lucrative city contract without bidding for it?' Whether you ask that question by e-mail, telephone, in person or by carrier pigeon, the answer is pretty much yes or no."

WHO'S ON THE OTHER COMPUTER?

Suppose you get a telephone call from a source who tells you he or she is an expert in some field or an eyewitness to something. This source offers you information about an issue or event. Are you going to take that information and write a story without contacting any other sources?

Of course not. You're going to do other reporting; if you have reason to wonder if the person is who he or she says, you will ask if other sources have heard of the person. You probably got a telephone number from the caller, too, so you can call back and verify that the call was on the up and up.

You should treat e-mail messages in the same way. If you get a tip from someone by e-mail, check it out with other sources and try to verify whether the person is who he or she says. You don't have to telephone every source you reach by e-mail, but use common sense. Is it someone whose name shows up on mailing lists you monitor, so you're pretty sure of who he or she is? Does the person's e-mail address indicate he or she works for a university or a government agency, as he or she says? And does what he or she say jibe with what other sources say? You may want to ask the person some more questions by e-mail, try to get to

A Question of Ethics

If you are going to conduct interviews by e-mail, do all you can to make sure the person on the other end of the computer connection knows you are a reporter working on a story. Make this clear before you ask a source questions over the Internet, just as you would for a regular interview.

This is easy to forget if you get caught up in a debate on a mailing list—or on a newsgroup message board or a chat line, two other Internet resources for finding and "talking" with people. It's also easy for other people to forget you're a reporter. If you identify yourself once as a journalist during an online debate but never do it again as you follow the debate through many strings of messages, you may unintentionally be deceiving the debaters. Make sure it's clear all the time that you are a reporter. If you decide to use comments made during an ongoing debate, make sure the person who made the comments knows who you are and what you are doing.

Often, you're not going to simply quote from a mailing list or newsgroup message anyway. Why not contact the person yourself and ask questions? Then there will be no misunderstanding, and you'll get fresh information and quotes.

Electronic mail and mailing lists are tools to reach people. But there are real people at the other end of those messages you find in your e-mail box every day. Treat them just the way you treated the city councilor you talked to after the meeting last night or the fire victim you interviewed at the hospital, with the same honesty, compassion, and healthy skepticism.

an online directory for the place where the person supposedly works, or phone the person.

Don't be extraordinarily suspicious of e-mail contacts; just be as cautious as you would be with any new source of information.

Chapter 5

EVERYBODY'S TALKING: USENET NEWSGROUPS AND INTERNET RELAY CHAT

After the U.S. House of Representatives voted to repeal a ban on assault-style weapons in March 1996, three people hotly debated the issue across cyberspace. One said that during a hearing the member of Congress sponsoring the repeal had displayed "uncontrollable rage," perhaps demonstrating why stricter gun control was a good thing. A second person disputed this, saying it was a congressman testifying against the repeal who had gone on an "infantile tirade." And a third person stated that he couldn't understand why the vote upset anybody; he didn't see any problem with repealing the ban.

At the same time, people who were cities or states or countries apart were consulting one another on all sorts of subjects: Why the Federal Aviation Administration had ordered airlines to check picture IDs of people holding plane tickets; whether it was legal to listen in on cordless telephone conversations; how easy it would be to sue a neighbor because he refused to remove the branches of a tree hanging over someone else's yard; equipment for blind ham radio operators; how people with chronic fatigue syndrome could get the most help from their doctors; how best to view Comet Hyakutake during the next few nights.

All these people could "talk" to one another because they were on the Internet, communicating through Usenet newsgroups.

With Usenet, you can ride a cyberspace bus full of thousands of people and listen in on such conversations, find people to interview for stories, and gather information on thousands of subjects. Sometimes the conversations are silly; sometimes they turn ugly. Bill Loving, computer-assisted reporting editor for the *Minneapolis Star Tribune,* says the discussions often seem like a cross between talk radio and barroom arguments.

But he also says newsgroups are good resources for finding people and learning what folks and issues and problems and solutions are firing them up. Most often, you'll find the conversations you can drop into will be starting points for a story or for interviews.

WHAT IS USENET?

Usenet is a collection of thousands of discussion groups, all organized around particular topics. As with online mailing lists, you subscribe to newsgroups so you can listen in and join the conversations. But you use a newsreader program, not your e-mail program, to do this. And you don't get hundreds of messages in your e-mail box once you've subscribed. Instead, you use the newsreader program to call up whichever conversation you want to check out; then you can switch to another discussion group or quit the program.

Think of a subject, and it's a pretty safe bet that some newsgroup discusses it. Some newsgroups deal with serious topics, such as epilepsy (alt.support.epilepsy) or computer security problems (comp.security.misc) or freedom of information (alt.freedom.of.information.act) or the environment (sci.environment) Then there are others that discuss less weighty subjects, such as alt.sports.football.pro.chicago-bears or alt.food.mcdonalds.

HOW THE NEWS GETS AROUND

When you work with Usenet newsgroups, you're again using client/server programs. Your newsreader program is the client, going after the messages, called articles, that you want to read in a particular newsgroup. You choose which newsgroups you want to read by subscribing, using the newsreader program. You can unsubscribe at any time, too.

When you subscribe to a newsgroup, your newsreader program adds it to a list it keeps of groups you subscribe to. The articles posted to those newsgroups don't come to your e-mailbox; they go to a computer called a news server that's part of the network your host computer is connected to.

There are news servers around the world linked to the Internet. Each day, these computers exchange the articles that have been posted to various newsgroups, enabling you and other Usenet users to read them no matter where the articles originated.

When you start up your newsreader client program, that program retrieves, from the news server, articles posted to the newsgroups you subscribe to. You can then read them or save them or reply to them.

Each computer network with a news server has a news administrator who decides how long articles get stored on the server before they are tossed out. Some newsgroups are very active, and hundreds of articles are posted to them each day, so they can't all be saved forever.

WHAT'S IN A NAME?

Different types of newsgroups are arranged in categories called hierarchies. Each hierarchy is concerned with a particular subject area or type of discussion group, and the name of a newsgroup tells you which hierarchy it belongs to and tells you something about the group. Mailing lists carry names like CARR-L or BEACHES-L, but newsgroups carry names with two or more parts separated by periods, such alt.movies.silent or rec.music.phish. The first part of a newsgroup name tells what hierarchy the group belongs in; the rest describes subcategories that exist within that hierarchy.

Some common hierarchies include the following:

alt	alternative groups, various topics
biz	business, marketing
comp	computers
misc	matters that don't fit into any other category
news	about Usenet
rec	hobbies, games, and recreation
sci	science
soc	social groups
talk	discussion about politics and various issues

You may not have access to all the existing newsgroups; your host computer system's news administrator decides what groups will be available on that system. There are strict procedures for setting up a mainstream newsgroup, including a vote by newsgroup users. But anyone can set up an alternative, or **alt** group, without following such procedure. So alt groups are often seen as less formal and less official, and sometimes news administrators decide not to make some alt groups available on their systems.

As with mailing lists, some newsgroups are moderated; a moderator decides which messages get posted to the group and which do not. And some newsgroups post messages in digest form.

You'll also discover groups in the **clari** hierarchy, with names such as such as clari.biz.industry and clari.news.crime. These groups are offered by a private company, ClariNet Communications Corporation, and they provide actual news and feature stories from organizations such as Reuters and the Associated Press. An organization must pay to carry these newsgroups on its network, but if you have access to them, it won't cost you anything to read the articles.

GETTING IN ON THE TALK

To get into Usenet, you'll use whatever newsreader program your host computer runs. The one you'll look at in this chapter is a program for shell account users called "rn." There are others, including "nn," "trn" and "tin," and you can use graphical programs such as the World Wide Web browser Netscape for reading Usenet. (See Chapter 8.)

To start up rn, you simply type in the program's name at your computer prompt:

```
rn
```

What you'll get next is a list of newsgroups you are subscribed to, if any, and a count of how many messages there are in the group.

You subscribe through your newsreader program by typing **g** and the name of the group:

```
g alt.support.epilepsy
```

After that, when you get into your newsreader program, you will be told how many messages are waiting in each group you subscribe to.

The list will look something like this:

```
unread news in news.announce.newusers     57 articles

unread news in rec.roller-coaster         12 articles

unread news in misc.kids.computer         24 articles
```

The program will also look to see if there are new groups you haven't subscribed to—it checks a file, .newsrc, that lists the groups you've subscribed to—and it will ask you if you want to subscribe to new ones:

```
Newsgroup rec.music.phish not in .newsrc--subscribe? ynYN
```

If you answer yes, you'll be asked where, in your .newsrc list, you want this group placed. Hit your return button, and the new group will be placed at the end of your list.

If you do not want to subscribe, type **n.** Sometimes there's a huge list of newsgroups here, so if you hit the shift key and **n** or **y**—the capital **N** or capital **Y**—you can take care of all of these in one fell swoop.

WHAT TO READ FIRST? WHAT TO READ NEXT?

After you've gone though this procedure, you'll be asked if you want to read articles in the first newsgroup you're subscribed to.

```
11 articles in news.announce.newuses--read now? ynq
```

If you type **n,** the newsreader program will move to the next newsgroup; if you choose **q,** you will be quitting rn. If you type **u,** you unsubscribe to the newsgroup.

If you type =, you'll get a listing of all articles, showing the subject headings, like this one from rec.roller-coaster:

```
26576 Re: Where to go coasting in Central Florida

26577 Re: CP Question (yes, another one!)

26578 Re: How do we get wimps to try coasters????

26579 Universal Studios Hollywood

26580 Re: The Case For Over-The-Shoulder Restraints

26581 The case against over-the-shoulder restraints

26582 Cedar Point Trip

26583 Re: rec.roller-coaster FAQ, part 3/3: lists and
statistics

26584 Re: The case against over-the-shoulder restraints

26585 Re: ACE recent mailing-Did I miss something????

26586 Mermaid Parade

26587 PGA Update (Batman?)

26588 Re: Cedar Point Trip

26589 Re: GA Scream Machine SFGad Got New Wheels!!
```

To read a particular article, you type in the number listed next to it. If you wanted to read about the Mermaid Parade coaster, you'd type in 26586.

Instead of requesting a directory, you can type in **y,** and you'll be presented with the first message or article in the group.

You can now read the articles one by one by continuing to type in **n.**

To save a message, type **s** and a name for the file you want it saved as. A copy of the article will be stored in your directory, as part of your account on your host computer.

WHATCHA READING?

The headers on newsgroup articles don't look exactly like the ones on e-mail messages. They look more like this one:

```
Article 145447 (123 more) in misc.consumers:
From: millhoo@haha.net
```

```
Newsgroups: misc.consumers, alt.privacy

Subject: Re: New FBI Access To Credit Files Raises Concern

Date: 24 Mar 1996 14:45:22 GMT

Organization: University of Myown

Lines: 10

NNTP-Posting-Host: annex-p11.tdi.net

Mime-Version:
```

Some rn Commands

=	get a directory of the messages, showing the subject headings
y	read the messages starting with the first one
n	go to the next article in the newsgroup
^N	(control N) jump to the next article in the thread
k	kill all the articles in this thread, so you don't have to read them
c	mark all the articles in the newsgroup as read, so you don't have to deal with them
h	get onscreen help—this will show you additional rn commands
q	quit rn
s	filename-save the article—a copy will be placed in your home directory

CAR in action

When a reporter at the *New York Times* was researching how hospitals and insurance companies were forcing women to leave the hospital within 24 hours of giving birth, Usenet led the reporter to some sources.

Stephen Miller, assistant to the *Times*'s technology editor, discovered a newsgroup on parenting where several women were discussing their pregnancies. He posted a request for people the reporter could interview and got many useful responses. One woman even sent along documentation, including letters to her doctor and her lawyer, to go along with her story, says Miller.

```
1.0Content-Type: text/plain; charset=us-ascii

Content-Transfer-Encoding: 7bit

X-Mailer: Mozilla 1.22 (Windows; I; 16bit)
```

After the header comes the body of the article and perhaps a signature.

You don't have to pay attention to every line in the header, but some will help you figure out what's going on with an article. The From line will give you the e-mail address of the person posting the article. The Newsgroups line will tell you to which groups the article was posted—and maybe point you to some other pertinent newsgroups. The Subject line will help you decide if you even want to read this article. If the information in that line begins with Re: and then a subject, you know the article is a reply to an earlier posting about the subject. The Date line will tell you how old the posting is; that might be important, especially if the posting concerns an ongoing news event, and it's possible circumstancs have changed or new information has come to light since the article was posted.

JOINING THE CONVERSATIONS

You will probably use a newsgroup by posting a query or message asking people to contact you so you can interview them for a story.

To look for a newsgroup discussing a particular topic, start up rn and type in **l.** You'll receive a list of all the newsgroups offered by your computer network. The problem with this is the list will be very, very long, and it is organized alphabetically by hierarchy. Another way to find groups is to search using the **l** command. You choose a keyword that describes the topic you are investigating. If you were working on a story about gun control, you might start a search like this:

```
l guns
```

and you'd get back a list that could include rec.guns and talk.politics.guns.

If you needed to interview people about creating an amicable divorce, or about the effects of divorce on children, you could search this way:

```
l divorce
```

and get back the name of a group, alt.support.divorce.

If you were writing about how your state legislature was trying to pass a law making it difficult for anyone to get information about others using driver's license records, you might find that a keyword such as license won't work.

There are lots of types of licenses, so that category is too broad. "Drivers' licenses" might be too narrow to have a whole discussion group devoted to it. You'll have to experiment. You might think in terms of a broader issue your subject falls under. For this story, searching with the keyword "privacy" may bring results. With the search

```
l privacy
```

you'll find groups such as alt.privacy and comp.society.privacy.

There are other ways to find newsgroups. You can always post to a newsgroup or mailing list and ask about others if you're stuck. There are also many books out that list newsgroups and mailing lists. There also are sites on the World Wide Web where you can search databases to find newsgroups that discuss particular topics, such as the Liszt site (http://www.liszt.com) and the tile.net site (http://www.tile.net).

FINDERS KEEPERS

News filter services can help you find useful nuggets in the pile of articles posted to newsgroups each day. These software programs find articles containing keywords you designate and send them to your e-mailbox. You might choose keywords that relate to your beat, or you might ask the program to watch for the name of your city or state in messages.

One such service, called SIFT (Stanford Information Filtering Tool) is offered free by Stanford University in partnership with InReference, Inc. You can find it on the World Wide Web at http://www.reference.com.

Before you start using a news filter, read any information provided online about the service so you'll know exactly what and how the program searches.

POSTING AN ARTICLE

To create a message and post it to a newsgroup with rn, you first quit the rn program, then type the following command at your host computer's prompt:

```
Pnews
```

This starts up a text editor program so you can compose a message, similar to what you do with your e-mail program. One common text editor is called Pico. With this program, you get several prompts to take you through the process. Fill in information if necessary and hit the return key to keep moving through the prompts.

First, you get asked which newsgroups you want to post to:

`Newsgroup(s):`

You'll see information about where your message is originating, and then you'll be asked how widely you want your article distributed:

```
Local organization: local

Organization: local

State: nh

Multi-State Area: ne

Country: usa

Continent: na

Everywhere:<null>(not "world")
```

`Distribution ():`

You can choose to send your article only to computers on your local network—or broaden the range. If you are asking for information about the American legal system, for example, it wouldn't make sense to send your query all over the world. You'd want distribution only in this country. You'd type in **usa.**

After you set the distribution area, you'll be asked for your subject line:

`Title/Subject:`

As with mailing list message subjects, you should put something specific and interesting and concise here, so your message gets noticed and read.

You'll then get a message that says the following:

```
This program posts news to machines throughout the organi-
zation. Your message will cost the net hundreds if not
thousands of dollars to send everywhere. Please be sure you
know what you are doing.

Are you absolutely sure that you want to do this? [n]
```

Probably the answer to this is **y,** or yes. And it isn't really going to cost thousands of dollars.

`Prepared file to include [none]`

Use this only if you have another computer file you want to attach to your message. If you do, type the file name in here.

Then you'll be asked if you want to send the message, edit the message, check spelling, or abort the message. You'll type in **s** to send, it'll wing its way through cyberspace, and you can sit back and wait for replies.

The newsgroup news.announce.newusers offers useful information for first-time newsgroupies.

MORE NETIQUETTE

Before you post a message to a mailing list or newsgroup, it's a good idea to hang around or "lurk" for a few days, so you get to see what sorts of topics are actually discussed by the subscribers. You're likely to get nothing but nasty replies if you send a message asking about something subscribers think is inappropriate for their list or group.

Some angry messages have come over a couple of the journalism mailing lists complaining about students' postings. If you send a message basically asking the list or newsgroup members to do your homework for you, you will probably get flamed. (Flames are articles or messages in which the writer says something critical about someone else.) This doesn't mean you shouldn't ask questions or offer your opinion. But think about what you are asking or saying before you send the message. Ask yourself: Is this a reasoned response? Is this a fair and clear question? Am I asking for a tip—or am I hoping someone else will do all my research?

In replying to a message or query, consider whether it makes sense to send a reply to all subscribers of the group, or just to the person who wrote the original message. Sometimes you should post to the whole list or group, because your message will be helpful to many. But you can also send an e-mail message to one person, using the electronic address you see on the original article.

TALKING BACK

You can also reply to messages on a certain subject or thread, rather than creating a new message on a new subject. If you type **f** or **F** while you're reading one article in a newsgroup, you'll get a document for typing in your follow-up article, with the header showing the subject line already filled in. If you use **F**, the document you're presented with will also include the article you are replying to.

If you want to send a message only to the author of the article you are reading, use **r** or **R** (**R** will put the original article in your message).

CAR in action

How much can you learn about a person just by reading his Usenet postings?

A lot.

Jonathan Gaw, staff writer at the *Minneapolis Star Tribune,* wrote a story about how easy it is to dig up information about individuals using the Internet. Someone was picked at random from Minneapolis-area Internet users and agreed to let the newspaper compile information about him. Gaw found that the man had posted about 75 messages on the Internet, many to newsgroups such as rec.food.drink.beer. From those messages, Gaw was able to learn what the man did for a living, where he worked, where he had gone to school, where he went to the theater, what beer he enjoyed most and that he liked humorist Garrison Keillor. And there was more.

"He has strong opinions about the quality, or lack thereof, of salad bars, wouldn't trade in his Macintosh for Bill Gates' fortune, feels that Indiana is a 'socially repressive state' and last fall vacationed in Paris and Rome," writes Gaw.

Messages to newsgroups and to some mailing lists are archived online, so people can search for past postings. That's a good thing for journalists to remember when they post messages.

The Internet offers various ways to gather information about individuals, including resources on the World Wide Web that search archives of Usenet messages for ones sent by a particular person. (See Chapter 8.) One such search tool is Deja News, at http://www.dejanews.com. With this tool, you can search for messages that mention a certain subject or for messages posted to newsgroups by a particular person.

JUST THE FAQs, MA'AM

One useful aspect of Usenet newsgroups is the existence of FAQs (pronounced fax), which are documents that offer answers to frequently asked questions. Actually, you'll find FAQs concerning various resources on the Internet, but Usenet FAQs give you information about specific newsgroups and about the subjects and issues and problems discussed on those newsgroups. Kenton Robinson, formerly a reporter for the *Hartford* (Conn.) *Courant,* often used newsgroup FAQs for background when working on features. "Sometimes I'd have a week to become an expert in something," he said during a panel at the CARROCK conference held by the National Institute for Computer-Assisted

A Question of Ethics

As with messages you send to a mailing list, if you post an article on a newsgroup seeking information and people's replies, don't forget to identify yourself as a reporter, and make sure anyone who answers your message understands you are working on a story. It's easy to slip into a conversation on the Internet, but you have to treat this as you would any other gathering where you might overhear information. If you were at a party and a bunch of people started running and screaming "Get that guy!" you would probably use that quote and not attribute it to anyone in particular. But you wouldn't have a lengthy conversation with someone, without telling him or her you are a reporter, and then identify and quote that person in a story.

If you see a comment in a newsgroup article and want to use it in a story, you've got to contact the writer, explain what you are doing, and ask permission. Often you'll want to contact the writer of the quote and ask that person some questions, instead of using a stale quote.

Reporting and Investigative Reporters and Editors in the fall of 1995. "The FAQs are a great way to do that."

For example, a FAQ for the sci.med.aids newsgroup starts out by explaining the group's mission:

```
Welcome to the sci.med.aids, the international newsgroup
on the Acquired Immune Deficiency Syndrome (see Q1.1 'What
is sci.med.aids?' for more details). This article, called
the sci.med.aids "FAQ", answers frequently asked questions
about AIDS and the sci.med.aids newsgroup. The FAQ is
posted monthly to sci.med.aids and related newsgroups. If
you are new to sci.med.aids, please read it before posting
articles or responses.
```

Later the FAQ lists the topics it covers, including the following:

```
Section 1. Introduction, General Information, and FAQ
Administrative Details

Q1.1 What is sci.med.aids?

Q1.2 Discussion topics.

Q1.3 Sci.med.aids distribution.

Q1.4 Periodical Postings on sci.med.aids (please
contribute)
```

Q1.5 Subscribing and unsubscribe to sci.med.aids.

Section 2. How to prevent infection.

Q2.1 How is AIDS transmitted?

Q2.2 How effective are condoms?

Q2.3 How do you minimize your odds of getting infected?

Q2.4 How risky is a blood transfusion?

Q2.5 Can mosquitoes or other insects transmit AIDS?

FAQS

One place you'll find FAQs is on the newsgroups themselves; often they're posted regularly along with other articles sent to the group. The newsgroup

---

CAR in action

Bob Sablatura, a reporter with the *Houston Chronicle,* says he often posts messages to newsgroups so he can track down sources or get other information. He sometimes "listens in" on discussions to find story ideas, but he's also had good luck getting information. When he needed the mailing address for Neil Armstrong, the former astronaut who once walked on the moon, he found traditional sources weren't helpful: "He's a very reclusive man now," says Sablatura. But Sablatura found a Usenet group that discussed space exploration, posted a message, and within minutes had responses from three people who sent him Armstrong's mailing address and, in one case, his telephone number.

When he was reporting on the Environmental Protection Agency's Superfund projects, Sablatura got stuck while trying to find the Bay Area Network in California. He posted a message to an environmental newsgroup and soon had his answer

Sablatura says there's still not enough good, solid information on the Internet. "It's kind of like prospecting for gold," he says. "You can find it out there on the Internet, but when you find it it's flakes, not a whole gold mine." But he believes more and more useful information will be placed online in the coming months and years, and that the Internet is a tool all reporters should know how to use.

news.answers offers FAQs and related information, so you can subscribe to that group to get FAQs. You can use anonymous FTP (see Chapter 6) to get FAQs, and you can search the World Wide Web (Chapter 8) to find them.

IRC—JUST CHATTING

Internet relay chat is another resource for contacting people. With IRC, you can "talk," in real time, with a virtual living room full of other people on the Internet at the same time you are. You type messages to them and they type back, and the communication is almost instantaneous. You can also just hang around and listen in. IRC works on the client/server model, with IRC servers around the world connected to each other. You tell your IRC client which chat discussion you want to join, and it makes the connection for you.

With IRC, there are different channels, rather than newsgroups, that you can join. Each channel has its own name, usually beginning with the # or pound sign, like this:

`#rockmusic`

Some channels are meant for discussion of certain subjects, such as #Windows 95; others are open to whatever comes up while participants are chatting away.

CHAT SESSIONS

If your computer network offers IRC, all you have to do to start up the program is type **irc** at the system prompt. If you don't have access that way, you may be able to get to a remote IRC client using an Internet tool called Telnet.

CAR in action

When the Alfred P. Murrah Federal Building in Oklahoma City was bombed on April 19, 1995, reporters monitored IRC channels including #oklahoma, where they could find out what people were saying about what they saw and felt and heard and about possible perpetrators.

(See Chapter 6.) Some sites that allow public access limit the number of IRC users allowed or the hours of use.

When you sign onto an IRC channel, you'll be asked to pick a nickname with up to nine characters. Chat participants show up on your computer screen as nicknames, not real names. What you'll see on your screen during a chat session will be these names and the remarks each participant makes during the session.

You may be automatically dumped into a particular chat channel, or you may get a blank screen when you start up the IRC client. Then you will need to specify a channel. To join a particular channel, use the join command and the channel name. IRC commands always begin with a slash mark:

`/join #rockmusic`

Once you've joined a channel, the remarks and actions of chat participants will scroll across your screen; at the bottom of the screen you'll type in your remarks or commands to change channels or list channels or some other action. (IRC is not case-sensitive.) The next to last line on the screen shows your status on the channel; for example it will tell you the name of the channel you're participating in.

WHAT'S ON THE SCREEN?

When someone types a remark, you'll see it on your screen like this:

`<Soho>I don't know exactly how to get to Boston from here.`

The word between brackets is the nickname of the "speaker," and the rest is what this person is saying to everyone else on the chat channel.

You type your messages in the bottom line on the screen. The message you type in won't show a nickname in front of it when it shows up on your screen.

You may also see information messages like this one announcing that someone else has joined the chat channel, preceeded by ***.

`***Moonman has joined channel #rockmusic.`

And you will see lines describing actions of the "speakers," like this one:

`*Soho shakes his fist.`

Some IRC commands

The commands you use will be preceeded by a /:

/quit	to quit IRC
/help	to get help
/help newuser	
/list	to get a list of IRC channels
/list #rock music	to get information about a channel
/join	to join the conversation
/leave	leave this channel

You can also have a private conversation with just one person on the channel. Type in the command /**msg,** the person's nickname, and the message you want him or her to get:

`/msg Soho This is the message I want delivered privately.`

You'll still see all the other chat on the screen, but your message will go only to Soho.

FINDING THE RIGHT CHANNEL

You can find lists of channels through anonymous FTP (see Chapter 6) or by subscribing to the newsgroup alt.irc.

Chat is fun and can bring you into contact with useful sources, but you'll find a lot of gossip on the channels; you'll find gossip on Usenet too, of course. You should verify information you get from people through IRC or Usenet just as you would information or tips you got via telephone or through an in-person interview.

There are other disadvantages to IRC. People work under nicknames, and sometimes conversations are full of junk and hard to follow, especially if much of what you see on the screen is messages indicating that various people are joining and leaving the channel.

As with mailing lists, you have to remember that the people you reach through newsgroups and chat channels are a self-selected group. They are computer-literate and already interested enough in the subject you are researching to go online and discuss it—but that doesn't mean they represent society at large. You may need to combine online sources with others to get the whole picture.

Warning!

The day after the Alfred P. Murrah Federal Building in Oklahoma City was bombed, a message was posted to an Internet newsgroup supposedly frequented by members of militia groups. The message said, in part, "If this turns out to be a bomb, expect them to tie it to the militia.... Expect a crackdown. Bury your guns."

Many major news organizations quoted the comment as an example of how militias were spreading their extremist messages via the Internet. But the posting was a joke, sent to the newsgroup by a student at the University of Montana. Many reporters didn't bother to track down the author of the message.

One editor did send the student e-mail, asking if he'd speak to a reporter. The student wrote back, explaining that he was kidding when he posted the message.

Two days after that, a message from a Tim McVeigh, in which the writer described himself as a "Mad Bomber," was found on America Online. Again, news organizations quoted the message, saying it came from Oklahoma City bombing suspect Timothy McVeigh. But that message turned out to be a joke too. America Online told any reporters who asked that the message was created after McVeigh had been arrested, so it couldn't have been posted by him.

Don't make assumptions about postings you find in cyberspace. Contact people who speak out online to find out who they are and where they got their information.

Chapter 6

TRAVELING THROUGH CYBERSPACE: TELNET AND FTP

You're working on a computer in Montana. You need to check something in the federal budget for a story you're doing on your state's federal subsidies. But the budget is stored on a computer in Washington, D.C. So you have to fly there to get it. Or you have to call someone, tell him or her what you need, and hope that person gets it right.

Or ... you can try a different type of traveling, through cyberspace, using two Internet resources: Telnet and anonymous FTP.

These allow you to log onto computers somewhere else on the Internet, as if you had accounts on those computers, and to read or gather information stored there. Some Telnet sites let you download information into your own computer; anonymous file transfer protocol sites are set up to let you do exactly that. They open collections of data all over the world to you.

This includes government information—archives of documents, surveys, reports, speeches, legislative hearings and bills; scientific information, including the most up-to-date earthquake reports and satellite pictures; and information about health and medicine, the environment, business, polls, politics, agriculture, technology, music, and more. You can search library catalogs at many Telnet sites, and FTP can bring you software as well as text and pictures. These are two more powerful tools for finding story ideas and information you need to make your stories complete.

By the time this book is published, some of the Telnet and FTP sites mentioned may have gone the way of the dinosaurs. Many computer systems have moved their information to a Gopher or to the World Wide Web. When you try a Telnet or FTP address, you may find the resource doesn't exist; you may find the information in a Gopher format, or on a World Wide Web page. You may be given new electronic addresses so you can FTP, Gopher or Web surf to the information you want.

But there are still resources you can't get to any other way, particularly if you've got limited Internet access. And you'll come across Telnet and FTP sites while working on the World Wide Web, so you need to know what they are and why they're useful.

In this chapter you'll learn to use Telnet and FTP with a shell account; in Chapter 8 you'll see how to use these resources with a graphical Web-browsing program.

TEST-DRIVING TELNET

With Telnet, you need to know the address of the computer you want to get to and the correct login. The user ID you use as a login for your own host computer won't work because with Telnet, you're transporting yourself into a different computer system that doesn't recognize that login. If you don't know the correct login—and many resources that list Telnet addresses also give you the login—you might try **guest** or **visitor** or **public;** sometimes they will get you into the public area of a remote computer system.

Besides taking you to sources of information you might not be able to reach, or reach easily, Telnet can help you if your host computer system doesn't offer a particular Internet resource. You can often use Telnet to reach a system that does, then use the resource while logged into that other system. For example, if your host system doesn't offer Internet Relay Chat, you might use Telnet to connect to a computer system that does. (This isn't the best way to do use IRC, but if it's the only way for you, you can try it. It isn't the best way because sometimes these remote computers are very busy and may limit the number of users at any one time.)

WHAT'S THE NUMBER?

As you've seen, host computers on the Internet are identified by names, like zippo.com—but each also has a unique IP, or Internet protocol, number. When you use Telnet or FTP, you may see a string of numbers come up, instead of the letter name you expected. The numbers are split into four parts separated by periods, like 123.45.67.89. You can use either the number or the name. If you type in the letter name and get connected but a number name comes up, don't worry; as long as your computer did what you wanted it to, you are all set. If you try to get to a computer using the letter name and it doesn't work, try the number instead.

LET ME IN

To use Telnet with a shell account, at your system prompt type in the command for Telnet and the address of the computer you are trying to reach:

```
telnet computeraddress
```

Say you want a list of publications concerning free speech. The law library at Columbia University is a great place to start, but you can't take a train to New York today. So you go online to CU-LawNet, a service provided by the Columbia Law School Public Information Service. The computer address is dessert.law.columbia.edu. Type in the Telnet command and the address, then hit your return button:

```
telnet dessert.law.columbia.edu
```

You'll see several messages:

```
Trying 128.59.176.83...

Connected to dessert.law.columbia.edu

Escape character is '^]'
```

What all this means is that your Telnet client is trying to reach computer 128.59.176.83 (the number for dessert.law.columbia.edu) and then has made the connection. You should pay attention to the escape character, **control-**], because if you get stuck in the middle of doing something on that other computer, the escape will get you out.

The login for this Telnet site is lawnet, so you type that in at the prompt, and you get a welcome screen that says this:

```
Welcome to CU-LawNet, a Columbia Law School Public Infor-
mation service...

First we need to know what terminal type you are using. If
you are dialing in to us, you are most likely using a
vt100.

If you are coming in from a machine in the student lab or
another law school network connected machine, you most
likely are also a vt100 type terminal.

The system will try to determine the type of terminal it
thinks you are using: "TERM = (vt102)"

If the choice displayed is correct, just press Return:
otherwise enter TERM = (vt100)-
```

It was easy to log into this remote computer, but there is a new wrinkle; this remote computer wants to know what type of terminal you are working on. Remember, your host computer thinks you have a "dumb terminal," so the remote computer will too—but it needs to know what type so it can display

FIGURE 6–1

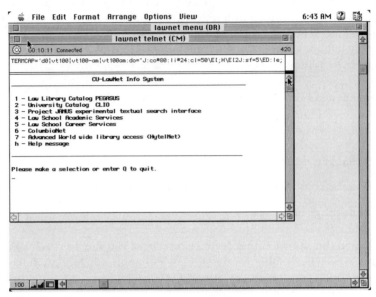

A menu listing resources available through CU-LawNet, an online Columbia Law site you can get to using Telnet.

information in a way that your "terminal" will understand. If you aren't sure what type of terminal your computer is pretending to be, try vt100; it's a common type. Some sites won't ask. Once you've told the remote computer what terminal type you've got, you get a menu of choices like the one in Figure 6-1.

Telnet sites will not all look exactly like this; you are moving to different computer sites each time, and sites can be set up in different ways. But with each site you will go through a login procedure and see some sort of welcome message and screen explaining the information and resources available to you at that site. At the bottom of the screen, you'll see what commands you can use during your Telnet session. These will be different at different Telnet sites too, but there's usually online help if you get stuck. For instance, if you type in **h** when you see the LawNet welcome, you'll get information on what each of the menu choices will give you.

You've now logged into a remote computer system. You can, by following onscreen commands, make use of all the information and services that system makes public. That's the magic of Telnet.

With CU-LawNet, you see on the screen a menu and numbers. To use the law library catalog, type in 1, and you'll get another menu of choices:

PEGASUS   Columbia Law Library

The On-Line Catalog of the Columbia Law School Library

A>**AUTHOR**

T>**TITLE**

S>**SUBJECT**

W>**Words in Corporate Author, Title or Subject**

D>**CONNECT to Periodicals Index and Other Library Catalogs**

C>**Call Number/Document Number**

R>**Reserve Lists**

I>**Library Information**

J>**DISCONNECT**

    Choose one (A,T,S,W,D,C,R,I,J)-

This menu allows you to search the library's online catalog. You may have seen this same type of screen if your school library catalog is online. You make a choice, type in a keyword or two, and wait while the computer pulls up what it has in its catalog that matches. For example, If you choose **S** to search by subject and then type in "free speech," you'll get a listing of catalogued resources in the law library that deal with that subject, like the listing in Figure 6-2.

FIGURE 6–2

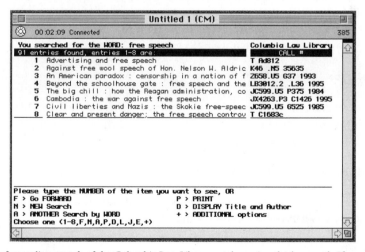

Results of an online search of the Columbia Law Library catalog using the keywords "free speech."

You can type in the number of an entry and get more information, including the date the item was published, the author's name, and where in the library it's located. Now you might be able to get a particular publication through an interlibrary loan.

You can't get the text of books or articles stored in the library online, but now you'll know what to look for or where to look for them. If you're seeking the name of an expert on a subject, searching through an online catalogue might be a quick way to find it.

Look again at the main menu for CU-LawNet. Item 7 allows you to work with something called HYTELNET. With this, you can reach many other libraries and online sites, so it's a good one to remember. You can get to HYTELNET through the Web now and through other Telnet sites.

TELNET COMMANDS

Telnet is fairly simple, then, to carry out. You use the Telnet command to get started, also typing in the computer address, and then use the login when you get to the Telnet site. Sometimes you will have to specify a port along with the address. Some Telnet servers offer more than one type of service, so each service is assigned a port. The port will be a number you add at the end of the address, like this:

```
telnet some.computer.with.port 10334
```

Once you log onto another computer through Telnet, you'll follow the commands you see onscreen.

There are a few other universal commands you might need: **open, close,** and **quit.**

If you go to your system prompt and type in **telnet** without an address, you'll get another prompt that looks like this:

```
telnet>
```

This means you've started the Telnet client program but you haven't told the program where to go. Now type in **open** and the computer address, and your client will take you there.

```
telnet > open epaibm.rtpnc.epa.gov
```

If you are in the middle of a Telnet session and want to leave one site and go to the next, you can use the **close** command

```
close

telnet>
```

You'll get the Telnet prompt, and you can use the **open** command to go somewhere else. This way, you don't have to keep going back to your host system's prompt every time you want to try a new site. You can switch from one site to another to another....

When you are really ready to end a Telnet session, use **quit.** You can also always use the escape character (**control-]**) and **quit** if you get stuck in the middle of doing something you suddenly think you don't want to.

KEEPING A RECORD

You'll want to keep track of useful Telnet sessions. Your communications software will let you log or capture everything that comes across your screen into a text file on a disk that you name. Check your software help information or talk to someone who can explain how your communications software does this.

FINDING TELNET SITES

You can search Gopherspace or the World Wide Web to find Telnet sites, and many books list them.

TAKE-OUT—GETTING COPIES OF FILES FROM OTHER COMPUTERS INTO YOURS

What if you know there's information on some other computer that you want for a story, and you need to have that data in your computer, so you can use it? Then you may need FTP—File Transfer Protocol.

This resource lets you log onto another computer, as you can with Telnet, but it also lets you download or copy files from the remote computer to your own computer—you can get the information, free, and save a copy to read or analyze as background for a story. The files you download can be documents, photographs, even software programs.

With many FTP sites, you don't need to know a different login for each site; you can use a login of **anonymous** to get to all the information available to the public. Once you log in, you can download information into your own computer to use as background for interviews and stories.

THE ABCS OF FTP

You need an FTP site address to get started, just as you needed Telnet addresses. So you give the FTP command:

```
ftp sitename
```

and hit enter.

Once you get to the site, you'll use anonymous for your login and hit enter again. You'll be asked for a password; use your e-mail address.

Look at one FTP session. You start by typing in the FTP command and the address, in this case, the address for the Internet Wiretap FTP site, where you can find a lot of government information:

```
ftp wiretap.spies.com
```

Next you get this message:

```
Connected to wiretap.spies.com

220 wiretap FTP Server (Version wu-2.4 (6) Thu Dec. 7
16:49:08 PST 1995) ready.

Name (ftp.spies.com):
```

At this name prompt, type in **anonymous.** You'll get another message:

```
331 Guest login ok, send your complete e-mail address as
password.

Password:
```

After you've answered that prompt, you'll get a welcome, and you'll be able to search for the file you need.

MOVING DIRECTLY THROUGH THE DIRECTORIES

Files on FTP servers aren't just piled into one list you can search and pull from. Instead, files are organized into directories and subdirectories. You might work on a computer system that works the same way or that uses file folders you can put into other file folders to keep things organized. To find a particular document at an FTP site, you need to know what directories and subdirectories to look under.

Think about it this way. Say you're storing documents having to do with a series you're working on about the way your city government works or doesn't work. So you've got three documents having to do with the city budget, one with last year's budget in it, one with this year's, and one with the proposed budget for next year; you have four documents having to do with spending on the schools, six on police, and three on the fire departments, and lots more. To keep track of these, you might put all three fire department files, called FIRE.EQUIPMENT, FIRE.PERSONNEL, and FIRE.MISC in one folder or directory, called FIRE.DEPARTMENT, then create a directory or folder for the schools and another for the police, and so on. Then you might put these folders or directories all into one directory called BUDGET.SERIES.

To track something down in this hierarchy of files, you'd first find the main directory, BUDGET.SERIES; ask for a directory of that directory and get the listings for schools, fire, and police; choose the fire directory and ask for a listing and finally get to the three documents you've stored there. You started with the main, or *root* directory, BUDGET.SERIES, and moved through subdirectories to find the documents you wanted.

You're going to do the same thing at FTP sites. You'll follow a path, or pathname, from main directory to subdirectories to get to the file or files you want. Take them one by one.

If you FTP to wiretap.spies.com and log in, then type in **dir,** you'll get something that looks like this:

```
200 PORT command successful.

150 Opening ASCII mode data connection for /bin/ls.

-total 121

-rw-r--r—1 root wheel 497 Mar 29 23:16 .cache

-rw-r--r—1 root wheel 1593 Mar 29 22:44 .cache+

drwxr-xr-x 2 wiretap daemon 512 Jul 1 1993 .cap

-rw-r--r—1 wiretap daemon 65 May 4 1993 .comment

-rw-r--r—1 wiretap daemon 320 May 11 1993 .files

-rw-r--r—1 wiretap daemon 78 Apr 23 1993 .jughead

-rw-r--r—1 wiretap daemon 874 Apr 24 1993 FEATURES

-rw-r--r—1 wiretap daemon 791 Apr 23 1993 README

drwxr-xr-x 3 wiretap daemon 1024 Jan 12 20:08 Releases

-rw-r--r—1 wiretap daemon 638 May 5 1993 SUBMIT

-rw-r--r—1 wiretap daemon 29170 May 11 1993 gov.index

-rw-r--r—1 wiretap daemon 82019 May 11 1993 library.index
```

Don't panic! You'll understand this in a moment. The first letter of each line in this directory tells you if the listing is for a directory or a file—the listings that start with *d* are directories, and everything else is a file.

You don't need to worry about the other letters on each line. What you do want to look at is the number right before the date—this tells you about how big the file is, in bytes, or for a diretory, tells the total size of the items in the directory, also in bytes. The larger the file is, the longer it will take to download and the more space it will take on your host computer system (or yours). You'll get some sense, after you've tried a couple of transfers, of how long everything takes.

The date will tell you when the file or directory was uploaded, and the last part is the name of the directory or file.

If you can find a README file or an INDEX file, you might want to download those—they will tell you about the site and what's there. In the case of this FTP site, the very first directory you find lists some files you can retrieve, including gov.index and library.index, as well as a couple of directories of files.

You might decide you want the gov.index file, but wait. Before you issue the **get** command, you need to tell the client and server what format you want the file transferred in.

BIN OR ASC

There are two basic modes you'll use to transfer files: ASCII or binary. ASCII is for transferring text files; binary is used for everything else, such as picture files. If you aren't sure what type of file you are transferring, use the binary mode—text will still translate fine.

If you want to download the index and you believe it is text, at the FTP prompt type in **asc** or **ascii:**

```
ftp> asc
```

You'll get another prompt, and you can now get the file:

```
ftp> get gov.index
```

The program will transfer this file and tell you when it's completed its job.

If you wanted to transfer a bunch of files that, say, had "gov" in their name, you could issue this command:

```
mget gov*
```

FTP Commands

To navigate you need to know a few commands:

dir or **ls** to get a directory of directories and/or files.

cd to move to the next directory down from the root directory or directory you are working in

cdup to move back up one directory

get to copy a file to your computer

mget to copy several files to your computer all at once

The asterisk tells the computer to find files with names like "gov," so it would pick up gov. index, gov.speeches, gov.reports or whatever.

After you issue the **mget** command, the computer will prompt you after each file comes up to make sure you wanted it. This is a useful command if you are dealing with files that have huge long names and you don't want to type them in and risk typos. Just use **mget** and the wild-card asterisk, then tell the computer **no** until it reaches the file you are after.

Many sites will have a pub directory where the files available to the public are stored, so that's another place to start looking if you're not sure exactly where you want to go.

AN FTP SESSION

Suppose you've gone to wiretap.spies.com knowing that there's a history database and you need some background for a story you are doing. You know you need to look in the directory named US-History. Use the **cd** command:

```
cd US-History
```

and you'll get another directory list:

```
-rw-r--r—1 root wheel 2124 Mar 30 00:07 .cache

-rw-r--r—1 root wheel 7043 Mar 29 02:26 .cache+

drwxr-xr-x 2 wiretap daemon 1024 Jul 1 1993 .cap

-rw-r--r—1 wiretap daemon 1422 May 3 1993 .files

drwxr-xr-x 3 wiretap daemon 512 Jan 13 23:11 Naval

drwxr-xr-x 3 wiretap daemon 512 Jan 13 02:49 Pre-WWII

drwxr-xr-x 4 wiretap daemon 512 Jan 12 18:27 Vietnam

drwxr-xr-x 3 wiretap daemon 512 Jan 12 22:48 WWII
```

More Netiquette

Many sites ask that you not try to download files during regular business hours, usually considered to be 6 a.m. to 6 p.m. This is because it takes a lot of computing power to download files, and during business hours the computer system is probably busy doing lots of other things. Since it's simple for a system's operator to decide not to let people have anonymous FTP access to information, it's best if you try to stick with these rules.

```
drwxr-xr-x 3 wiretap daemon 512 Jan 12 19:43 WWII-AF

-rw-r--r—1 wiretap daemon 18579 Mar 30 1993 arms1775.txt

-rw-r--r—1 wiretap daemon 21018 Mar 30 1993 artconf.txt

-rw-r--r—1 wiretap daemon 9273 Mar 30 1993 decind.txt

-rw-r--r—1 wiretap daemon 5775 Mar 30 1993 emancip.txt

-rw-r--r—1 wiretap daemon 18114 Mar 30 1993 federal.10

-rw-r--r—1 wiretap daemon 11812 Mar 30 1993 federal.51

-rw-r--r—1 wiretap daemon 37066 Mar 30 1993 foia.req

-rw-r--r—1 wiretap daemon 42141 Mar 30 1993 germany.sur

-rw-r--r—1 wiretap daemon 23801 Mar 30 1993 greenvil.txt

-rw-r--r—1 wiretap daemon 26768 Mar 30 1993 japan.sur

-rw-r--r—1 wiretap daemon 1642 Mar 30 1993 mayflow.cp

-rw-r--r—1 wiretap daemon 5987 Mar 30 1993 monroe.doc

-rw-r--r—1 wiretap daemon 2266 Mar 30 1993 neut1793.pr

-rw-r--r—1 wiretap daemon 5112 Apr 2 1993 open1.not

-rw-r--r—1 wiretap daemon 11831 Mar 30 1993 orders.fun

-rw-r--r—1 wiretap daemon 17301 Mar 30 1993 ordinanc.nw

-rw-r--r—1 wiretap daemon 13258 Mar 30 1993 paris.txt

-rw-r--r—1 wiretap daemon 11340 Mar 30 1993 resolves.cc

-rw-r--r—1 wiretap daemon 3130 Mar 30 1993 transmit.txt

-rw-r--r—1 wiretap daemon 25261 Apr 22 1993 u2.txt

-rw-r--r—1 wiretap daemon 51614 Mar 30 1993 us-const.txt

-rw-r--r—1 wiretap daemon 5725 Mar 30 1993 virginia.dec
```

From here, you could download any of the text documents or go into the directories for World War II or the Vietnam War and see what you could find, depending on what you need for your story.

When you get one of these files, you are following a pathname:

```
directory/subdirectory/file
```

or

```
pub/US-History/virginia.dec
```

There's online help at FTP sites too. At this site, if you type **help** at the FTP prompt, you'll get a list of commands you can use.

On what roads do police nab the most speeders? Bill Loving, com-
puter-assisted-reporting editor at the *Minneapolis Star Tribune,* used
FTP to look for an answer to that question. He wanted a database of
speeding tickets from the Minnesota State Highway Patrol. Loving
said the database was too big to put on floppy disks, and other computer equipment the newspaper and police had didn't match up to
facilitate a transfer from one computer system to another. So he
asked the police to put the database on the agency's FTP server. Several days later, Loving downloaded the data to the newspaper's computer in about 20 minutes, using FTP. With that information, he said,
the newspaper's reporters will do many stories, such as one on the
roads where the most speeding tickets are given out.

FILES COMPRESSED AND DECOMPRESSED

In Chapter 3, you learned about compressed files. (See page 30.) At FTP sites,
you'll see the same sorts of files. Some will be straight text; you know that
because the file names will end with the extension *txt.* Others will be compressed using special software, and you'll need software to decompress them so
you can read them.

FINDING FTP SITES

You can find sites through many Internet books and by searching on the World
Wide Web. You can also use a program called Archie to search through FTP
space to find files stored at various sites.

FINDING FILES WITH ARCHIE

Archie supposedly has nothing to do with the cartoon character, though after
Archie came Veronica and Jughead, two ways to search Gopherspace. (See
Chapter 7.) With Archie, you can specify keywords or parts of words. Archie
searches a database of files available on FTP servers throughout the Internet,
looking for filenames that match the word pattern you designate. It isn't hard
to use Archie, but you need to set parameters for your search, and figuring those
out takes a little time.

If your host program doesn't offer Archie, you can employ Telnet to reach an Archie server and then start searching. Use Telnet to go to archie.rutgers.edu, log in using the word **archie,** and you'll get an Archie prompt to begin searching:

```
archie>
```

Don't start yet! You need to tell Archie how you want your search done and how you want the results. At the prompt, issue the show command so you can see a list of options for your search:

```
archie> show
```

The list will look confusing. But if you pay attention to just a few variables, they'll make your searches more useful.

This is what you'll get with **show:**

```
# 'autologout' (type numeric) has the value '60'.

# 'compress' (type string) has the value 'none'.

# 'encode' (typec string) has the value 'none'.

# 'language' (type string) has the value 'english'.

# 'mailto' (type string) is not set.

# 'match_domain' (type string) is not set.

# 'match_path' (type string) is not set.

# 'max_split_size' (type numeric) has the value '51200'.

# 'maxhits' (type numeric) has the value '100'.

# 'maxhitspm' (type numeric) has the value '100'.

# 'maxmatch' (type numeric) has the value '100'.

# 'output_format' (type string) has the value 'verbose'.

# 'pager' (type boolean) is not set.

# 'search'c (type string) has the value 'sub'.# 'server'
(type string) has the value 'localhost'.

prog stuffit

# 'sortby' (type string) has the value 'none'.

# 'status' (type boolean) is set.

# 'term' (type string) has the value 'vt100 24 80'.
```

The things to pay attention to are the **mailto,** the **maxhits,** the **pager, sortby,** and **search.**

Mailto allows you to put in your e-mail address so you can mail the results of your Archie search to yourself. If you want to do this, issue the command

```
archie> set mailto youremailaddress
```

Maxhits limits the number of items Archie searches for and displays; most of the time you will probably want to limit this, maybe to 10 or 15; if you don't, you may get a huge list that scrolls across your computer screen for what seems like forever. The command is:

```
archie> set maxhits 10
```

The pager determines whether Archie gives you a scrolling screenful of the hits, or whether it delivers them one page at a time, with you hitting the space bar to look at the next page. If you are doing a long search, you'll want the pager on, so you can slowly go through your search results:

```
archie> set pager on
```

Sortby allows you to tell Archie to put the results of your search in a certain order:

```
archie> set sortby none
```

This tells Archie not to sort the results of the search. You have other options for sorting, including **filename** (alphabetically by filename), **host name** (alphabetically by name of computer host), **size** (size of file), and **time** (from most recently modified file to least recently modified file).

The other variable you have to deal with has to do with the type of search—do you want Archie to search only for sites with the exact word you've designated or for files that include that word? If you want exactly that word, set the search option for an exact match, and type in the sought-after word with precise capitalization.

```
set search exact
```

If you want Archie to find files with names that include the word and not to pay attention to whether a name is lower- or upper-case, use the **sub** option:

```
set search sub
```

Now you're ready to ask Archie to search.

CAR in action

When can jaywalking land you in jail? When you don't have enough money to pay your fine. That's one of the things Michael Berens of the *Columbus* (Ohio) *Dispatch* discovered when he reported and wrote a series of stories, "Cash Register Justice." He discovered that thousands of Ohioans were serving jail time for crimes that weren't legally punishable by jail, simply because they could not afford to pay fines, while some people accused of more serious crimes went free. Berens used several online resources to gather information for his stories. With FTP he gathered background information from the National Institute of Justice Statistics and reports from the Government Accounting Office (GAO). He also ordered paper copies of the National Institute's reports using e-mail and learned about the GAO's latest reports through the GAO's daily e-mail service.

RESULTS OF ARCHIE'S SEARCH

Say you want to find online newspapers or information about them at FTP sites. Set your search parameters, and, at the Archie prompt, type in the keywords

```
archie > find newspapers online
```

You'll get a list of items that look like this:

```
Host sun.rediris.es (130.206.1.2)

Last updated 14:47 20 Jan 1996


Location: /docs/internet/Resources

FILE -r--r--r—99350 bytes 15:00 28 Feb 1995 newspapers_
online.lit
```

Archie has found a file on the computer named sun.rediris.es (IP number 130.206.1.2.). The path through the directories to the file is docs/internet/Resources, and the file is called newspapers_online.lit. You can FTP to the site and find this and download it now, if you wish.

Many FTP sites also allow you to upload files, using **put** and **mput** commands. Often there will be a particular place you can upload files so a system operator can look them over and evaluate them to see if they really should be posted on the site.

> **Warning!**
>
> Gathering information from computers around the world is not with-
> out perils. Any piece of data online was, at some time, typed into
> some computer by a person, and people make mistakes. Government
> Telnet and FTP sites aren't immune to erroneous information. So use
> your reporting common sense when using what you pull out of
> cyberspace. Verify what you find with other sources.

WHAT TO TAKE WITH YOU ON YOUR JOURNEYS

Feel like a world traveler yet? Your trip isn't over. You've toured Telnet and FTP sites; next, you'll learn how to tunnel through Gopherspace and surf the World Wide Web.

Though each online resource operates a little differently, some computer and information-gathering skills translate from one to another; you can build on what you've already learned. You worked with compressed files, for example, on bulletin board systems; you've seen them again at FTP sites. You've used computer addresses to get where and what you want; you'll use them again with Gopher and the Web. Telnet sites offer menus of choices; so do Gopher sites. And while you search particular online resources in different ways, everything you learn about focusing searches and choosing keywords will help you find jewels of information no matter where in cyberspace you look.

Chapter 7

GOPHER: MENUS BY THE MILLIONS

The answer: Gopher.

The question: What fuzzy rodent shares its name with a tool that brings you online information about NASA, schoolchildren and computers, new AIDS treatments, and chocolate-chip-and-dried-cricket cookies?

Gopher is another resource for finding information in the vast, confusing library of the Internet. It's easier to use than Telnet or FTP; you don't need to know a login or password, and sometimes you don't even need the address of the computer you want to reach. You can search Gopher servers around the world using a keyword or phrase, and quickly get a list of resources culled from different online sites. You can save or download files from these resources, moving from one to another without needing to knowing where you're going. Gopher does all the work for you behind the scenes.

With Gopher, you can locate files and databases and search library catalogs. You can start Telnet and FTP sessions or link to the World Wide Web. And the information available on Gopher servers ranges widely, from business and economics to travel to Congress to science:

- From the Gopher for the Education Resource Information Center, ERIC, you can learn what's going on in classrooms around the country and about government studies and programs concerning education. The Gopher address is ericir.syr.edu.
- The Library of Congress Gopher, at marvel.loc.gov, allows you to search that library catalog and others and connects you to many other U.S. government resources.
- NASA gophers, such as the one at nic.nasa.gov, offer NASA news including descriptions of repair work done on the space shuttle and a schedule of shuttle launches.
- Information about cancer and AIDs research and treatment is available on the National Institutes of Health Gopher, gopher.nih.gov.
- The Iowa State Department of Entomology EntoGopher, at gopher.ent.iastate.edu, features Tasty Insect Recipes, including Chocolate Chirpie Chip Cookies and Banana Worm Bread. (You never know when you might need an insect recipe.)

As with Telnet and FTP resources, you'll find that some information once stored on Gopher servers has been moved to the World Wide Web. The Web is growing, but Gopherspace is not. Sometimes, though, information on the Web is not as complete as that on a Gopher. Some people prefer Gopher because they find the World Wide Web's graphics and photographs frivolous and time-consuming to bring up on their computer screens. With Gopher, you'll see only text, plus icons if you use a graphical Web browser with Gopher. (See Chapter 8.)

RODENT IN CYBERSPACE

Gopher is a client/server program developed at the University of Minnesota, home of the Golden Gophers sports teams. Gopher servers all over the Internet contact one another and share resources, so you can move easily from information on one computer to information on another computer. Gopher presents information as menus or lists of directories and files. The files can be text, binary files, sound, and pictures.

Gopher works rather like this. Imagine there's only one restaurant in your town, a steakhouse. You get a menu listing every item that restaurant makes in its kitchen, including sirloin steak, teriyaki steak tips, grilled chicken, and baked potatoes. All of this sounds good, but what you really want tonight is Chinese food, or spaghetti, which that restaurant doesn't make.

You're in luck, though. That one restaurant is connected magically to the Chinese restaurant and an Italian restaurant two towns over. So the steakhouse menu also lists everything you can get at those other restaurants. You order Chicken Amazing and pork fried rice, and the steakhouse relays that order to the Chinese restaurant, which makes your food and delivers it to the steakhouse.

Gopher is better than this, of course, and makes more sense. You'd have to wait a while for your meal to be driven from one restaurant to another, but Gopher works almost instantly. Besides, you could drive to the Chinese restaurant, but if you need information that's on a computer two countries away, you need Gopher.

SLIPPING INTO A GOPHER TUNNEL

To begin a journey in Gopherspace, you need to start up a Gopher client program and make contact with one Gopher server. There are many programs; the one you'll learn about in this chapter is a client you can use with a shell account on a host computer system.

If your host system has its own Gopher server, you can get to it by typing in the gopher command at your system prompt:

gopher

If this doesn't work, you can get to a Gopher server somewhere else in Gopherspace by typing in the command and a computer address, such as the one for the ERIC server:

gopher ericir.syr.edu

Hit your return button, and you'll get to the Gopher. You'll see on your screen a list or menu that looks like the one in Figure 7-1.

This menu represents resources available on the ERIC Gopher, such as the bibliographic database listed as menu item 11. It also represents links to other Gopher servers, such as menu item 18, "Gophers and Library Catalogs."

Wherever you Gopher to, you'll get a menu that looks something like this. You can retrieve files from these menus and reach other Gopher servers.

WHAT'S ON THE MENU?

It's easy to make sense of a Gopher menu. Look again at the ERIC menu. At the top of the menu, you see the Gopher server's address. At the bottom right, you see this notation: **Page : 1/2.** This means the menu has two pages, and you're looking at the first one. To move to the second page, hit your space bar. To move back to the first page, hit **b.**

At the bottom of the menu, you'll see two commands you can use. Typing in **?** will produce a list of commands you can use to navigate through menus. Typing **q** will end your Gopher session.

FIGURE 7–1

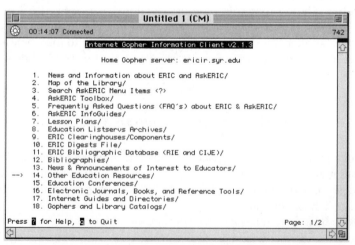

The main Gopher menu for the Education Resource Information Center, ERIC. The Gopher address is ericir.syr.edu.

There are 18 numbered menu items on this page of the menu. You can tell what type of item is listed by looking at the symbol or symbols at the end of the menu listing. Some of the ones you'll see most are these:

- A slash, or /, means the item is a directory, rather than an individual file. Remember that when you explored FTP sites, you saw that files on an FTP server were kept in directories. Often, to get to a file you wanted, you had to move from a main directory to a subdirectory to another subdirectory, following a designated path, to find the file you wanted. Gophers use the same sort of hierarchical system to store information; sometimes you will have to move through several directories on a particular Gopher server before you get to the file you want.
- If you find nothing at the end of a line, that's a text file you can look at and save.
- BIN means it's a binary file.
- TEL means if you choose that item, you start a Telnet session automatically.
- If you see , you know that menu item provides a resource you can search, using keywords.

Look again at Figure 7-1. Except for item 3, all of the items on this menu end in slashes, so they all represent directories. Item 3 allows you to do a keyword search of information on this Gopher.

Usually, when you reach the main menu of a gopher, you'll find an item that gives information about the Gopher. On the ERIC Gopher, it's item 1, "News and Information about ERIC and AskERIC." This listing may help you figure out where information on the Gopher server comes from and how you can credit it in a story. It may also tell you whether this Gopher really offers the information you need.

Gopher Glitches

You will run into some problems with Gopher. First of all, you may try a Gopher address only to get the message "Connection refused." Don't take it personally. This can mean that the Gopher is too busy to accept your connection or that the server or computer network is down temporarily. The best thing to do is to try again later. You might also get messages that say "Host name unknown" or "No information in file." Again, a computer or network may be temporarily down or information may have been moved to another site. You can try again later or try a different Gopher resource.

Choosing from the Menu

Items on a Gopher menu are numbered, and an arrow appears next to the first item. You can choose an item from the menu in a couple of ways. First, move the arrow, using your arrow keys, until it's next to the item you want, then hit return or the right arrow key.

Second, type in the number of the item. This is particularly useful if you're working with a very long menu.

Remember that with FTP, you moved from a main directory through subdirectories to get to files. With Gopher, you move from a main menu to submenus until you get to files. So each time you choose an item on a Gopher menu, you move either to a new menu or to a file.

For example, suppose you choose item 14, "Other Education Resources," from the main ERIC menu. What you'll get is another menu that looks like Figure 7-2. Most of the items on this menu end in slashes, so they are directories. Item 17 will start a Telnet session with a NASA resource. Choose item 1, "U.S. Department of Education," and you'll get another menu with only five listings:

```
U.S. Department of Education

    1. U.S. Department of Education/

    2. A Teacher's Guide to the U.S. Dept. of Education

    3. Goals 2000/
```

Figure 7-2

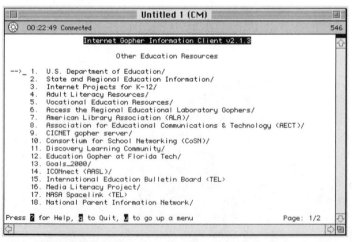

A Gopher menu obtained by choosing one item from the ERIC Gopher (see 7-1). This menu lists links to Other Education Resources, including the U.S. Department of Education Gopher (menu item 1).

4. School-to-Work,Vocational and Adult Education (OVAE)/

5. Schoolwide Programs–Chapter 1 / Title I (ESEA)/

Guess what—you've just traveled from one Gopher server to another, without pause. You are now working on the server for the U.S. Department of Education. One of the beauties of Gopher is that all you have to know how to do to navigate is to choose an item from a menu. The program does the rest of the work, making contact with the right computer and listing the available information and resources for you, so you can switch from one Gopher to another with ease.

(You can, of course, go directly to the U.S. Department of Education Gopher by using the **gopher** command and the server address, gopher.ed.gov, at your shell prompt.)

FETCH A FILE

No matter what Gopher server you end up on, what you'll usually want from Gopher is a file of information, not just a menu. You keep working through menus until you find one.

If you choose item 1, "U.S. Department of Education," from the last menu you pulled up, you'll see yet another menu. One of the items listed is "Updates on Legislation, Budget and Activities of the Department." Choose that, and you'll finally get to a menu, like the one in Figure 7-3, listing some files (you'll know they're files because there's no symbol at the end of the listings).

FIGURE 7-3

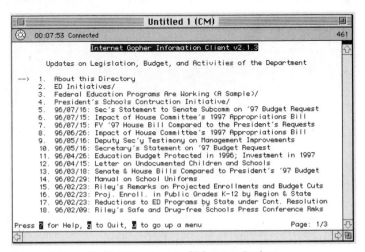

A menu of files available on the U.S. Department of Education Gopher.

Now if you need information on school uniforms, or Title I, or drug-free school programs, you can read the text, save copies of the files, or e-mail copies to yourself.

WORKING WITH FILES

To work with a file on Gopher, all you need to do is follow commands displayed at the bottom of your screen or commands you can learn about by typing in **?** for help. You'll get a new Help list showing the commands for saving, downloading, printing, and other tasks, as in Figure 7-4. Type in the right command and follow any onscreen prompts that pop up. That's it.

For example, to send a copy of the file to your e-mail box, type in **m.** You'll get an onscreen prompt asking you to type in an e-mail address, as in Figure 7-5.

To download a file, type in **D.** You'll get a prompt asking which protocol you want to use. (For a reminder on downloading protocols, see Chapter 6, page 93.)

MARKING A PLACE IN GOPHERSPACE

Online help, onscreen commands, and prompts and menus. That's Gopherspace. It's pretty easy to move around, almost too easy. You can get lost in Gopherspace. If you tried to map it, you'd be able to show particular Gopher servers, where information resides—but the paths between them would not be

FIGURE 7–4

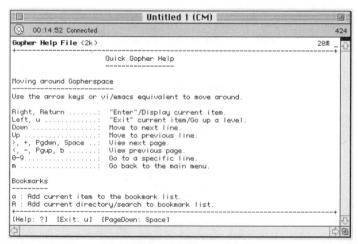

An onscreen list of Gopher commands. Type "?" while navigating Gopherspace to get this list.

FIGURE 7–5

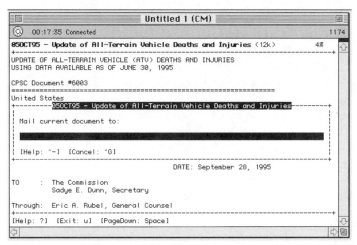

The box and prompt you get onscreen when you type in "m" to e-mail a copy of a document you find on a Gopher.

> **Warning!**
>
> If you have an account on a host computer, you may not be allowed to download or save items to that computer. One option is to e-mail files to yourself. That way, you can then read them, save them, or print them the way you do other e-mail.

so simple to draw in, because you can get to one particular Gopher server from many other places, and by routes direct and indirect. And Gopher doesn't tell you how it gets somewhere, any more than the gopher in your lawn does.

It can be frustrating trying to keep track of where you've gotten and how you got there, if it's a place you might want to go to again. So Gopher offers you a way to mark your place and quickly find it again.

If you find a Gopher location you want to reach again, type in the letter **a.** This allows you to create a "bookmark." You'll be asked to type in a name for the bookmark; make it something you will recognize again, something indicative of the Gopher site or the file you've found. Then hit the return key. That's it. Gopher has saved that in a bookmark file. Now when you want to go to the same place again, type in the letter **v.** Gopher will produce a list of your bookmarks. Choose the one you want, hit enter, and Gopher will take you directly there.

If you type in an uppercase **A** instead of **a**, an entire Gopher menu or a database query will be added to your bookmark list.

To delete a bookmark, type **v** and then, when the list comes up, choose the entry you want to delete and type in **d** and hit enter.

JEWELS—GOPHERS BY SUBJECT

If you already know that a particular Gopher server has information you need, you can go to that site and retrieve it. But since there are thousands of Gopher servers on the Internet, you won't always know exactly where to go or what site name is the right one. Gopher provides resources that make it easier to find information you need, and one of these is Gopher Jewels.

Many Gopher menus include a Gopher Jewels item. This resource separates Gopher servers in subject categories and provides instant links to the resources, so you don't have to know the addresses of the servers. If you are covering a certain beat, say health or economics, you can go to Gopher Jewels and link to Gopher servers specializing in that subject area.

A Gopher Jewels menu will have listings like these:

```
Gopher-Jewels

       1. GOPHER JEWELS Information and Help/

       2. Community, Global and Environmental/

       3. Education, Social Sciences, Arts & Humanities/

       4. Economics, Business and Store Fronts/

       5. Engineering and Industrial Applications/

       6. Government/

       7. Health, Medical, and Disability/

       8. Internet and Computer Related Resources/

       9. Law/

      10. Library, Reference, and News/

      11. Miscellaneous Items/

      12. Natural Sciences including Mathematics/

  ->  13. Personal Development and Recreation/

      14. Research, Technology Transfer and Grants
          Opportunities/

      15. Search Gopher Jewels Menus by Key Word(s) <?>
```

On this menu, items 1 through 14 have slashes next to them, so these are all directories, while item 15 is a search resource that lets you search the Jewels

---

Gopher commands

q   Quit, or exit, a Gopher, after being asked if you are sure you really
want to quit.

Q   Quit, or exit, a Gopher without being asked.

s   Save a file to your home directory.

u   Move back up one directory.

=   Get information on where an item on a Gopher menu actually
resides; you have to be looking at a menu, with the arrow next to
the item you are curious about, when you type this in.

m   If you type in **m** while you are looking at a Gopher menu, you will
be taken back to the main menu of the Gopher you began your
Gopher session with.

m   If you type in **m** while you are looking at a file, you will get a box in
which you can type in an e-mail address, so you can e-mail the file.

D   Download a file—you cannot download a menu.

P   Print the file.

a   Add a bookmark.

A   Add a Gopher menu or a database query to your list of bookmarks.

---

menus using keywords. You can choose one of the numbered items and work
through directories until you reach a file you want, or you can try a keyword
search.

To work through the directories, you might choose item 13, Personal Development and Recreation. You'll get another menu that looks like this one:

```
Personal Development and Recreation

        1. Employment Opportunities and Resume Postings/

 ->     2. Fun Stuff & Multimedia/

        3. Museums, Exhibits and Special Collections/

        4. Games

        5. Jump to Gopher Jewels Main Menu/

        6. Search Gopher Jewels Menus by Key Word(s) <?>
```

Choose item 2, Fun Stuff & Multimedia:

```
Fun Stuff & Multimedia
```

        1. Aviation/

        2. Bicycling/

        3. Fantasy/

        4. Games/

        5. Gardening/

        6. Humor/

        7. Magazines/

        8. Music/

        9. Pets/

       10. Pictures/

       11. Recipes/

       12. Restaurants/

   -> 13. Sports/

       14. Television & Film/

       15. Fun Stuff & Multimedia (misc)/

       16. Jump to Gopher Jewels Main Menu/

       17. Jump up a menu to Personal Development and
           Recreation/

       18. Search Gopher Jewels Menus by Key Word(s) <?>

The menus go on and on, until you get to the servers and files you want.

VERONICA AND JUGHEAD

Gopher Jewels sorts out some of the sites and information for you, but if you're not sure what subject to look under, it might take you awhile to find something useful.

There is another way to search Gophers. You used Archie to search for FTP sites; with Gopher, you have Veronica and Jughead. Both of these search for keywords that occur in the menu titles of items on Gopher servers. Veronica searches servers all throughout Gopherspace; Jughead searches only the one server you are working on at the time you do your search.

The names? Some say Veronica stands for Very Easy Rodent-Oriented Net-Wide Index of Computerized Archives, and Jughead for Jonzy's Universal Gopher Hierarchy Excavation and Display. Others, including Harley Hahn, author of *The Internet, A Complete Reference,* say that these explanations came after the names appeared and that the names do not stand for anything. Regardless, they are useful search tools.

To do a Veronica search, you have to find a Veronica server. If you go to a Gopher main menu and choose the menu item that says "Other Gopher and Information Servers," you'll often get another menu with an item that says something like this: "Search titles in Gopherspace using Veronica." Choose that, and you'll get another menu that looks like the one in Figure 7-6.

This looks like a lot of gobbledygook, but basically it's a list of options for your Veronica search. At the end of each menu item, you see letters enclosed in parentheses. Those represent names of Veronica servers. You can choose any one of them. You're offered a choice of servers because sometimes one server will be too busy to deal with your request for information. You can then try the same search with a different server.

Another choice you have is whether you want Veronica to give you only a list of directories with your keywords in them, or any type of Gopher resource, be it a directory or a file or whatever.

You might want to find only directory listings dealing with environmental issues, so that from there you can choose a directory that looks helpful. But if you don't know whether directories are what you want, or you want Veronica to search everything in Gopherspace, choose the search that will "find ALL gopher types" or "Search Gopherspace."

Jughead searches will offer similar options—but for one particular server rather than all servers in Gopherspace.

You choose a Veronica server for your search the same way you choose any item for any Gopher menu. You'll get a prompt asking you to type in keywords for the search.

FIGURE 7–6

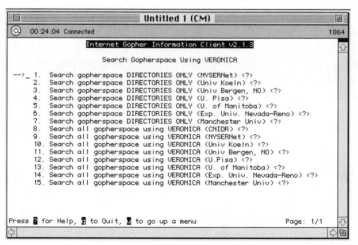

A menu of Veronica servers you can use to search through Gopherspace for particular Gopher directories and menu items.

LET'S GET LOGICAL

You learned about keyword searching of databases using the Boolean opera-tors **and, or,** and **not** in Chapter 3. (See page 37.) You can do the same sort of search with Veronica and Jughead.

For example, if you start a Veronica search by typing in the words "juve-nile crime," Veronica assumes you intend the word "and" to join the two, and it then looks for menu items that include both the words "juvenile" and "crime." You'll find that many Internet resources assume the **and** operator unless you state otherwise.

But say you want menu items that include either of two or more words. You have to tell Veronica that you want to search for "crime **or** trials." Now Veron-ica will search for titles that have either of those words, or both.

Or you want to know about crime—but you are not looking for statistics. You tell Veronica to search for "crime **but not** statistics"—and that's what you'll get (although crime is so general that you are likely to get vast numbers of items, so narrow it down.).

You can use an asterisk as a wild card when searching. If you tell Veronica to look for "journalism," you'll get items with that word in it but only that word. You won't get titles with the word "journalists." But if you tell Veronica to get "journal*," it will search for any matches including "journalists" and "journal-ism." You can use the asterisk only at the end of a word.

You can also use parentheses to narrow your search. The parentheses tell Veronica to treat the words within the parentheses as one item. Suppose you did a search for "juvenile crime or trials." Veronica would search for "juvenile" and "crime" or for "trials," but not "juvenile" and "trials." But if you put the query together this way

```
juvenile and (crime or trials)
```

it will search for "juvenile crime" or "juvenile trials."

Jughead works the same way. Not every Gopher server offers Jughead searching, but it's useful if you know you need to search only a particular Gopher and not all the Gophers across cyberspace.

For example, say you want information on public schools and how many of them provide their students access to the Internet, because you are working on stories about the need for new technology in your local schools. From the ERIC Gopher you went to the U.S. Department of Edu-cation Gopher; why not do a Jughead search of that Gopher, rather than searching all of Gopherspace? The U.S. Education Gopher main menu lists a Jughead search. If you choose that menu item, a box will appear where you can type in your keywords. You type in **Internet access,** hit enter, and wait for your search to conclude. Jughead comes up with a new menu con-taining one listing:

```
Search all U.S. Department of Education Menus using JUG-
HEAD: Internet access

-> 1. 95/0203: Students With Little Access to Internet
   (4K)
```

You can now read this report or save it to your computer account or mail it to yourself.

WHAT YOU SEE IS WHAT YOU GET

What Veronica does is create a whole new Gopher menu for you, with items that include the keywords you specified. This menu didn't exist anywhere until you started the search; it's custom-made for you. And the items on the menu may exist on different servers all over the world. All you have to do is choose a menu item and hit the return key. You'll go right to the directory or file you chose, no matter where in Gopher space it "lives."

Suppose you were looking for information about students' legal rights. You could choose the NYSERnet Veronica server, and a search of all Gopherspace, and type in "students' rights" as your keywords. It might make more sense to use a wildcard, to type in "student* rights," so you'd get anything with "student," "students'" or "students'." (See Figure 7-7.)

If you hit your return button after typing in the words, the search would begin. The result would be a menu like the one in Figure 7-8. These directories and files could be from Gopher servers all over the world.

CAR in action

Gopher can be useful for quick checks of facts, if you know how to search. Ivan Weiss of the *Seattle Times* recalls using Gopher while he was copy-editing a local columnist's piece. The writer discussed a local Bloomsday celebration, in which a bar was featuring the Irish whiskey Old Bushmill's because it was mentioned in James Joyce's *Ulysses*." Weiss didn't think the writer had the name of the whiskey right. He went online, searching the World Wide Web, and came upon a Gopher site containing the full text of *Ulysses*. He searched the chapters one by one until he found the right name. It was Bushmill's, not Old Bushmill's.

From start to finish, his search took three to four minutes, said Weiss.

FIGURE 7–7

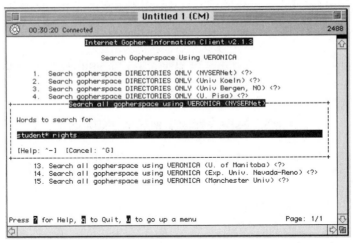

The box and prompt you get when you choose a Veronica server. You type in your keywords and start the search.

FIGURE 7–8

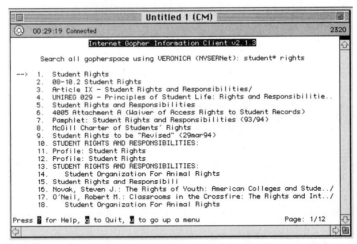

Results of one Veronica search using the keywords "student* rights." You can click on any of these menu listings to get to the actual Gopher item, no matter where on the Internet it is stored.

WHERE DOES THIS INFORMATION COME FROM?

If Veronica pulls up a file you're interested in, but you can't tell from reading the file where it came from or who created it, try the = command. You can use

FIGURE 7-9

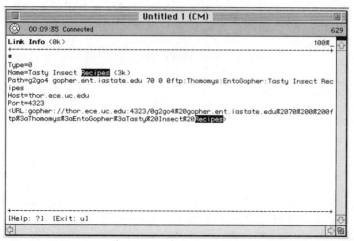

Information about a Gopher menu item, including the name of the item and the address of the Gopher where it can be found.

A Question of Ethics

Because Gopher does things invisibly, taking you from here to there with just a keystroke, it is sometimes difficult to know where the information you see on your screen comes from.

Ethical conduct includes being accurate and thorough in reporting, and that means you need to know that information you're using comes from a reliable source. You also need to attribute some information, identify sources for readers, and give credit where credit is due, just as you would with information you got from a source not on the Internet.

Verify data you get from Gopher. And use the = command to figure out where information comes from. Some Gopher sites provide e-mail addresses so you can contact people who created the sites. They might be able to help you figure out where information comes from.

this command only when you have a menu of items; it won't work if you've got a file onscreen.

What you'll get is information about the host computer and the path through Gopherspace that Veronica took to get to the menu item, like the screen shown in Figure 7-9. Then you can contact the host server and look for menu items about the server or the data stored there.

Sometimes, of course, the document you pull up or a Gopher server you go to will also give you that information.

ONE MORE WAY TO SEARCH

Some Gopher servers will offer you another option in your searches: WAIS, or Wide Area Information Servers. These resources allow you to search particular databases using keywords, the way you search with Veronica and Jughead. But WAIS searches through the text of documents in the databases, not just the titles.

You can do a WAIS search from a Gopher if you find a menu item labeled something like "WAIS" or "WAIS Based Information." Choose this option, move through menus, and you'll eventually come to a list of WAIS databases. The Washington and Lee University Library Gopher at liberty.uc.wlu.edu, for example, has links to WAIS databases including speeches made by President Clinton, documents from the Occupational Safety and Health Administration, bills in Congress, and Supreme Court decisions.

You can choose one database from the list just as you choose any item from a Gopher menu. You'll then get a prompt asking you to type in keywords. Hit your return button, and the search will begin. The result will be a list of files containing your keywords. You can view the files or e-mail them to yourself.

CAR in action

It was a fishy story from the start, and Whit Andrews turned to the Internet and Gopher Jewels for help.

Andrews was a reporter for the *Munster* (Indiana) *Times* when he first used the Internet for reporting. He'd heard that a species of fish called ruffe was endangering the perch population in northwest Indiana. Perch were important to the economy there, both because there was commercial fishing of perch and because tourists came to Indiana to fish for and eat perch. Ruffe weren't native to this country, and Andrews wanted to know something about them before he tried interviewing scientists for his story.

He did a search using Gopher Jewels and found research papers placed on Gophers by Sea Grant researchers.

"I read this information," says Andrews, "and then I knew my stuff before I talked to scientists. This [type of research] really helps when you are talking with scientific sources. You're not asking stupid questions, not saying 'Tell me again where this fish comes from.' You can focus on the questions that will result in valuable quotes. This improves the quality of the story but also reduces the amount of time you spend on research."

He has also used e-mail and ProfNet for stories. When he needed to talk to experts about the perch population dropping in Lake Michigan, he sent a query to ProfNet. "Not only did I get the major perch researchers for the area, but I also heard from people who could talk about aquaculture, about farming perch. And they put me in touch with the only aquaculture firm in the United States producing perch," says Andrews. "I ended up with a great story."

Chapter 8

AN INFORMATION EXPLOSION: THE WORLD WIDE WEB

When news breaks or an interesting story surfaces these days, many journalists head to the World Wide Web.

When TWA Flight 800 crashed after taking off from New York on July 17, 1996, Web sites offered President Clinton's reaction and data about TWA, the Boeing Company's 747, and the Federal Aviation Administration. The FBI even set up an online site to to provide a hotline telephone number and e-mail address so members of the public could reach the agency with any information they might have about the crash.

When a truck bomb exploded on June 25, 1996, outside a complex that housed U.S. Air Force personnel at the King Abdul Aziz Air Base in Dharan, Saudi Arabia, reporters turned to the Web for maps of that country, photographs of the bomb site, and press releases from the State Department.

While athletes were diving and leaping and running during the 1996 Summer Olympic Games in Atlanta, Web surfers found quickly updated competition results, photographs, and interviews with athletes.

As scientists debated whether a meteorite showed evidence that life once existed on Mars, journalists could view photos of the planet taken during NASA space missions; read *The Martian Chronicle,* an electronic newsletter about Mars exploration from NASA's Jet Propulsion Laboratory; and find, if they did a keyword search of the Web, the lyrics to David Bowie's song "Life on Mars?"

And reporters with some free time on their hands (after deadline, of course) could meet the Vermont dog who predicts earthquakes, read movie reviews written in rhyme, listen to music from James Bond flicks, and check Monty Python sites to determine just how much Spam there is in Spam, sausage, Spam, Spam, Spam, bacon, Spam, tomato, and Spam.

The World Wide Web is the fastest growing part of the Internet. There you'll find government agencies, nonprofit organizations, businesses, newspapers such as the *Los Angeles Times* and the *New York Times,* magazines, photographic archives, cartoons, directories, and much more. There are databases you can search on topics ranging from aviation to Congressional actions to environmental regulations to missing children to nonprofit organizations to speedtraps.

For journalists, the Web is becoming a good way to get information quickly for stories done on deadline, to gather databases for major investigative projects, to put information and events in a context, to see what other journalists are writing about, and to stay on top of what's happening with computers and online publishing.

WHY THE WEB?

Although some of the sites on the Web will dazzle you with brilliant graphics, the Web, like other Internet resources you've learned about, is still only one more tool to use when you need an expert or some information. What sets it apart from other online resources is that it is relatively easy to navigate; it's growing by leaps every day; on the Web you can find not just text or software, but also graphics and pictures, sound and video; the Web is where online publishing is blossoming.

And then there's the main reason for the Web's popularity: One site on the World Wide Web can lead you, with a keystroke or two, to hundreds of other sites on computers around the world with information related to whatever you are investigating. There are simple ways to do keyword searches so you can get information connected to a particular story or beat.

H IS FOR HYPER

The Web works this way because information is stored on Web servers as *hypertext,* using a special programming language called Hypertext Markup Language, or HTML. With HTML, information is set out in documents called pages, with links, called *hyperlinks,* to other pages embedded in it. A page looks like a document you might create in your word processing or graphics program—it will have text on it, and it may have graphics, photographs, or comics or drawings. Look at the home page for the online *New York Times,* for example. (See Figure 8-1.) This page includes section headings you can click on, using your mouse, to get to other Web pages with news stories and more photos.

A home page is the starting point for a World Wide Web site. This may be the place where someone puts the main and most important information, or it may be just a table of contents, listing various things you can get to from that page. It may also include links to pages or files of information on other sites.

FIGURE 8–1

The New York Times home page on the World Wide Web, viewed with Netscape.

NOT-SO-MISSING LINKS

Suppose you are reading a news story about three people who had to be rescued after they were caught in a storm while trying to climb Mount Washington in New Hampshire. This main story is on the front page of your paper. There are three sidebars to this story, all of them inside the paper, so "refers" or blurbs referring you to these other stories are boxed with the main story. One blurb tells you there's a story on page 6 about this being the ninth time people have had to be rescued from Mount Washington this year; the second tells you there's a story on page 7 about hypothermia, which two of the climbers suffered from; the third blurb tells you another story on page 7 features the people who do such rescues and the training they receive.

Now, imagine this same story in hypertext on the World Wide Web. You'd have text (you could have photographs too, as with a regular, ink-rubbing-off-on-your-hands newspaper). Within the text of the story, certain words are highlighted, underlined or set in a different color than the rest of the text. These words would be hyperlinks to other Web documents. The word "hypothermia" might be highlighted; after you click on the word, up on your computer screen would come a document about hypothermia, its effects and treatment. The word "rescue" might be highlighted; one click and you'd see a story about rescuers.

The documents on hypothermia and rescuers wouldn't have to be on the same computer as the one about the Mount Washington incident. They could reside on two different computers halfway around the world. And you don't have to know that, or the addresses of the other computers, or even that there are other computers to know about. All you have to do is click, and read, and click again. One Web page can contain many such links to text, graphics, sounds, and video (so you'll see the term "hypermedia" too) on computers all over the world, but the finding is done invisibly—all you have to do is get to one Web page and start following links. You can get to sites in Israel or Japan or Canada, Florida or California or Maine, just by clicking on the screen.

BROWSING AROUND

Before you can get anywhere on the World Wide Web, you need a computer program called a browser. The Web works on the client/server model you've encountered with other Internet resources. Your browser program is the client that transmits your commands to World Wide Web servers holding the information or links you want.

If you are working with a SLIP/PPP account (see Chapter 2), you will use a graphical browser to navigate the Web; this type of program will display graphics and photographs. If you have a shell account and are working through a remote host with terminal emulation software, you can still surf the Web, but your client will be a character-based browser. With this type of browser, you see only text onscreen. The *New York Times* page you looked at before was located with a graphical browser, Netscape; in Figure 8-2, you see what you get when you go to the same site using the text-based browser "lynx."

There are various browser programs available; with some, you can get access to Usenet newsgroups; use Gopher, FTP, and Telnet; and send and receive e-mail. This chapter will show you the basics of lynx and Netscape Navigator for the Macintosh.

MORE ADDRESSES

When you began using e-mail you deciphered e-mail addresses; with Telnet, FTP, and Gopher you used site names to tell client programs which computers to contact. With the World Wide Web and browser programs, you will use URLs, or Universal Resource Locators. URLs look a little different than other addresses, but you are using them to do the same thing—to tell your client program where on the Internet to go. For example, **www.boston.com** is the address for the *Boston Globe* Web page. To get to it, you would type into your computer a command telling it to use the hypertext transfer protocol for the World Wide Web:

```
http://
```

FIGURE 8–2

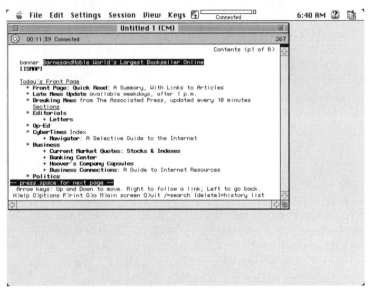

The low graphics version of The New York Times Web page, viewed with lynx.

That protocol is the set of instructions a computer program follows to deal with hypertext.

After the double slashes, you'd put in the Web address:

`http://www.boston.com`

The **com** suffix tells you this is a commercial site. If you saw **edu** there, you'd be at an educational site; if you saw **org** there, a nonprofit organization. The domains are the same as those you learned about with e-mail addresses. (See page 49, Chapter 4.)

Sometimes you'll have a more complicated address to deal with. When you looked at files on an FTP site, you followed a path name from directory to subdirectory to file. You'll do this with URLs too. For example, the Hot News/Hot Research page, put together by David Shedden, researcher and archivist for the library at the Poynter Institute for Media Studies, and Nora Paul, Poynter's library director, includes links to Web sites and pages connected to breaking news events. The page can be found at this URL:

`http:www.poynter.org/hr/hr_intro.htm`

While **www.poynter.org** is the name of the computer site, the first **hr** refers to a directory containing the file you're trying to get to. You'll sometimes see a number of directories listed in an address, nested together. The last part of the address, **hr_intro.htm**, is the name of the file you want. Some addresses don't have that part; you'll have to get to a Web page and find a link to the exact file you are looking for.

The Web is case-specific; it matters whether letters in an address are upper- or lower-case.

JUST BROWSING

The basics of navigating the Web are the same no matter what browser you use: You can move from Web page to Web page by choosing links embedded in each page, or you can tell your browser to "go to" a certain address; save text to a file on your computer or in your account on your host computer; mail documents to yourself or to others; move back and forth between places you've visited fairly easily; and bookmark places you know you'll want to return to again and again. With the character-based program lynx, you'll use your arrow keys and other keystrokes to navigate and work with documents on the Web. With Netscape, you'll use your mouse to click on links and icons and pull down menus.

LYNX EXAMPLE

Take a look at how lynx and the Web work. Say you want to go to the Thomas page offered by the Library of Congress. It's a good resource for information

---

Web Glitches

Unexpected things can happen while you are trying to get somewhere, and none of them necessarily mean you did anything wrong. When you get an error message, though, first make sure you've typed in the URL correctly. The computer can only do what you tell it to do, not what you wish it would do.

You may get a message saying the server you want to contact is busy and you should try again later. Sometimes you just can't get into a site at a particular moment because so many others are trying to get there too.

You also may find that the site or file you're seeking doesn't exist or that the address has changed. The Web is a work in progress and will continue to be so; everything definitely does not stay the same. If you are trying an old address, you may get a message that tells you the new address. If not, there are ways to search for the site you want, as you'll see later in this chapter.

on Congress and legislation. The URL is **http://thomas.loc.gov.** At your system prompt, you type in the following:

```
lynx http://thomas.loc.gov
```

You've now told the host computer you want to use the lynx program, that you are using the protocol for hypertext documents (http://), and that **thomas.loc.gov** is the site address. All Web URLs start with **http://.** Now hit your return button, and wait.

At the bottom of your screen, you'll see messages: one telling you that your host computer is trying to contact the one you designated in the URL, and then, if the connection is successful, that information is being received from that site in bytes. Finally, you'll be presented with a computer screen that looks like the one in Figure 8-3. This is the Thomas home page.

It's all text; any word or phrase that is in darker type than the rest is a hyperlink to a different Web document. At the top right, you see a notation indicating that what you are looking at is page 1 of three pages. Don't get confused. What you are looking at is only one *Web page,* but this one Web page consists of three screenfuls (or pages) of information, which you can scroll through. To scroll down, hit your spacebar; to scroll back up, hit the hyphen key.

At the bottom of the screen in Figure 8-3 is a list of lynx commands. With lynx, you use your keyboard's arrow keys to move from link to link on one Web page, or to follow links from one Web document to another. To move from link to link, up and down, on one Web page, you can use the up and down arrows. To follow a link to a different Web page, choose or highlight the link by using your up or down arrow keys, then hit your right-arrow key. To move backward one link, use the left arrow.

FINDING INFORMATION WITH THOMAS

The Thomas site, like many others on the Web, offers databases you can search using keywords. You get to those databases by choosing links from this home page. You follow links from one Web page or document to another until you find what you want. Just as you worked through hierarchies of menus with Gopher, you work through hierarchies of Web pages and links with the Web.

Look at Figure 8-3 again. You see the title for the page: "THOMAS: Legislative Information on the Internet," and a bit of information about the page: "In the spirit of Thomas Jefferson, a service of the U.S. Congress through its Library."

Underneath these, you see a list of choices you can make from this home page: About THOMAS, Congress This Week, Bills, Congressional Record, Committee Information, Historical Documents, The Legislative Process, and U.S. Government Internet Resources. All of these choices are in bold-face type; they

FIGURE 8–3

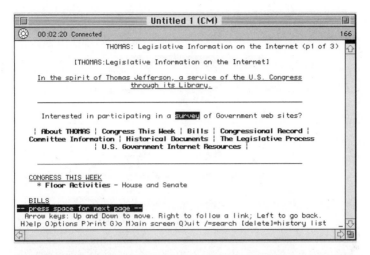

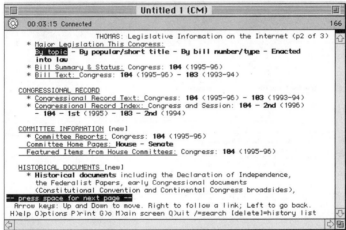

The home page for THOMAS: Legislative Information on the Internet, viewed with lynx.

represent hyperlinks, so if you click on any one of these, you'll get a new Web document onscreen.

Below these is a listing of the same categories, but with details about the information each one represents and with the categories broken down into more specific categories.

Want to check out something in the Constitution of the United States? Use your down-arrow key to move to the link at the top of the Thomas page labeled "Historical Documents," and hit your right-arrow key. You'll move, via this hyperlink, to a new page like the one in Figure 8-4. This page offers other

FIGURE 8–4

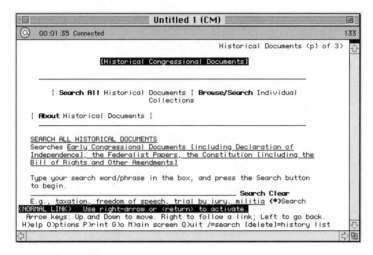

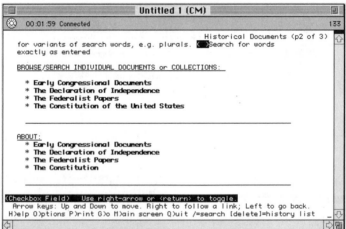

The Historical Congressional Documents page of the THOMAS Web site. Here you can do a key-word search or browse through historical documents such as the Declaration of Independence.

links and options, including a keyword search of the historical documents stored at this Web site. Further down the page, there's a link for "The Constitution." Choose that and you'll get yet another page, like the one in Figure 8-5. Again you get options, including keyword searches. Once again choose the link for "The Constitution of the United States" under the Browse category on this page, and, finally, you'll get a new page, like Figure 8-6, with the text of the Constitution.

This is how hyperlinks and World Wide Web pages work, no matter which browser program you use. You get to one page, choose a link, and follow it to

FIGURE 8–5

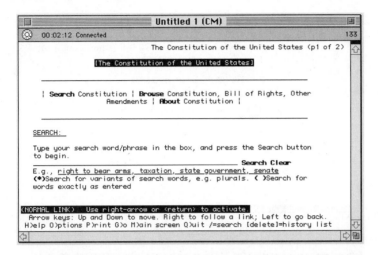

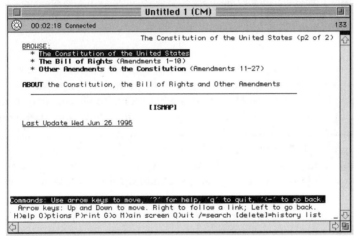

The Constitution of the United States page of the THOMAS Web site.

another page, then choose another link and follow it until you get to information you need.

SAVING AND MAILING: OTHER LYNX COMMANDS

When you're working with lynx, you'll see at the bottom of the screen, like the one pictured in Figure 8-7, a string of commands you can use with lynx. Type **H** and you'll get onscreen help, showing more available commands available; all you need to do is follow the onscreen help and prompts. Type **P** and

FIGURE 8–6

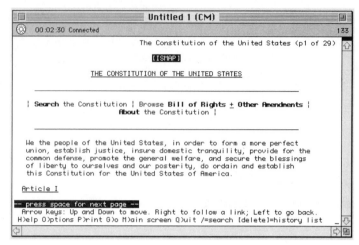

The text of The Constitution of the United States, as stored on the THOMAS site. You can key-word search through this text.

you'll see a page listing choices for working with a Web document: save a copy to a file on your host computer, mail a copy to yourself or someone else, or print out a copy. Each choice will be listed as a hyperlink; to choose an option, you'll use your up and down arrow keys to move to the right listing, then your right-arrow key to start the process.

If you elect to save a copy of the document, you'll be prompted to type in a file name. Your host computer system may not let you save files on it; if so, e-mail a copy to yourself by choosing the mail option. You'll be prompted to provide an e-mail address.

Lynx Tip

When you first start working with lynx, pay attention to which arrow key you're hitting. If you see two bold-faced links on a Web page side by side (in a horizontal listing) it makes sense to use your right-arrow key to move from the left link to the right link, except this would be wrong. The right-arrow key always means you want to follow a particular link; you can't use it to move from link to link on one onscreen page. It will take a little while to get used to this. At least it's easy to move backward when you've followed a link you didn't mean to follow—just hit your left-arrow key.

FIGURE 8–7

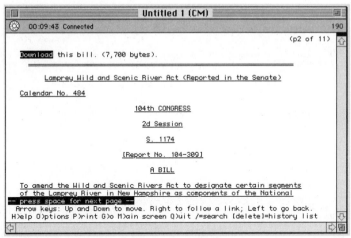

A screen showing text of a bill being discussed by Congress, viewed with lynx. Commands for navigating with lynx are listed at the bottom of the screen; if you type "H" you get more onscreen help.

If you need to download a file you find on the Web using lynx, hit **d.** You'll be asked to choose a downloading protocol. (For more on downloading protocols, see page 32, Chapter 3.)

TOO MANY PAGES, TOO LITTLE TIME

You've seen how easy it is to get lost while moving from Gopher to Gopher. Web surfing can be even more addicting and more dizzying. You're likely to start on one page and surf through twenty more before you look up. Luckily, browsers offer ways to keep track of where you've been, to remind yourself where you are, and to mark places you want to get back to, as you did with Gopher.

With lynx, if you hit your backspace key, you'll see a history page, which lists all the Web pages you've visited during the current lynx session. The listings will be live links, so you can choose one if you want to travel back to a particular page.

Type = to get an information page. This will give you the name and URL of the file you have onscreen and the link you've selected.

To mark a page for future lynx sessions, you can create a bookmark. While looking at the page you want to bookmark, type in **a.** You'll be asked to give the bookmark a name. Once you do that, it's saved in a bookmark file like the one in Figure 8-8. To view the file any time you're working in lynx, type in **v.** The bookmark listings are live links; you can follow them to the marked Web pages.To delete an item from your bookmark file, highlight the right one and hit **r.**

FIGURE 8–8

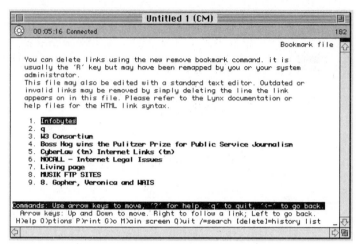

A bookmark file created with lynx. Each listing is a live link to a Web page.

Those are the lynx basics. And all the tasks you carry out with lynx you can also do with a graphical browser. The differences come in the way Web pages look and the way you carry out the tasks.

THE GRAPHIC DETAILS

Since you use a graphical brower with a SLIP/PPP account, you'll have the software program on your own computer and start it up from there. You'll still make your connection to the Internet through your host computer and log on with a login and password. You'll be presented with a Web home page. Everything on the page will be in color; the links will be the words that are in a different color from other text on the page. Sometimes icons or photographs on a page also will work as links.

With a graphical browser, you'll work not just with hypertext, but with hypermedia: text and lots of other digitized information including sound, pictures, and video. For example, at a 1996 Summer Olympic Games site, you might have seen still pictures of the track and field events, watched a video of Carl Lewis's medal-winning long jump, and listened to an interview with Lewis.

A NETSCAPE SESSION

With Netscape, you'll see a Location bar on the first home page you pull up. You can type a URL into that box, then hit your return key. A new Web page will show

CAR in action

"I have found the Internet so convenient that I routinely check it for any story I happen to be working on, to see if there are relevant documents or data that will enhance the story."

That's Patrick Lee, talking about using the Internet to cover his beat. Lee, a business reporter for the *Los Angeles Times,* often finds useful data on the World Wide Web. When he wrote about a U.S.-China trade dispute, he downloaded export and import information from the International Trade Administration Web site. He got the Boeing Company's financial report to shareholders when researching a story about Boeing and China. When he was assigned to cover widespread power blackouts in the western United States in the summer of 1996, he was able to pull from the Web the U.S. Department of Energy's report to the president on a July 2 blackout. He downloaded data on county business patterns, in a spreadsheet format, from the U.S. Census Bureau's Web site and loaded it into a database management program. With that, he says, he was able to select statistics to describe Los Angeles business and economics in a number of stories.

Lee says it's important to become familiar with search techniques for online resources, to know what you are looking for, and to know where the information you find comes from. And he says he spends no more than an hour on any story searching the Internet for information; he also does plenty of "old-fashioned" interviewing and researching for stories.

The Internet offers a wealth of information for business reporters, says Lee, including government economic, employment, census and other kinds of data, and financial documents, both from the the Securities and Exchange Commission and from private companies.

But Lee doesn't use the Internet for things he can get more easily on the telephone, "such as a live comment from a human being," or by fax, such as a brief report.

up on your screen. If you typed in the URL for Thomas, **http://thomas.loc.gov,** you'd get the Thomas home page, just as you did with lynx. But with Netscape, that page will look like Figure 8-9. You can now delete the Thomas page URL and type in another if you want to surf to a different Web page.

With Netscape, at the top of the screen, you see a menu bar; each menu offers you choices of actions you can take, such as saving a file or getting some online help. Next you'll see a toolbar with buttons; each of these allows you to

FIGURE 8–9

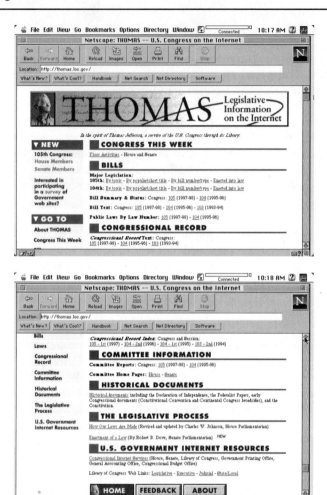

The home page for THOMAS: Legislative Information on the Internet, viewed with Netscape.

take certain actions while working on the Web. Under the Location bar are buttons linked to specific resources on the Web.

MAKING A MOVE

The listings on this Web page in bold, different-colored type represent links, the same links you saw on the Thomas home page using lynx. What do you do when you want to follow a link from this page? Using your mouse, position the pointer

lynx commands	
q	quit the lynx program
h	help—this will give you a list of available commands
down arrow	move to the next hyperlink on a Web page
up arrow	move to the previous link on a page
right arrow	follow a link to another Web document
left arrow	return to the previous document (move backward one link)
g	Type this in while you're working in lynx and you'll be able to type in a new URL and quickly switch to a new Web site.
a	This allows you to add a link to your bookmark file.
v	brings up your bookmark file
r	removes an item in your bookmark file.
backspace key	This shows you a history page, listing the different URLS you've visited during the current lynx session.
=	gives you file and link information, so that if you follow a link to a document, you can figure out where in cyberspace that document resides
/	allows you to search the Web page onscreen using key-words
Control-**g**	stops a document transfer

(it will turn into a tiny hand when you move it across a link on a Web page) on a link, and click once. At the very bottom of your screen is a status bar; here you'll see messages about the progress of the program as it goes out to find the computer you've specified and to bring the Web page to your screen. At the top right, where the box with the **N** is, you'll know the computer is working on your request because white streaks will move through the blue sky in the box while the search for the Web page goes on.

If the linkup is successful, the page will come to life before your eyes, with the graphics building or loading a little at a time. When the building of the page is complete, you'll see "Document: Done" in the status bar. It takes longer for graphics than for text to be transmitted, so pages with very fancy graphics can take awhile to come up onscreen completely.

Now, if you want to go back to the page you were at just before this one, you can simply click on the **Back** button at the top of your screen. If you want to go forward again after that, click on the **Forward** button. The **Home** button will take you back to the home page you started with. If you decide that you don't want to see the Web page that's currently building onscreen, click on the **Stop** button to halt the process.

ANOTHER TURN WITH THOMAS

You've already looked at the "Historical Documents" offerings on Thomas. At this site you can also search a database of legislative bills, using keywords. To do that, click "By topic" under the Major Legislation heading on the Thomas home page. You'll get another page of live links, listings of subjects such as air pollution and labor. If you click on the "Bill Summary & Status" link on this page, you'll be presented with a search page like the one in Figure 8-10.

Suppose you worked in New Hampshire and wanted to know about any bills dealing with your state. You could type in "New Hampshire" as your search phrase. Click on the page's search button, and the search would begin.

The results would be presented as a list of hyperlinks, of course, like the one in Figure 8-11. From that page, you could click on any link to get to the text of a bill.

A NETSCAPE SAVE

When you find text on a Web page you want to save, you can use one of the Netscape menus to do so. Go to the File menu and choose *Save As.* You'll be prompted to type in a name for the copied file; click on **OK** and the copy will be saved on your computer. You'll get only the text, but usually that's what you are going to be interested in anyway. You give the file a name, hit **Return,** and a copy is saved on your computer.

There's a mail option on that menu too, if you want to mail the document to yourself or somebody else. You'll be prompted to type in an e-mail address.

If you find binary files, such as software programs, that you want, you'll often be able to download them with only a click of your mouse on the icons or listings of the files.

MARK THAT PAGE

To create a bookmark with Netscape, all you've got to do is go to the Bookmarks menu and select *Add a Bookmark.* When you want to go to a place you've bookmarked, pull down the menu and select the bookmark; each listing is a hyperlink.

To follow the history of where you've been during a particular Netscape session, look under the *Go* menu. There you'll see a list of the names of the sites you've visited, all of them links. Go to the Window menu and choose *History,* and you'll get a list of the sites you've visited with their URLs.

FIGURE 8–10

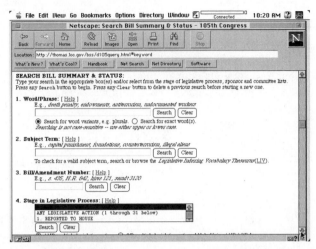

The search page on the THOMAS site. You can search, using keywords, through U.S. House and Senate bills. You can also search for legislation sponsored by a particular member of the House or Senate.

FIGURE 8–11

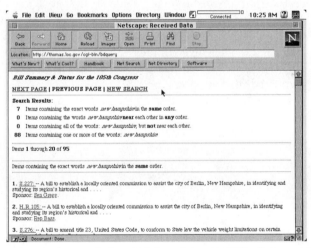

Results of a THOMAS search using the keywords "new hampshire." The listings are all live links to other documents.

LOST AND FOUND

If the Web is so huge, how can anybody ever find anything he or she wants? E-mail, mailing lists, and newsgroups help; often journalists post queries to NICAR-L or CARR-L asking where they might find information. You'll find books that list

A Question of Ethics

The Web is glitzy and fun, and there's so much information out there. Ethical reporting means being thorough, so learning to use the Web is a part of that.

But ethical reporting also means being careful about borrowing information and being fair. If you use someone else's ideas or information in a story, attribute what you use.

Also, be wary of taking everything on a Web site at face value. Remember to treat the information you get online the same way you would treat the information you get offline, with the same respect and the same skepticism. That means, first, that you think about who has created the site and who has put up this information. It's pretty easy to set up a site and put a document up on the Web; you don't have to have special training or particular expertise. Do the people who created this Web site really know the subject they're discussing here? Do they have a hidden agenda? Are they reliable sources of information? Usually at a site there are ways to get in touch with the people behind it. Often you are going to want to do that. Are these people really experts? Are they pushing one side of an argument? Do you need to verify information and see if there are people out there who disgree with it? (Probably.)

Second, remember that databases, computerized and otherwise, sometimes contain incorrect information. So if the information doesn't add up, check it out. The computer doesn't do this for you; it just presents lots of information. It doesn't make judgments on right or wrong, on good or bad information; it just sends it along when you ask for it. You've still got to analyze and ask questions and interview and double-check with other sources. What the online world does give you is more information, instantly, than you've ever had before, and more access to more people than you've ever had before. That's valuable, but the computers don't do your job. They are tools to help you do yours better.

various online resources, such as Bruce Maxwell's *How to Access the Federal Government on the Internet,* and Web sites where journalists and others have compiled links to useful Web pages, such as The Beat Page, put together by Shawn McIntosh of the *Dallas Morning News* (**http://www.reporter.org/beat**).

There are also search tools that help people navigate the Web. These include searchable directories that sort Web pages into subject categories, and search engines that allow you to hunt, using keywords, for links and Web pages. Some of these tools will also find Gopher and FTP sites; some search archives of Usenet newsgroups. They make it easier—not always easy, but easier—to find what you need.

Search resources aren't all created equal, and they don't all do exactly the same thing. It's important to know *how* and *what* a resource searches. Some search the full text of Web pages, while others search only titles, headings and descriptions of Web sites. Some search through more Web URLs than others.

Search engines such as AltaVista **(http://www.altavista.digital.com)** create databases of URLs with automated programs, called spiders or crawlers, that search throughout cyberspace for information about Web pages and files. When you use such a search engine, you are searching through the database that one of these programs created.

With Web directories like Yahoo! **(http://www.yahoo.com)**, what you actually search is a database compiled using descriptions of documents and Web sites written by the people who created the sites or by the directory staff.

Sometimes, a directory is linked to a search engine, so you have access via one Web site to both types of tools.

To search, you go to the home page of a search resource and type in your keywords, then click an onscreen button or link to start the search. The search tool comes up with as many matches as it finds for those words and creates a page listing matches. The listings are all hyperlinks, so you can click on them to go directly to the listed Web pages.

Some tools rank the results of a search for relevancy to your keywords. They might consider one Web document more relevant than another, for instance, if your keywords appear more times or appear higher up on the page in one document than in another.

At a search resource's home page, you can often find information about what the resource searches, how it conducts searches, how it ranks results for relevancy and how often its database of Web pages is updated. Look on that page for links labeled "search," "hints," "options," "advanced searches," or anything that might provide information about the search tool.

A SAMPLER OF SEARCHERS

If you're seeking information on a general topic such as music or computers, an index or directory like Yahoo! at **http://www.yahoo.com** may be the place to start. Yahoo! organizes Web sites by subject area; when you pull up the Yahoo! home page, you'll see a list of subjects including arts, business and economy, entertainment, government, recreation and sports, and society and culture. Each subject heading is a link that will take you to a more specific subject listing. If you choose the entertainment link, for example, you'll get a page of listings including books, comics and animation, food and eating, movies and films, and trivia. Each of those listings is a link too. You can work through Yahoo! pages by subject, from most general listing to most specific.

Yahoo! also lets you search using keywords. It searches only titles on Web pages and short descriptions of what is on a Web site, and it produces a page full of links to the Web sites it locates that include your keywords. The links are listed under subject headings, in alphabetical order by heading.

If you've got a more specific, or more obscure, topic to research, a search engine that searches the full text of Web pages such as Opentext, at **http://index.opentext.net,** may be more useful. Opentext searches 1.5 million Web pages, and it locates FTP and Gopher sites as well as Web pages. The results of a search will include links to the resources Opentext finds as well as the URLs and brief descriptions of each.

And if you're seeking an expert or just someone to interview about a particular subject, you may want a search engine that will search the archives of Usenet newsgroups, such as Deja News at **http://www.dejanews.com.** (Some resources that search the Web also search newsgroup archives.) You can search for messages on a certain topic with Deja News; you can also locate messages posted by a particular person. You'll get back a list of messages; the list will include the date each message was posted, the subject, the newsgroup it was posted to and the author's e-mail address.

ONE SEARCH

New search resources pop up everyday. You'll want to try several out and decide which ones you like best.

AltaVista, at **http://www.altavista.digital.com,** is a search engine created by Digital Corp. The company says AltaVista searches the full text of more than 21 million Web pages and articles from more than 14,000 Usenet newsgroups. You can use Boolean search operators with this resource. The results of an AltaVista search come onscreen as a page of listings, each of them a link to the resource AltaVista found. AltaVista also provides the URLs for the resources.

If you go to the AltaVista home page, you'll see a box where you can type your search terms. A search for "endangered species" would result in a page like the one in Figure 8-12. Scroll down the page and you'll see listings concerning the Endangered Species Act, endangered species and the Great Plains states, endangered species and the St. Louis Zoo, and more. Each of these listings represents information on a different World Wide Web server; this list, created especially for you based on your keywords, connects you to any one of them with just a click of your mouse.

If you chose the first item listed, you'd get onscreen a new page, with a new URL, called the Living For Endangered Species page. That page offers links to the U.S. Fish and Wildlife Service Endangered Species page and to a page for The Raptor Center. Choose the raptor link, and you get to page listing links for all sorts of information on raptors, including the care and feeding of injured birds. And the linking goes on.

FIGURE 8–12

Results of an AltaVista search with the keywords "endangered species."

BRINGING A SEARCH INTO FOCUS

Many Web search tools allow Boolean searches. (For more information on Boolean searches, see page 37, Chapter 3, and page 116, Chapter 7.) Using the Boolean operators **and, or,** and **not,** you can narrow your searches and often make the results more useful.

Some search tools also let you use the operators **near** and **adj.** With **near,** you can set up your search so that two terms, say "budget" and "cuts," must appear *near* each other on the page, and you can usually specify *how near,* say, no more than five words apart.

With **adj,** if you set up a search for "American adj Indian," you are specifying that the pages the search tool locates must include those two words right next to each other, in that order. With some search tools, putting quotation marks around the phrase you are looking for will have the same effect as **adj** does. Without **adj** or the quotation marks, the search engine would find pages including the words American and Indian, but not necessarily pages that tell you about American Indians.

All search tools *do not* offer the same options for searching. So before you begin typing keywords and sending search requests off into the vastness of the Internet, read on the search tool's home page everything you can find about how to conduct a useful search.

NOT WHAT YOU WERE LOOKING FOR?

A search with resources like AltaVista can be a fast way to find useful information. Without these resources, the Web would be terribly difficult to use; you'd have to find things by hit or miss. But searches can also be a waste of time; you won't always find something you need or pages that discuss exactly the subject you are investigating. If the search resource you used lists the items found in order of relevance to your search terms, and you don't find what you need in the first few pages of matches, it doesn't make much sense to go through the next 200 items.

Practice searching with different resources and realize that if you have no luck after trying several search engines and different keywords, it may be time to go offline for the information you need.

FINDING FOLKS

There are people finders on the Web, too, directories and services that let you search by name for people. One such service is Switchboard, at **http://www.switchboard.com.** This service's database is copied from published directories and other public sources of information. You can get addresses and telephone numbers with Switchboard.

CAR in action

The death of the police officer been ruled a suicide. But then the coroner's inquest ruled it a murder. The police had been investigating for almost a year, and now reporter Bob Sablatura of the *Houston Chronicle* was trying to find out whatever he could.

Reading through the autopsy report, he found mention of stippling around the gunshot wound, which might give clues to what happened. He went online, searched the Web with the keywords "forensic" and "stippling," and found a New York forensic scientist who not only had posted articles he had written about gunshot wounds but also about the effects of such wounds and the different types of stippling that occurred.

"This all took me 15 minutes or so," says Sablatura. "If I had tried to find this information without electronic access, I could have spent months and months without finding it."

Another people finder is the Yahoo! People Search, at **www.yahoo.com/search/people.** You can search for telephone numbers and addresses, e-mail addresses and people's home pages on the Web.

The Web and Other Internet Resources

Graphical browsers allow you to get to other Internet resources from the Web. The look of an FTP or Gopher site reached this way is different than ones you've seen so far, but you still get to information by working through hierarchies of files or menus.

To open a Telnet session from the Web, using Netscape, type the Telnet command and the computer address into the Location box, in a slightly different way than you've done before:

```
telnet://sitename
```

With a Web browser, the computer address will always be preceeded by **://**.

Hit your return, the Telnet connection will be made, and you'll log on just as you would if you used Telnet off the Web. And you'll again use keystroke commands the computer system you've logged onto understands.

FTP with Netscape

FTP with a Web browser is easy. You type in the **ftp** command and sitename into the Location box:

```
ftp://wiretap.spies.com
```

You looked at this FTP site using lynx. With Netscape, the site would look like Figure 8-13.

You see names of directories, preceded by file folder icons, and names of files, preceded by page icons. Next to the listings for files, you can see how big the files are and the date each was last changed. To move down in a directory, click on the file folder icon; you'll move to a page showing the next subdirectory. To view a text file, click on it. Each of these listings acts as a hyperlink.

You can save or e-mail information from an FTP site the same way you'd save or e-mail text from a Web site. If you find a binary file you need to download, you can click on it to begin the file transfer.

Gopher with Netscape

You'll get a similar page display if you use Gopher with Netscape. Type in the URL for a Gopher:

FIGURE 8–13

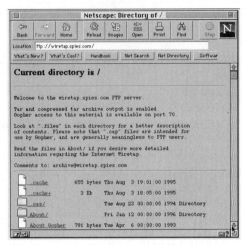

The wiretap.spies.com FTP site as viewed with Netscape. You navigate by clicking on folders (directories) and page icons.

FIGURE 8–14

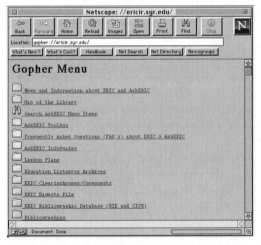

The Gopher for The Education Resource Information Center, ERIC, viewed with Netscape. You navigate through Gopher menus by clicking on folder and page icons.

gopher://ericir.syr.edu

This brings up a page like the one in Figure 8-14. Again, you'll see file folder icons denoting directories; the telescope icon identifies a resource you can use to search a database. To move through the menus on the Gopher, you click on file folder icons; to look at a text file you click on a page icon. You can save text from the Gopher too using the *Save As* option from Netscape's File menu.

You use icons and buttons to work with e-mail and Usenet newsgroups through Netscape too; look under the Window menu for items to start up e-mail or newsgroup work. Graphical browsers like Netscape offer you a way to work with different Internet resources without stopping during an online session to switch programs.

A WIDE WORLD, BUT NOT THE WHOLE WORLD

Journalists have been calling the Internet, and especially the Web, a vast wasteland for years. That is changing. There is more and more useful information to be found, from databases to maps and charts to people you can interview. And it's growing and changing.

But be forewarned: You will not find everything you want out there in cyberspace. While many states now put information on the Web, and even some cities and towns, you're not necessarily going to find something about your community's waste treatment plant, or the local candy factory, or the mayor.

CAR in action

Whit Andrews was working at the *Times* in Munster, Indiana, when he heard Congress was considering a bill with 19 riders that would affect enforcement of air and water regulations. He went online to the Thomas Congressional World Wide Web page, where he could read the entire bill and riders.

"I was able to determine from reading the bill and the 19 riders which ones would have an impact on our area," he said. "Then I was able to take the story out of being a Washington conflict and put it into the realm of what this means for Lake County, Indiana."

What it meant, he found, was that these rules would damage a local oil refinery, that the riders would bar the federal government from proceeding with Superfund cleanup projects in the area, and that the bill and riders, if passed, might prevent the federal government from pursuing action against a local sewage plant.

Through the Thomas Web site, Andrews had immediate access to the bill and riders and could track them through Congress. Then he was able to tell his readers just how seriously all of this would affect them.

What you will find are federal and sometimes state databases, tips from other journalists, maps and weather information, scientific information, museums, library catalogs, journalism organizations, newspapers, people's pets, novels, and comics. The best way to learn to make good use of the Web is to surf it for a while, trying some searches and following links to the good and the weird. It's a tool well worth exploring and understanding.

It's also important, though, to keep the Web and everything else online in perspective. This is only one part of your research for a story. If you can't find something online, don't assume the information or opposition or place or person doesn't exist. Combine computer-assisted research with telephone calls, interviews, observation, and even reviews of paper records to make sure you don't miss something. Getting the whole story is what great reporting, online or off, is all about.

Chapter 9

IT'S COMPUTERIZED, BUT IT'S NOT ONLINE, PART I: INFORMATION ON CD

What's smaller than a breadbox but holds more information than a stack of telephone books?

A compact disk. Where once you might have found a dictionary, telephone book, and street directory on a reporter's desk, you now may find CDs with information about people, businesses, science, sports, medicine, literature, the environment, finances, and the highways and byways of the United States.

CDs with Information

If you have a CD-ROM drive on your computer, you've opened up a whole new reference library for yourself. Library Director Nora Paul of the Poynter Institute for Media Studies, in her online "Computer Assisted Research: A Guide to Tapping Online Information," says some CDs offer much more information than print versions of the same databases, and low cost makes them a good choice for many newspapers trying to beef up their reference libraries.

She also cautions that here may be a lag in the updating of the CDs, so information online may be more up to date. The way you search for information can vary from one CD to another, so you have to learn different search techniques. But there is on-disk help to learn how to search and how to print out what you find.

CD Memory

"CD-ROM" stands for *compact disk, read-only memory*. While the technology exists to write information to CDs, right now you're only going to be concerned about reading the information that's on there. And one of the things that sets CDs apart from computer disks is how much information they can hold.

CAR in action

When a man in Akron, Ohio, climbed into a Cessna that he owned with four other people in a flying club and took off, flying aimlessly, air traffic controllers in Cleveland and Youngstown, Ohio, and Erie, Pennsylvania, tracked him. At about 1:15 a.m., he plunged to his death into the Shenango River Lake near Clark, Pennsylvania. The police had been preparing to arrest the man and charge him in connection with a hit-and-run accident before he took off.

The *Herald* of Sharon, Pennsylvania, needed information fast. A reporter was sent to the scene and told to get the tail number of the plane. With that, staffers were able to ask the Federal Aviation Administration the right questions and pull unofficial information on the plane from an aviation page on the World Wide Web. Then they used a CD-ROM telephone-listing database to find the registered owner of the plane and many of the pilot's next-door neighbors. And all of this was done on deadline.

John Zavinski, director of graphics and technology at the *Herald* (he says this means he's in charge of "weird coding and things that buzz, whir and hum"), says CD phone databases are frequently used by reporters at the Herald. Once, a reporter needed to track down a former local steel executive who was supposedly under house arrest; the reporter didn't know in which house, since the executive owned three. Searching with the CD for variations of the executive's name, staffers found a number and reached his answering machine in suburban Washington, D.C.

A competing newspaper ran a story about a man, supposedly from the local Hempfield Township, who had found his long-lost sibling with a CD phone database. Zavinski says unfortunately that paper didn't check a database for the address of the story's subject. The Herald discovered that "the man was from another Hempfield nowhere near here," he says.

The amount of space data takes up on a disk or computer hard drive is measured in bytes. A 3.5-inch high-density floppy disk can hold about 1.4 megabytes; a CD-ROM can hold about 600 megabytes.

CDs offer searchable databases of different types. Some are Yellow Pages–type listings; some offer bibliographic information on articles so you get the title of a article, the date, the publication it appeared in, and other such information, but you have to get the article from another source; some offer the full text of articles.

WHAT'S ON TAP?

There are CDs with databases of information on hundreds of subjects. In Paul's online guide, at http://www4.nando.net/prof/poynter/chome.html, you'll find a hypertext link to a list of useful CDs put together by Kathleen Flynn, coordinator of Electronic Services at *U.S. News & World Report.*

CDs used in newsrooms include all sorts of directories, reference works, and collections of information. James Derk, computer columnist for the Scripps Howard News Service and computer editor for the *Evansville* (Indiana) *Courier,* says that in his newsroom, for example, reporters work with CDs containing millions of business and residential listings, including addresses and telephone numbers; encyclopedias; electronic atlases that include street-level maps for the United States; information about toxic substances released into the air, water, and land by manufacturing plants; census information; data about over-the-counter and prescription drugs; the complete text of hundreds of literary works; the budget of the United States; criminal justice statistics; stories from daily newspapers across the country; and databases concerning music, sports, cinema, historical government documents, U.S. foreign affairs, marriage records, and business.

Because they hold plenty of data and allow searches for particular information using a person's name or other keywords, CDs are a great resource for journalists working on deadline and off.

Chapter 10

FINDING MEANING WITH SPREADSHEETS AND DATABASE MANAGERS: AN INTRODUCTION

Bubba the beagle. Twenty-four missing Mazda Miatas. Two hundred fifty thousand dollars for the fire department.

None of these scraps of information means much by itself. But you can put the power of your computer to work and find meaning in such bits of data. Using computer programs called spreadsheets and database managers, you can sort through thousands of pieces of information like these, sum up hundreds of numbers, or compare statistics and records, looking for patterns or trends that indicate something significant is happening.

If you find one dog in your city named Bubba, it won't matter much to a reader—unless he or she is having trouble choosing a name for a puppy. But if you find out seventy-eight dogs in your city are named Bubba, and twenty of them are owned by the same person, you might have the beginnings of a feature story dog lovers and others would enjoy.

You won't be able to tell readers much about how safe it is to park downtown if all you know is that ninety-five cars were stolen last year in your city. But if you can find out where the cars were parked when they disappeared and whether the number of cars stolen last year is more or less than the number stolen in other years, you've got a compelling story of love and loss and cars to tell.

And if the fire department's budget increase is a lot more or less than other departments are getting, you'll have a few pointed questions to ask city officials before you write about what this budget means.

Spreadsheets and database managers can help you figure all this out. They give you reporting power because these programs can carry out thousands of calculations in seconds and quickly sort and group information so you can see what might be significant and what might not.

Journalists use these computer-assisted reporting tools for all sorts of stories:

- William Casey, director of computer-assisted reporting for the *Washington Post,* used computer analyses to gather information for stories showing only one in four homicide cases in Washington, D.C., resulted in convictions; about the reasons residents in the poorest areas of metropolitan Washington lacked access to doctors and basic medical care; about how mail delivery in the Washington area was improving but wasn't as good as residents and postal officials wanted it to be.
- The *Atlanta Journal & Constitution* was able to tell readers that what hospital patients paid for services in Georgia didn't necessarily correlate with costs or quality. Instead, it had more to do with what kind of doctors practiced at a particular hospital and with hospitals' competition for patients.
- Reporter David Danelski of the *Press-Enterprise* in Moreno Valley, California, used a spreadsheet to record information about a group of teens and their weeklong carjacking spree. He sorted the information by date and time so he had a chronological record of the spree; this also helped him identify teens the police had not named in press releases. He included court information in his computer database and was able to track what happened to members of a particular gang who were involved in twelve separate criminal cases.
- Journalists at the *News-Press* in Fort Myers, Florida, analyzed information for a feature story showing which homes in their area had the highest appraised value; a local Congressman owned the second-highest appraised home.

One of the greatest benefits of such computer analysis is this: You don't have to rely on what officials tell you about the data you've got, whether it's a city budget or aircraft safety records from the Federal Aviation Administration. You can create a computer database, if one doesn't exist, and you can examine the raw information yourself.

Then, armed with what you've discovered, you can complete interviews and other research, and turn out in-depth stories based not just on anecdotal information but also on the actual records.

To make the most of these software programs, though, you are going to have to learn some new jargon, some new ways of thinking about information, and some math.

STRENGTH IN NUMBERS

The world is getting more complex every day. Readers are bombarded with information, some of it statistics, and making sense of it isn't easy. But making sense of it is a vital job journalists can tackle if they know how to work with and compare numbers.

There are many computer whizzes out there doing complicated statistical analysis. But you don't have to start with that. This book will show you how to do some basic calculations and to sort information to look for patterns and surprises, using spreadsheet and database management programs.

In the past, for example, a city manager or mayor might propose budget figures for the next year, tell reporters how much of a total increase that budget would represent over the current year's, and then explain that she was going to have to raise taxes to pay for the budget. The reporters could look over the budget, in its daunting, multipage form, but often they didn't have the time or inclination to study the budget further. In fact, on deadline a journalist could probably do very little with an unwieldy budget, except maybe to explain the big picture and look at a few individual parts, maybe the school budget and the fire budget.

If you were one of those reporters, you might rush back to your office and write a story that gives the budget totals for various city departments. You might leaf through a few pages to see if anything unusual jumps out at you, then explain how much the budget has increased over the past years, then report what the mayor said about the budget and the coming tax increase, and move on to your next story.

But if you have a spreadsheet program—and if you are really lucky, you might even get the mayor to provide the budget on a computer disc, already in a spreadsheet—the computer can help you analyze the budget, check what the mayor says versus what the budget says, and maybe even figure out what the story should tell readers and what questions you should ask city officials.

WHAT'S IN A DATABASE?

You can use a spreadsheet or a database manager to create and analyze a database, which is a collection of related information, usually put into some uniform format. A database can come in computerized form or paper form. A telephone book is a database; a library card catalog is a database. A collection of records of who works for your school system is a database; so is a file of information about hazardous chemicals. And if you put information about a crime spree or property appraisals or school employees into a spreadsheet or database management program, you are creating a database.

What you can do with a database when you're working on a story doesn't have to be complex. Eventually you may learn to perform sophisticated statistical analysis with complicated collections of data, but you can begin with your story idea, knowledge of a few basic things spreadsheets and database managers can do, and some questions.

INTERVIEWING THE DATA

Asking questions is key. Don't approach spreadsheet or database work as something totally removed from all the other reporting you've been doing. It's not.

How does your usual reporting process go? You get a story idea. You try to find background information by checking in the newspaper's morgue or library (or maybe you're a savvy reporter who knows how to use online sources to get information), and you figure out which sources to interview and what questions to ask. You ask those questions, and you write your story.

Now add a step before the interviewing. You have a database. It might be a budget; it might be records of crime in your state, categorized by city and type of crime; it might be hospital records showing the number of cesarean deliveries your area hospitals perform. Before you interview people for your story, "interview" the database. Use your computer to sort out the information, find what's most interesting or most important or surprising. Ask questions and use the software to get the answers.

For example, consider that budget the mayor handed out. What do you need to know: How much is this budget going up from the past year's? Which departments are getting increases, and how big are the increases? Which departments do not benefit from this budget? Which city services are eating up the most money? Is the tax increase really necessary?

Once you figure out your questions, all you have to do is put those questions into a format that your spreadsheet program or database program can understand. The program will do the calculations and give you the answers.

This type of questioning helped Michael Berens of the *Columbus* (Ohio) *Dispatch* when he wrote a series of stories, "Cash Register Justice." He discovered that thousands of Ohioans were serving jail time for crimes that weren't legally punishable by jail, simply because they could not afford to pay fines. Berens, who used spreadsheets and database managers to report the story, says, "I had all of this raw data about who was going to jail. I asked questions of the data. It's in interviewing the data that you find the real answers." He asked why so many people charged with minor offenses such as jaywalking or failing to register a pet were going to jail; he asked whether people charged with more major offenses were getting out of jail more quickly than others; he asked how many times drivers bypassed mandatory jail sentences for drunken driving by paying fines.

WHAT TO LOOK FOR

When you ask questions of the data, you are looking for trends, patterns, or anything that raises more questions than it answers. This computer analysis gives you more in-depth knowledge about your subject, more to ask about, and more to report. And anything that makes you more knowledgeable about your subject has to be good for you, your paper, and your readers.

Using computers, you'll also be able to analyze records you might not have been able to before, because there are so many of them. Berens said, "The 'Cash Register Justice' series would have been impossible to do with paper records. [With the computer,] I'm able to sift through hundreds of thousands of cases and look for patterns and trends, especially patterns that the court would rather I not see."

Much of this type of analysis is being done with enterprise projects, which are major stories that take weeks or months to complete. But as more journalists become proficient in such analysis they are also tapping into databases for stories they have only few days to work on, or even for breaking stories completed on a tight deadline.

HARD NEWS AND FEATURES

Not every story lends itself to this type of investigation. If you have only a few numbers to deal with or a few calculations to work on, you'll probably find it's faster to do them by hand or with a calculator.

But if you have hundreds or thousands or millions of records to work with, you'll want to use a spreadsheet or database manager. If you need to see if there's a pattern or trend in all that information, or if you need to sort out and keep track of lots of text or numbers, use a spreadsheet or database manager.

Many stories that reporters use this type of computer-assisted reporting for are about serious subjects, such as Duff Wilson's *Seattle Times* stories about children dying while in state-approved foster care. You can also use these reporting techniques for features, such as the dog-name story. And once you've got some databases available in your newsroom, you may even find you use them for some deadline stories. For example, if you have a database with the names and addresses of city employees, you might use it when the police log reveals that someone you think works for the Department of Public Works has been arrested and charged with receiving stolen property.

GETTING STARTED

When you begin your reporting, think about what resources and sources you need to tap into, just as you do when you begin any reporting project. Ask yourself some questions: Who is the expert on this subject, or will have information about this? What information do I need to know, and which person, agency, or resource can provide it? How can I find out who has the power to change the situation or event or trend I'm reporting on? How can I find out who is most affected?

Next, you'll use your knowledge of online reporting tools to see if there's helpful information online, and you'll contact the people who have other data, perhaps in computerized form, that will help you report the story.

When you have gathered information and put it into your computer, you can start asking questions and getting answers with your spreadsheet or database manager.

SPREADSHEET OR DATABASE MANAGER?

Spreadsheets are good tools for keeping track of and organizing information and for analyzing budgets or any other numerical information. They can help you calculate quickly and easily (and over and over again), sort information so you can see trends or patterns, compare numbers, and create charts.

Database management programs can do these things too, but they can handle many more records than spreadsheets; the limit for a spreadsheet program is usually about 16,000 records. Database managers can quickly analyze millions of records and organize records into groups, also showing patterns or trends. A database manager can pull records out of a large database that match a criterion you specify, say, all the people in the city with dogs named Bubba. And with a database program, you can compare two or more databases, say one database listing all the people in your state who've been convicted of a felony in the last five years and another listing all the people teaching or working in your public schools. You can figure out how many people working in the public schools have been convicted of a felony in the past five years or how many people with drunken-driving convictions are teaching driving school, or how many . . . well, you get the picture. Often reporters use both, analyzing raw data with a database manager and then looking at smaller pieces of that data with a spreadsheet.

Learning to use these programs requires curiosity, patience, and a willingness to make mistakes. Once you get the hang of things, you'll probably be hooked, and you'll keep on learning more sophisticated ways of using these programs.

And just as there are resources you can go to for help with online research, so too is there help available for learning to use these programs. There are journalists out there who have done lots of this kind of analysis of databases; if you get stuck, they may be able to help. Journalists who have done certain types of analyses often are glad to share what they've learned.

Michael Berens of the *Columbus Dispatch* says you should start by learning just what you need to know to do a particular story; you don't have to understand every aspect of every program right away—or maybe ever. The simplest analysis can be done with a spreadsheet, and he says there are hundreds of stories that can be done using that tool.

Plenty of books explain spreadsheets and database management programs and math; there are computer tutorials for learning to use these tools, too.

Finally, keep in mind that any information you can gather and analyze should help you figure out where the center of your story lies, what's important about the subject for readers, what the numbers or other data mean. But numbers are usually not the story—the people represented by the numbers are the story. The more numbers you gather, the more important it's going to be to talk to people and visit places and figure out how to make those numbers come alive to your readers. Great interviewing and observation and powerful writing are more important than ever.

NUMBERS, NUMBERS EVERYWHERE

With spreadsheets and database programs, you're going to be concerned with several things: adding and subtracting numbers, of course; figuring out percentages; figuring out rates.

You need to do more with numbers than simply list them because by themselves they often don't mean very much or the meaning isn't clear. You can find meaning by comparing one number to another. As you learn about how to get spreadsheets and database managers to do what you want, you'll learn or relearn the math that will help you make sense of the information you've got in front of you.

VITAL STATISTICS

Suppose you know that there were 170 parking tickets given out on one street and 29 on another; you might assume that one street is more ticket-prone. But what if that street where 170 tickets were given out has space for 70 cars to park, while the one where 29 tickets were given out has space for only 20? Simply comparing the ticket totals won't give you an accurate or complete picture of what is going on. To compare such numbers, it makes sense to convert them into a rate of some sort.

There are three formulas that turn numbers into rates: percentage, percentage change or difference, and per capita. A spreadsheet or database manager program will do these calculations for you, but you need to be clear on exactly what you are asking the program to do.

PERCENT OF TOTAL

You have 25 bagels; four of them are onion bagels. Your roommate says you buy way too many onion bagels. You want to show him that's not true, so you compare the number of onion bagels to the total number of bagels. You want to figure out what percentage of your bagels is of the onion variety.

To figure out a percentage, you create a fraction by dividing one number by another, the smaller amount by the total. To determine your bagel answer, you need to know what percentage four out of 25 is. So the fraction you will use is 4/25 or four divided by 25. The answer is 0.16. Percentage is rate per 100, so multiply that number by 100. Of the bagels you bought, only 16 percent were onion.

For news stories, you'll use percent to figure out such matters as what percentage of parking tickets are given to city employees, or how big a chunk of the town budget goes to the police department, or what percentage of fires in your community are caused by arson.

PERCENTAGE DIFFERENCE

You and your brother each got 45 speeding tickets this year, so he's claiming he's as careful, or careless, on the roads as you are. But you know that last year you got 30 tickets, while he only got 20. You want to show him that his ticket increase shows his speeding problem has worsened a lot more than yours. You can do that by figuring out the percentage difference.

When you calculate percentage difference or percentage change, you are comparing two numbers and trying to determine the significance of the change from the first number to the second number. You got 30 tickets last year and 45 this year; the difference between those two numbers is 15. You want to know how much of a change, in percent, that is from your original ticket total of 30. So you create a fraction, 15/30, and get .50. Multiply that by 100 and you get 50 percent, which is how much your speeding ticket rate has increased over last year.

The difference in the number of tickets your brother got is 45 minus 20, or 25. Divide 25 by last year's amount, 20, and get 1.25. Multiply by 100, and you'll see he had a 125 percent increase in the number of tickets he got.

(Of course, you cannot assume from these numbers that both of you are speeding more. Other factors might be involved; you both might be traveling more roads that are more heavily patrolled by police, or your brother might have bought a red sports car that attracts more attention. Never assume anything. Just describe, in a story, what you know from the numbers, not what you guess.)

This type of comparison will help you determine which departments or employees benefit most from a new city budget. The mayor might say that two departments get the same benefit from a proposed budget because each will receive a $50,000 increase. But if one department's original budget was $50,000 and the other's was $300,000, they are not both faring the same, and the percentage difference will help show that.

PER CAPITA

If you compare numbers, say, of premature births or car accidents by city or state or county, the basic numbers may not tell the whole story. New York City might have 560 accidents a year and Podunkville might have 20. You'd assume that New York City was more dangerous—but if New York City has a lot more people (and therefore lots more cars on lots more streets), then just comparing those two numbers is misleading. One way to deal with that is to turn the numbers into a per capita rate. Per capita takes into account the population of a place. To figure out the per capita rate in this case, for example, you'd divide the number of accidents in New York City by the population of the city. You'd do the same with Podunkville, and then you'd have apples and apples to compare, instead of apples and grapes.

If the number of occurrences of something, such as accidents, is small, your per capita rate will be small too, like 0.0009. To make rates like this easier to compare, such statistics are often multiplied by 100,000. What you'd have here, then, would be 90 accidents per 100,000 people.

MOVING ON TO SPREADSHEETS

The next chapter will show you the basics of putting information into a spreadsheet as well as using it for calculations, including percent and percentage difference. Chapter 12 will show you some of the ways you can use a database management program.

Newspapers use various software programs. The instructions and illustrations given in this book for spreadsheets are for one of the most popular, Microsoft Excel, used on a Macintosh computer. Newspapers use others, too. Chapter 12 will include examples in Microsoft FoxPro.

LEARNING THE STEPS

If you've used spreadsheet or database management programs before, this may all seem easy. If you haven't, just take it one step at a time.

Beth Marchak of the Cleveland, Ohio, *Plain Dealer*'s Washington bureau sometimes works with college students on computer-assisted projects. She says that when she's confronted by students who are nervous about tackling such programs, she sometimes mentions the slogan on a relative's T-shirt: "Shut up and dance." In other words, Marchak says, just plunge in. Some of this work is not easy; constructing databases can be time-consuming, and learning to use the programs will take time and patience.

You'll probably make some mistakes; the best reporters sometimes do. If you're afraid mistakes you make in analyzing information will result in bungled stories, remember that the computer analysis is only the *beginning* of your reporting. You are still going to interview people about the numbers you arrive at, and you may even work with an outside consultant to get the numbers right; many news organizations do this. If your numbers seem wrong, you'll ask someone about them. If your analysis uncovers something so surprising that it makes you suspicious, you'll ask somebody about this too.

But the only way to learn this type of computer-assisted reporting is to try it. The band is playing; the dance floor is wide open.

Chapter 11

SPREADSHEETS: BY THE NUMBERS

It was a dark and stormy afternoon. I was looking out at the rain-swept street, remembering Paris. Behind me, I could hear the clacking of keyboards. The newsroom didn't look much like Paris. I didn't look much like Paris either. I sighed and turned back to my computer. I had a story to write. That's my job. I'm a reporter.

"Smythe!" my editor bellowed. "What have you got on that budget?"

Smythe, that's me. Marguerite Smythe. Rhymes with scythe.

Earlier that day the mayor of our city had given me a copy of her proposed budget for the coming year. I'd put it all into a spreadsheet program on my computer, nice and neat. Now I had plenty of questions.

How much was the city budget going up? How much in taxes would all of us poor slobs have to put up to pay for it? Which city department was going to get the most money? How come I hadn't had a raise in two years? Ah, well, I wasn't going to find an answer to that one.

But the first three—they were easy. The spreadsheet did it all, figured out the answers and spit them out. The budget was going up by $1.8 million. The fire department was getting the biggest chunk of the loot. And property taxes weren't going to go up much at all, just like the mayor had said—but every other tax was going to skyrocket.

Now I had lots more questions—to ask that mayor.

I'm a reporter. That's my job.

You can make spreadsheets sing too. Journalists use them to make sense of information in lots of ways:

- To do calculations, adding numbers or figuring out percentages or comparing rates. You could analyze budgets, campaign contributions, or a community's recycling rates, or compare annual property appraisals or the amount of traffic on certain roads, for example, using a spreadsheet.

- To sort numbers and text, putting items into alphabetical or numerical order, so trends, patterns, and changes over time can be seen. If you had records of city employees' overtime earnings, you could see who, in which jobs, made the most for working overtime, how much that overtime pay compared to those people's regular salaries, and how much the city's overtime payouts were increasing over time. You might use a spreadsheet to store information about court cases you were following or about a natural disaster in your community so you could quickly find what happened on a certain date or list every related event in order by date and time.
- To create graphs and charts so readers can visualize the changes represented by the numbers. You could create a column chart, for example, showing the differences between last year's budget figures and this year's for each city department.

BY THE NUMBERS

First and foremost, a spreadsheet is a way to keep track of information. You may have created a sort of handwritten spreadsheet in your notebook in the past. If you've ever drawn columns, labeled each column, and put some information in each, you've made a spreadsheet. Say, for instance, that you were trying to compare schools in your city. You might have many different pieces of information, such as test scores, lists of courses—required and elective, and so on. You'd try to get all this information on that page, putting the test scores in one column, the number of students in another, and so on. You might average the test scores and also figure out the student-teacher ratio.

A computer spreadsheet program can help you record, sort, and evaluate information. It can help you do it quickly, and it can easily handle hundreds of pieces of information in seconds. Another benefit of using spreadsheets is that you don't have to do every calculation individually, over and over again. So the spreadsheet can help minimize human error and the time it takes to find what you're looking for. It's a tool that makes this kind of analysis easier and faster.

Figure 11-1 shows you a spreadsheet with information from a database of dog licenses. Remember the dog Bubba? The information is listed by categories—dog owner's name, street, dog's name, dog's breed, and dog's age—and set out in a uniform way, so it's easy to go through.

You can put information into this format, then ask questions about the information. You have to ask those questions in a way your computer and spreadsheet program can understand, and that can mean typing in a mathematical formula or a particular command or choosing a command from a menu. But once you've done that, the computer will do the sorting and the calculating for you.

FIGURE 11–1

An Excel spreadsheet filled with dog license data.

BACK TO THE BUDGET

Consider a budget the mayor of your city might give you, as the mayor of reporter Smythe's city did. You wish the mayor had given it to you on a computer disk, already set out in a spreadsheet. If you can get information in some sort of electronic format, you can usually import it into your spreadsheet program in your computer. But your city government still works on paper. So you bring the budget—a database—back to your office to sort the information out.

These are the numbers:

EXPENDITURES	FISCAL YEAR 1996	FISCAL YEAR 1997 (PROPOSED)
City Council	$80,825	$104,875
City Manager	$160,770	$200,785
City Attorney	$122,955	$188,985
Community Development	$298,520	$338,520
Fire	$3,301,685	$3,801,120
Police	$3,989,250	$4,932,850
Public Works	$3,007,700	$3,604,920
Parks & Recreation	$1,556,950	$1,699,850
Total expenditures	**$12,518,655**	**$14,871,905**

REVENUES	FISCAL YEAR 1996	FISCAL YEAR 1997
User fees	$355,625	$756,195
Property taxes	$7,598,750	$7,640,990
Water & Sewer	$3,368,615	$4,583945
Utility taxes	$1,195,665	$1,890,775
Total revenues	**$12,518,655**	**$14,871,905**

The mayor has gleefully announced that because she has done such a great job with the budget, property taxes won't go up. The increase in taxes shown in the budget, she says, will be paid by new businesses that have moved into the community; residents won't see an increase in the property tax they pay for their homes.

Before you start figuring out what to ask and what to say about this budget, put it into a spreadsheet program. Begin by opening up a spreadsheet document in your computer. The one in Figure 11-2 was created in Microsoft Excel on a Macintosh computer.

In this chapter, you'll see some of the ways to use Microsoft Excel; sometimes there's more than one way to carry out a particular task with the program. Microsoft Excel commands will not always be the same as ones used with other spreadsheet programs, but you should be able to transfer the basics you learn here to spreadsheet sessions with a different program.

FIGURE 11–2

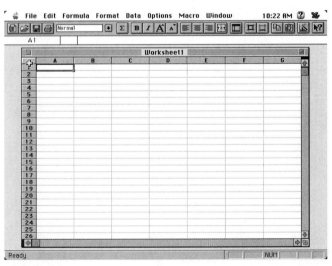

A blank Excel spreadsheet.

You work in a spreadsheet program by using pulldown menus, as listed across the top of the spreadsheet; by clicking and dragging with your mouse; and by clicking on buttons or icons in the tool bar at the top of the screen. There's more than one way to do some things; there are keyboard equivalents to some of the menu actions, for example. This book will show you one way; you can choose whichever method works best for you.

LITTLE BOXES

A spreadsheet is made up of rectangular boxes called cells. Each vertical stack of cells in the spreadsheet is called a column; each horizontal line of boxes is called a row; each row of related information is a record. Columns are labeled with letters, while the rows are labeled with numbers. You can put information into spreadsheet cells, and you can ask the spreadsheet to sort the information in a bunch of cells or sum up numbers in a column, and more.

To get this done, though, you have to be able to tell the spreadsheet program which cells you want it to work with. Each cell is identified by an address. The addresses are simple; the column letter and the row number make up a cell's address. So the top-left cell has the address A1, for column A, row 1. The next one down is A2, and so on. This is the same sort of grid and identifiers you've used when you've looked for a city on a map. Usually a map is divided into squares. Across the top of the map, running from left to right, the squares are identified by letters. Across the sides of the map, running from top to bottom, the squares are identified by numbers. You look at the map key and find that the place you want to go is in F4. So you move across the map to the F squares, then down to square 4. Spreadsheet cells are identified in the same way.

BOXING IT UP

Putting information into a spreadsheet is a little different than putting words into a word-processing document. When you start a document in a word-processing program, you put the cursor where you want to type words or numbers, and start typing.

With a spreadsheet, there are a couple of extra steps to go through. First, you've got to select the cell where you want the information to go to. You'll see that when you are working with the spreadsheet cells, the arrow cursor you are used to turns into a little cross, like this: ✚

You select a cell by putting that cursor in a cell and clicking on it. When a cell is selected, it will have a dark outlined box around it, as in Figure11-2.

Once you've selected the cell, you can type the information in—but it may not appear in the cell right away. It may first show up in the display or formula bar that runs at the top of the spreadsheet. With Microsoft Excel, the information shows up in both the cell and the formula bar. After you type the information, you can check to make sure it is correct, then hit enter or return. The information will be placed in the selected cell, and the select box will move to the next cell down in the column, so if you are typing a bunch of information into one column, you don't need to keep selecting the next cell with your mouse.

If you make a mistake in entering information, just select the cell you need to correct, type the right information into the display bar, and hit enter.

When all the budget information provided by the mayor is typed into a spreadsheet, it will look like the one in Figure 11-3.

When you enter information into a cell, you might find that the information is longer than the cell is wide. To make a column of cells wider, move the cursor to the vertical line separating two columns at the top of the spreadsheet, between the cells with the letter labels in them. The cursor will turn into a double-sided arrow that looks like this <-l->. Now, holding the mouse button down, drag the arrow cursor to the right until the column is as wide as you need it to be.

IN THE MONEY

All the numbers in the spreadsheet so far represent dollars, but there aren't any dollar signs here yet to show that. When you are entering information into a spreadsheet, don't worry about making sure numbers are formatted as dollars

FIGURE 11–3

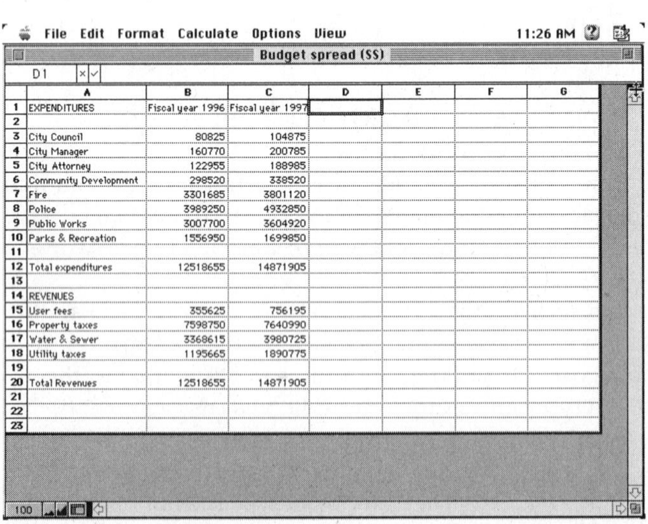

	A	B	C	D	E	F	G
1	EXPENDITURES	Fiscal year 1996	Fiscal year 1997				
2							
3	City Council	80825	104875				
4	City Manager	160770	200785				
5	City Attorney	122955	188985				
6	Community Development	298520	338520				
7	Fire	3301685	3801120				
8	Police	3989250	4932850				
9	Public Works	3007700	3604920				
10	Parks & Recreation	1556950	1699850				
11							
12	Total expenditures	12518655	14871905				
13							
14	REVENUES						
15	User fees	355625	756195				
16	Property taxes	7598750	7640990				
17	Water & Sewer	3368615	3980725				
18	Utility taxes	1195665	1890775				
19							
20	Total Revenues	12518655	14871905				
21							
22							
23							

Budget information in a spreadsheet, including expenditures and revenues for two years.

or a percentage or whatever. But once you've typed the numbers in, you can select or highlight all the cells with numbers you want changed into currency. You do that by placing the cursor at the left top corner of the first cell you want changed, and using your mouse, hold down the button and drag the cursor across all the cells you want to select. All the selected cells will turn black, except for the one you started with. It will stay white. (Don't make yourself crazy trying to turn it black; it is still selected.) You can select only cells that are adjacent to one another.

After you've selected the cells you want as currency, pull down the Format menu and choose *Number.* You'll get a dialogue box that gives you choices of format, including Currency, Date and Time. Click on Currency, click on OK, and the numbers in all the cells you highlighted will be presented as sums of money, with commas in the right places and dollar signs in front of each. (See Figure 11-4.)

INTERVIEW THAT INFORMATION

Once you have the numbers into the spreadsheet, you can begin interviewing your data, just as our fictional reporter Smythe did. What questions do you have about the budget? The first question you might want answered is this: How much of an increase is each department getting? The second: How much is each revenue source increasing?

FIGURE 11–4

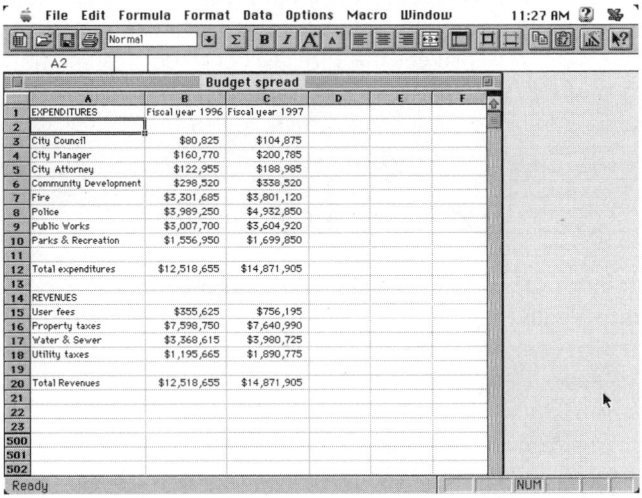

The same budget information shown in Figure 11-3 but in a currency format, with commas and dollar signs.

To get these answers out of the spreadsheet, figure out what mathematical questions you're posing. Say you want to know how much more money the city council will get this year than it got last year, if this budget is approved. How would you figure that out? You'd subtract the proposed 1997 number from the 1996 number. That's what you have to tell the spreadsheet to do.

But you don't type in those numbers to get the answer. Instead, you tell the computer to take the number in one cell and subtract it from the number in another cell. That's why the cell addresses are important. In this case, to find out how much of a budget increase the City Council is getting, you want to subtract the number in B3 from the number in C3.

These are the steps to follow:

- Select the cell where you want the answer to this subtraction problem to go. This cell will contain a formula, as opposed to a label or number. You'd probably want to first select D1, and type in a heading for the column, such as Change, then select the cell in column D that corresponds with the row for City Council.
- Tell the spreadsheet to subtract B3 from C3. You do this by typing a formula into the display box.

With Microsoft Excel, formulas always start with an = sign. If you don't put an = sign in the display box, the spreadsheet thinks you're typing information to be placed in a cell.

So you'd type in this:

```
=C3-B3
```

Then hit enter. The correct answer should appear in cell D3, as in Figure 11-5.

That's the basic way you get the spreadsheet to do a calculation. Select the cell where you want the final answer to go. Type in the mathematical formula. And hit enter.

COPYING THE FORMULA

Now, you want to do the same calculation with the other rows. You could do each one individually, typing in a new formula each time. But if you have 500 rows, you do not want to do that. A spreadsheet program is set up to make this kind of work easier.

You want to copy the formula in cell D3 all the way down so that each row has a yearly change calculation. So select cells D3 through D12 by holding the mouse button down and dragging across all those cells. (Remember, all the selected cells will turn black except for D3.) Then go to the Edit menu and choose *Fill Down*. Here's the beautiful thing. The spreadsheet uses the same

FIGURE 11–5

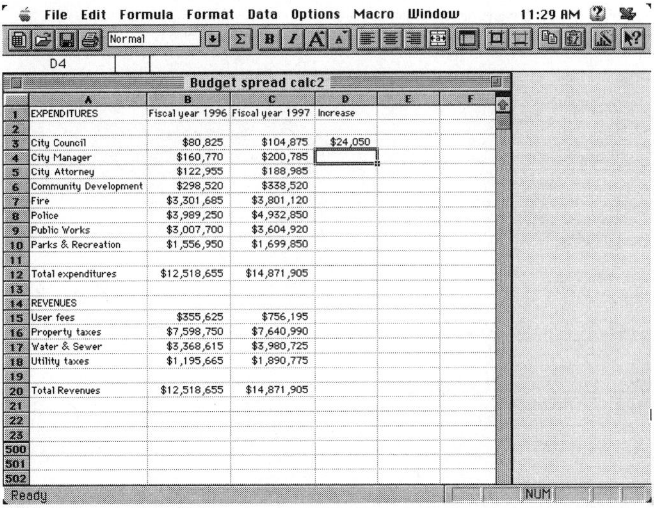

	A	B	C	D	E	F
1	EXPENDITURES	Fiscal year 1996	Fiscal year 1997	Increase		
2						
3	City Council	$80,825	$104,875	$24,050		
4	City Manager	$160,770	$200,785			
5	City Attorney	$122,955	$188,985			
6	Community Development	$298,520	$338,520			
7	Fire	$3,301,685	$3,801,120			
8	Police	$3,989,250	$4,932,850			
9	Public Works	$3,007,700	$3,604,920			
10	Parks & Recreation	$1,556,950	$1,699,850			
11						
12	Total expenditures	$12,518,655	$14,871,905			
13						
14	REVENUES					
15	User fees	$355,625	$756,195			
16	Property taxes	$7,598,750	$7,640,990			
17	Water & Sewer	$3,368,615	$3,980,725			
18	Utility taxes	$1,195,665	$1,890,775			
19						
20	Total Revenues	$12,518,655	$14,871,905			
21						
22						
23						
500						
501						
502						

A spreadsheet showing how to calculate increases in budget amounts from one year to the next.

basic formula, subtracting the number in B from the number in C, but it switches its calculation to incorporate the correct cells all the way down the spreadsheet to calculate the budget increases. It puts the answer to C4 - B4 in D4, and to C5 - B5 in D5, and so on. Now the spreadsheet looks like the one in Figure 11-6. In cases where there are no values for the spreadsheet to perform a mathematical calculation on, you'll see a value of zero; you can select that cell and delete the zero.

Now you've got an answer to one of your earlier questions. You can see that the Department of Public Works is getting the biggest absolute increase in terms of the amount of money, while the Community Development Department is getting the smallest increase. So now you have two new questions for the mayor: Why is Public Works getting so much more money, and why isn't Community Development getting more?

You can do the same calculation with the revenues, to see what's going to increase the most. You'll see that the biggest dollar growth is for utility taxes, while projected state aid will increase the least. So two things you'll ask the mayor is why the utility tax will be increasing so much, and why she thinks state aid is going to increase so little.

COMPARING ONE INCREASE TO ANOTHER

With a budget, or salaries, or other numbers, the increase from one year to another doesn't always tell the whole story. If two departments get the same

FIGURE 11–6

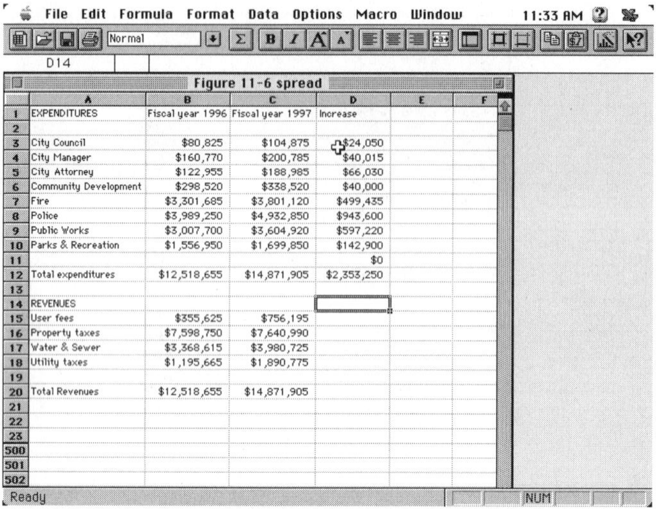

The budget increases in expenditures from one year to the next.

Warning!

Being able to copy formulas down a whole column in a spreadsheet is a great time-saver—imagine having to type in such a formula for 1,000 cells, or doing 1,000 such calculations with your hand-held calculator. If you had to do those calculations by hand, you very likely would make some mistakes; the spreadsheet won't. So spreadsheets can make your work more accurate.

The spreadsheet can only do what you tell it to do, not what you hope it will do. So it's very important that you get your original formula right. Double- and triple-check it yourself, and maybe have someone else look at it too.

Also, when working with any computer program always remember to save your work frequently. Most programs have an auto-save function.

---

increase, say $50,000, that doesn't mean they necessarily fared the same. If one department's budget was originally $125,000, and another's budget was $25,000, which department is going to be affected most by the new budget?

You can figure this out by calculating the percent difference, or percent change—comparing the original budgets of these departments with the budget increase each got. (See Percentage Difference, page 159.) (If the numbers seem confusing and you're not sure what to divide into what, try turning what you've got into a simpler problem. For example, Jim had 5 fish. He got 20 more. The increase was 20; what was the percentage difference? The change is 20 fish. So you divide 20 by the original number of fish, 5. That equals 4. Multiply by 100 to get the percentage—that's a 400 percent difference.)

Look at the mayor's budget and your spreadsheet. Which department is getting the best deal and which worse, if you look at the percentage differences? To find out, you need to use another spreadsheet formula. Select the cell you want the answer to appear in. Start with the percentage difference for the City Council. What are you going to ask the spreadsheet to do? You want it to divide the number in D3, the budget increase amount, by the amount in B3, the original budget figure. You use a slash for dividing, so your formula whould look like this:

=D3/B3

Hit return. You'll get the percent change or percent difference. Now copy the formula all the way up and check out the results, shown in Figure 11-7.

The city attorney's office is getting an awfully big increase, and so is the city manager's office. What's going on? Is the mayor expecting major legal problems in the coming year? Has she hired on relatives and friends to work in those two offices? What's the story?

Do the same calculation for revenues and you'll see that while the mayor may not plan to raise property taxes, folks in this city are still going to pay out

FIGURE 11–7

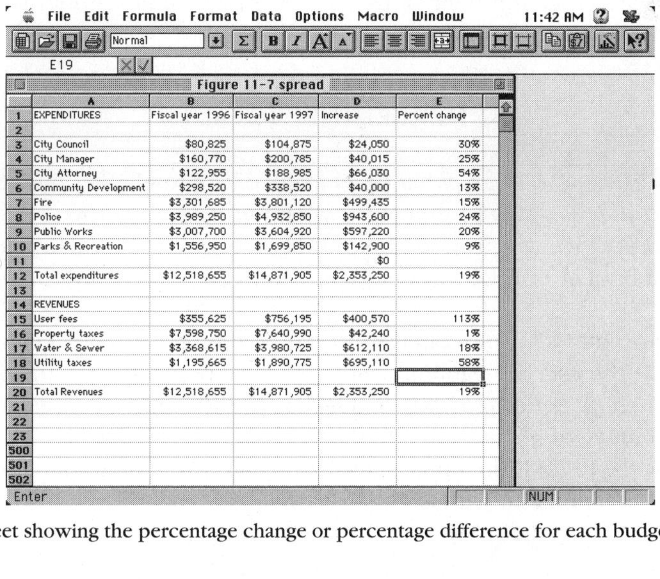

	A	B	C	D	E
1	EXPENDITURES	Fiscal year 1996	Fiscal year 1997	Increase	Percent change
2					
3	City Council	$80,825	$104,875	$24,050	30%
4	City Manager	$160,770	$200,785	$40,015	25%
5	City Attorney	$122,955	$188,985	$66,030	54%
6	Community Development	$298,520	$338,520	$40,000	13%
7	Fire	$3,301,685	$3,801,120	$499,435	15%
8	Police	$3,989,250	$4,932,850	$943,600	24%
9	Public Works	$3,007,700	$3,604,920	$597,220	20%
10	Parks & Recreation	$1,556,950	$1,699,850	$142,900	9%
11				$0	
12	Total expenditures	$12,518,655	$14,871,905	$2,353,250	19%
13					
14	REVENUES				
15	User fees	$355,625	$756,195	$400,570	113%
16	Property taxes	$7,598,750	$7,640,990	$42,240	1%
17	Water & Sewer	$3,368,615	$3,980,725	$612,110	18%
18	Utility taxes	$1,195,665	$1,890,775	$695,110	58%
19					
20	Total Revenues	$12,518,655	$14,871,905	$2,353,250	19%

A spreadsheet showing the percentage change or percentage difference for each budget item.

CAR in action

When John Archibald and Bob Blalock of the *Birmingham* (Alabama) *News* decided to look into their state's record for punishing repeat drunken driving offenders, they used a spreadsheet program to analyze data, including arrest reports, county demographic information, and information on individuals' driving histories and personal histories. They also obtained a database from the Department of Public Safety listing the worst drunken-driving offenders. But, according to "Investigative Reporters and Editors: 100 Computer-Assisted Stories," the database was incomplete, and the reporters had to fill in with information they got during visits to dozens of county offices and small communities where nothing was available in computerized form.

They learned that 110,000 people in their state had been convicted of driving while under the influence of alcohol in the past five years, and that Alabama law was not keeping drivers convicted of drunken driving—even drivers convicted more than once—off the roads.

Tougher legislation concerning DUI cases was passed after the series ran.

---

a lot because user fees are going to increase by a whopping 113 percent and other taxes are going up. What does the mayor have to say about that?

PERCENT OF TOTAL

Suppose you want to know what percentage of the total 1997 budget the city attorney's office is going to pull in, or what percentage of total revenues will come from user fees or property taxes. Then you are asking what percentage of the total budget or total revenues a line item is. (See Percent of Total, page 158.)

To figure out what percentage of total revenues that user fees would be, you'll divide the user fee figure in cell C15 by the revenue total, the number in C20 (Again, think of Jim and his fish. If he has 25 fish, and 5 of them are piranha, what percentage of his fish are piranha? You want to divide 5 by 25; it wouldn't make sense to do it the other way. The answer? 0.2, or 20 percent—unless he puts those piranha in with all the other fish.)

Select a cell for the answer, probably F15, and type in your formula:

```
=C15/C20
```

You then convert your answer to a percentage, using the Format menu and the *Number* option.

Now you want to do the same calculation for all the other revenue categories. But you can't just *Fill Down* with this formula. Here's why. Remember when you filled down with the formula C3 - B3, putting the answer in column D? The spreadsheet software knew that as it moved down in column D, it should move down in columns B and C too, so that it performed C4 - B4 and so on. But you don't want the spreadsheet to move down like that in this case; you don't want the number in the next cell, C16, to be divided by the value in C21, which is 0. You want every revenue category's total divided by the same number, the number in cell C20.

There's an easy fix. Tell the spreadsheet you want it to move down the column, but only with the first value. You want every number divided by the value in cell D20. You do this by using the $ symbol. The formula you should type in this time is:

```
=C15/$C$20
```

The $ signs anchor the C and the 20, so the spreadsheet knows it should always use the value in C20 as the base of the fraction, or the number to divide by. You can do the same calculation for the different city departments and their budgets, typing in a similar formula at the top of the spreadsheet and filling down.

The results are in Figure 11-8.

Any more questions for the mayor now?

SUMMING UP

Typing in formulas isn't the only way to get answers from your data with a spreadsheet. The programs also offer shortcuts called functions, which allow you to sum up or do other calculations quickly. You can use the Sum function to see if the mayor's total revenues and total expenditures are correct or to add up numbers in any category in a database. If you wanted to see if the mayor's revenue total for the year is correct, you'd select a cell in the spreadsheet with the budget figures, then ask the computer to add, or sum, all the revenue numbers for that year. In the formula bar, you'd type this:

```
=SUM(C15:18)
```

The = sign tells the spreadsheet you are using a formula or function, not just typing information into the spreadsheet. Sum explains what you want it to do; and the information in the parentheses tells the computer to use the information in cells C15 through C18. You could also select the cell to hold the answer, type

FIGURE 11–8

File	Edit	Formula	Format	Data	Options	Macro	Window			2:27 PM

F15   =C15/$C$20

Budget spread calc5

	A	B	C	D	E	F	AN	A
1	EXPENDITURES	Fiscal year 1996	Fiscal year 1997	Increase	Percent change	% of '97 total		
2	City Attorney	$122,955	$188,985	$66,030	54%	1%		
3	City Council	$80,825	$104,875	$24,050	30%	1%		
4	City Manager	$160,770	$200,785	$40,015	25%	1%		
5	Police	$3,989,250	$4,932,850	$943,600	24%	34%		
6	Public Works	$3,007,700	$3,604,920	$597,220	20%	25%		
7	Fire	$3,301,685	$3,801,120	$499,435	15%	26%		
8	Community Development	$298,520	$338,520	$40,000	13%	2%		
9	Parks & Recreation	$1,556,950	$1,699,850	$142,900	9%	12%		
10								
11								
12	Total expenditures	$12,395,700	$14,682,920	$2,287,220	18%			
13								
14	REVENUES							
15	User fees	$355,625	$756,195	$400,570	113%	5%		
16	Utility taxes	$1,195,665	$1,890,775	$695,110	58%	13%		
17	Water & Sewer	$3,368,615	$3,980,725	$612,110	18%	27%		
18	Property taxes	$7,598,750	$7,640,990	$42,240	1%	51%		
19								
20	Total Revenues	$12,518,655	$14,871,905	$2,353,250	19%			
21								
22								
23								
500								
501								

Ready   NUM

Percent of total figures (far right column) for each budget item.

=SUM(and drag the mouse across all the cells holding values you want summed. The program will type in all the cell addresses; all you have to do then is close the parenthesis in the formula.

Hit return, and you'll get the sum, as in Figure 11-9. You'll see that the mayor's revenue total is off by more than $600,000. Ah … something else to ask her about.

NOT JUST AVERAGE

When you are working with numbers in a database, sometimes you want to tell readers what the mean, or average, of those numbers is. The average can tell readers what, in a database of values, is a typical value.

A database of parking fines levied against city employees may list total fines for each person. But to give readers an overall sense of how much in fines these employees rack up, you might also tell readers the average amount of fines per person. One way to compare fine amounts, say the amount firefighters owe compared to the amount city workers in all other departments owe, would be to determine the average amount owed by each of these groups and compare those numbers.

You can figure the average by adding up all the values you've got, then dividing that sum by the number of values you added up. If you have 10 numbers in your database, you'd add them and divide the sum by 10. A spreadsheet can make this much simpler because you use the Average function, which will calculate the average of the values you select.

FIGURE 11–9

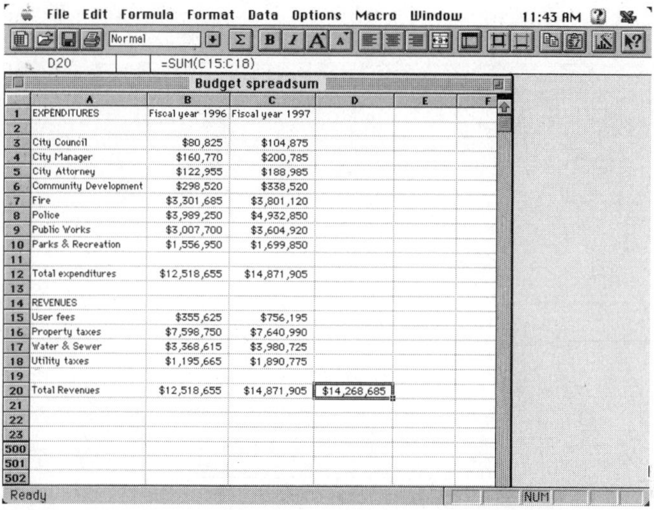

Example of how to use the spreadsheet SUM function to check budget totals.

Figure 11-10 shows a spreadsheet with information on parking fines. To figure out the average amount of fines, you'd select a cell for the answer, then type this into the formula bar:

=AVERAGE(C3:C32)

You've told the program to give you the average of the values in cells C3 through C32. The answer is $83.

Sometimes an average is misleading. If most values in the database you are looking at are similar, the average will give readers a sense of what the numbers mean overall. But if a few values are much higher or much lower than the rest, those values skew the average. In the parking fee database, for example, one person owed $500; the next highest fine was $250, and most of the fine amounts were $50 or less. The average, then, is higher than most of the fine totals; it's not truly representative of the actual fines. So it might make sense to use the median or the mode, rather than the average.

The median is the middle value, the value that half of the numbers fall above and half below. To figure the median for the parking fines, you type this into the formula bar:

=MEDIAN(C3:C32)

The answer is $50.

The mode is the most frequently occurring number in a string of numbers. To get this, you type in the following:

FIGURE 11-10

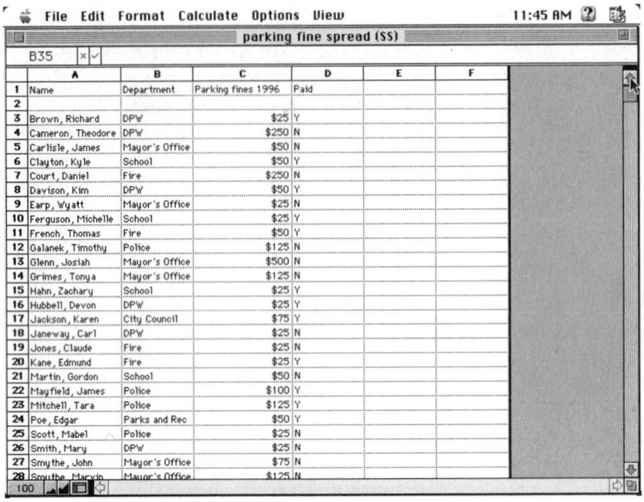

File Edit Format Calculate Options View   11:45 AM

parking fine spread (SS)

	A	B	C	D	E	F
1	Name	Department	Parking fines 1996	Paid		
2						
3	Brown, Richard	DPW	$25	Y		
4	Cameron, Theodore	DPW	$250	N		
5	Carlisle, James	Mayor's Office	$50	N		
6	Clayton, Kyle	School	$50	Y		
7	Court, Daniel	Fire	$250	N		
8	Davison, Kim	DPW	$50	Y		
9	Earp, Wyatt	Mayor's Office	$25	N		
10	Ferguson, Michelle	School	$25	Y		
11	French, Thomas	Fire	$50	Y		
12	Galanek, Timothy	Police	$125	N		
13	Glenn, Josiah	Mayor's Office	$500	N		
14	Grimes, Tonya	Mayor's Office	$125	N		
15	Hahn, Zachary	School	$25	Y		
16	Hubbell, Devon	DPW	$25	Y		
17	Jackson, Karen	City Council	$75	Y		
18	Janeway, Carl	DPW	$25	N		
19	Jones, Claude	Fire	$25	N		
20	Kane, Edmund	Fire	$25	Y		
21	Martin, Gordon	School	$50	N		
22	Mayfield, James	Police	$100	Y		
23	Mitchell, Tara	Police	$125	Y		
24	Poe, Edgar	Parks and Rec	$50	Y		
25	Scott, Mabel	Police	$25	N		
26	Smith, Mary	DPW	$25	N		
27	Smythe, John	Mayor's Office	$75	N		
28	Smythe, Marvin	Mayor's Office	$125	N		

Parking ticket information in an Excel spreadsheet.

=MODE(C3:C32)

The answer is $25, as shown in Figure 11-11.

Any or all of these values may help you explain the significance of the numbers you present to readers.

SORTING

Another way you can use spreadsheets is to sort information. You can do that with numbers or with text or with both. Sorting can help you figure out who is getting the biggest or smallest increase or what the most popular dog name in your city is or which police officer gives out the most parking tickets.

With the budget, for example, you might want to have your list of departments in order from highest to lowest percentage change. How do you do that?

First, you select all the cells in the spreadsheet that you want sorted. When you sort, it's important to highlight all the rows and columns that go together, not just the one column you want to sort by. For example, with the budget you'd select A1 through F9, not just Column E. If you don't do this, if you select only Column E, the spreadsheet may sort just that, but then the numbers in that one column won't match up with their counterparts in the other columns any more. The City Council percent change might be in the row with the Fire Department budget numbers, and so on.

FIGURE 11–11

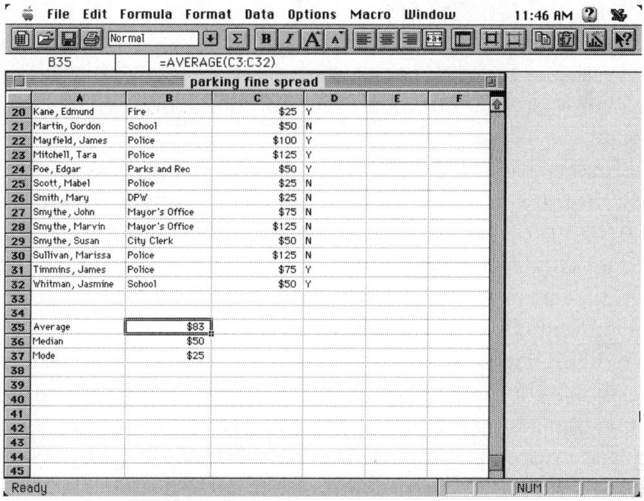

A parking fine spreadsheet showing the average fine and the median value and mode for the fines.

Next, you go to the Data menu and choose *Sort*. You'll get a dialogue screen that asks which column you want to sort by, and how you want it sorted, ascending or descending. If you are sorting by percent change, you want column E, and you want it in descending order, from largest number to smallest. Hit OK, and you'll see the expenditures are now listed differently than they were in the original, with the biggest percent difference at the top. This isn't so grand when you are only dealing with a few rows, but if you are dealing with hundreds, the sort command can quickly offer a revealing look at information.

DOGGONE THAT DATA

You can use sorting to learn something from a database of dog licenses, for a feature story. This kind of story has been done by many newspapers; some papers have used database manager programs to do it, because they had too much information for a spreadsheet program to easily handle. But you'll come across stories you can do using a spreadsheet that holds information in text form, such as dog names, addresses, or parking ticket offenses. You can use the Sort function for text just as you can for numbers; the records will be listed in alphabetical order.

Look back at Figure 11-1, the dog-license Microsoft Excel spreadsheet. To do a story using this or any other spreadsheet, you first interview the data. Who owns the most dogs in the city? (When you write your story, you'll need to remember that this

CAR in action

When an escaped prisoner flees across state lines, does he improve his chances of staying out of jail, even if police three states away catch him?

The answer Michael Berens came up with is yes. Berens, a reporter for the *Columbus* (Ohio) *Dispatch,* used spreadsheet and database management programs to analyze law enforcement information, including extradition cases, and discovered that hundreds of fugitives from other states were being arrested in Ohio and then released because other states weren't interested in spending the money to retrieve them. People convicted of robbery and drug offenses were getting away scot-free.

Berens obtained paper files on all the extradition cases for his county and created a computer database. He also got lists of defendants arrested on the charge of being a fugitive from justice and tracked the disposition of those cases. He interviewed more than 100 people. He detailed what he found in a three-day series, "Fugitives from Justice."

Berens says he started using spreadsheets and a Macintosh computer for reporting in 1988, and since then he's used computer-assisted reporting to create stories that have gotten national attention.

Berens says his first CAR project concerned police officers who owned crack houses. Berens says he tracked the real estate holdings of every member of the Columbus police force, discovering that some police officers owned more than $1 million worth of property each.

For that project, reporters computerized search warrants for every police search in the city. When they put together the database, one piece of information was missing—the day of the week of each raid. An editor suggested they add that information to the database, said Berens. And they discovered that the police department had never done a raid on the weekend, ever.

"We interviewed drug dealers at these houses," said Berens, "and they said 'Yeah, we know that, that's why we are only open on the weekends.'" After the stories ran, Berens said, the police department changed its policies on when it held raids.

He said he used computers to do analysis for stories about how many alcoholic drinks the vice squad was consuming every day while working undercover. That story was reported using the squad's expense reports. Some of the officers were buying up to 10 drinks a night, he said, and by computerizing the information from the expense sheets, Berens was able to break down what each officer

(continued)

(continued from previous page)

was buying. Then he was able to figure out where they were buying the drinks—the 10 most frequented bars were within walking distance of the vice squad headquarters, and had never been cited for code violations.

"It turned into a funny story," says Berens. "The vice squad members said they don't actually drink the drinks but pour them on the carpet. So then we started going into restaurants, looking at carpets, interviewing waiters. ...."

One of his most famous projects, says Berens, was a 1991 investigation into some unsolved slayings. Berens used computer analysis to document the existence of a serial killer at work across several states. He created a database, using a spreadsheet program and entering information about crimes, such as exactly where each body was found and what kind of hair and clothes the victim had. He said he was able to link the deaths of nine women in four states. After his stories ran, an Ohio task force was created to collect information using a national telephone hotline about the slayings.

For that story, Berens used online resources to search for stories from other publications. He downloaded articles to gather details about homicides and see if he could find a connection between cases.

This project demonstrates the power of a simple spreadsheet, says Berens, and the way some basic computer skills can help a reporter create important stories.

"Technically, that series took very little computer skill," Berens says. "But the computer gave me the organizational tool to bring home my point."

Berens says the computer analysis is the beginning, not the end of the reporting for stories: "The numbers help you figure out what the story is, but you've got to talk to people and show people in your stories." The best computer-assisted story, he says, is the one in which the numbers are invisible.

---

data only covers registered dogs—there may be other dogs whose owners haven't registered and licensed them.) What's the most popular dog name in the city?

You can get the answers to these questions with a sort. First, select the whole spreadsheet; you don't want to mix up your records. Choose *Sort* from the Data menu, choose to sort by owner's name, in ascending order, and see what happens. The results are in Figure 11-12.

Well, Mother Goose of Shoe Lane owns seven dogs, all golden retrievers. Nobody else has so many. You'll definitely want to interview her—and maybe her neighbors.

FIGURE 11–12

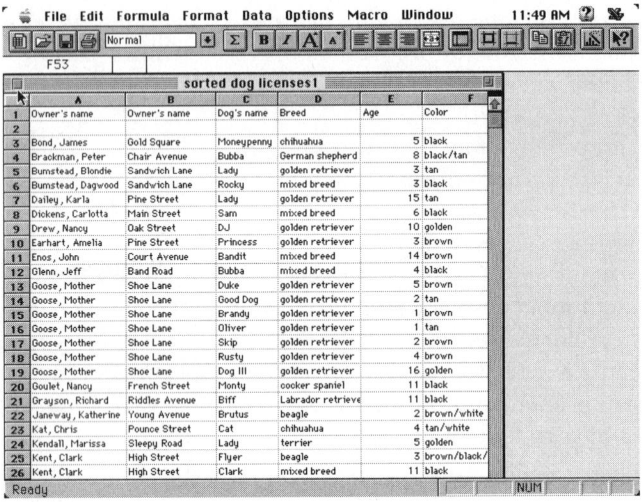

	A	B	C	D	E	F
1	Owner's name	Owner's name	Dog's name	Breed	Age	Color
2						
3	Bond, James	Gold Square	Moneypenny	chihuahua	5	black
4	Brackman, Peter	Chair Avenue	Bubba	German shepherd	8	black/tan
5	Bumstead, Blondie	Sandwich Lane	Lady	golden retriever	3	tan
6	Bumstead, Dagwood	Sandwich Lane	Rocky	mixed breed	3	black
7	Dailey, Karla	Pine Street	Lady	golden retriever	15	tan
8	Dickens, Carlotta	Main Street	Sam	mixed breed	6	black
9	Drew, Nancy	Oak Street	DJ	golden retriever	10	golden
10	Earhart, Amelia	Pine Street	Princess	golden retriever	3	brown
11	Enos, John	Court Avenue	Bandit	mixed breed	14	brown
12	Glenn, Jeff	Band Road	Bubba	mixed breed	4	black
13	Goose, Mother	Shoe Lane	Duke	golden retriever	5	brown
14	Goose, Mother	Shoe Lane	Good Dog	golden retriever	2	tan
15	Goose, Mother	Shoe Lane	Brandy	golden retriever	1	brown
16	Goose, Mother	Shoe Lane	Oliver	golden retriever	1	tan
17	Goose, Mother	Shoe Lane	Skip	golden retriever	2	brown
18	Goose, Mother	Shoe Lane	Rusty	golden retriever	4	brown
19	Goose, Mother	Shoe Lane	Dog III	golden retriever	16	golden
20	Goulet, Nancy	French Street	Monty	cocker spaniel	11	black
21	Grayson, Richard	Riddles Avenue	Biff	Labrador retrieve	11	black
22	Janeway, Katherine	Young Avenue	Brutus	beagle	2	brown/white
23	Kat, Chris	Pounce Street	Cat	chihuahua	4	tan/white
24	Kendall, Marissa	Sleepy Road	Lady	terrier	5	golden
25	Kent, Clark	High Street	Flyer	beagle	3	brown/black/
26	Kent, Clark	High Street	Clark	mixed breed	11	black

Dog license data, in a spreadsheet, sorted by dog owner's last name.

CAR in action

A famous groundhog, his shadow and some long winters.

Jennifer LaFleur, database editor at the *San Jose Mercury News* (she was training director for the National Institute for Computer-Assisted Reporting), and Rosemary Armao, then executive director of Investigative Reporters and Editors, used a spreadsheet to analyze sightings of Punxsutawney Phil, the Pennsylvania critter who gets his mug on TV every year on February 2, Groundhog Day, when a crowd of people shows up at his hideaway to wait for Phil to come out of his burrow. If it's a sunny day, and he ventures out and sees his shadow, supposedly there will be six more weeks of winter. If it's cloudy and he doesn't see a shadow, spring is supposed to be just around the corner.

The two journalists gathered Groundhog Day data, using February 3 issues of the *Punxsutawney Spirit* and the *Punxsutawney Plaindealer.* They discovered, after putting their data into a spreadsheet and graphing the times of groundhog sightings, that the groundhog sees his shadow 91 percent of the time, based on 97 years for which they could find data. They also learned that although for 110 years, times of Phil sightings had varied from 6 a.m. to 4:30 p.m, in the past 15 years, the sightings came between 7:20 and 7:50 a.m. Apparently, Phil was performing on cue, with a little help from some human handlers.

> **Warning!**
>
> When you are working with a spreadsheet or a database management program, before you do calculations or sort information, save a copy of the original data. Then if you accidentally delete information, or do a sort and later realize that you mixed up all the columns, you have the original to go back to. You don't ever want to get stuck having gone through a lot of trouble to get information, and then discover you have destroyed it all. You may think this will never happen to you, but computers crash and human beings make mistakes. So this bears repeating: Always keep a copy of the original data.
>
> You can sort the data, then save that sorted information as a new file, with a new name. You'll preserve the data in its original form, in the old file, and you'll have your sorted data too.

Now sort by dog name, column C. You'll find there are six Bubbas and five Ladys. And there are some odd names here. One guy has two dogs named Trout and Salmon. Is he the city's game warden? There's Prince Charles, a little royalty. And a couple of people have named dogs after themselves. There's Chris Kat, who lives on Pounce Lane and has a dog named Cat. And Good Dog—did Mother Goose run out of names?

PER CAPITA

Figure 11-13 shows rates of car theft in 20 cities. You want to compare the rates, to figure out which city has the most car thefts. To do that, you need to take into account the populations of those cities, because otherwise the comparison won't be fair; a city with 600,000 people is likely to have more car thefts than one with 50,000, just because there are more cars in the larger city. So you want to figure out the per capita rate of car thefts in each city. (See Per Capita, page 159). You do that by dividing the number of car thefts by the population of a city. Then you probably will multiply the number you get by 100,000, to get the rate per 100,000 residents.

To get the spreadsheet to do this, you need to use another formula. Select a cell for your first answer, cell D3. You want the spreadsheet to divide the information in cell C3 by the information in B3, then multiply it by 100,000. In Microsoft Excel, that formula will look like this:

```
=(C3/B3)*100000
```

The parentheses tell the program to do the division first, then multiply. Once you get that answer, you can fill down for the rest of the spreadsheet.

FIGURE 11-13

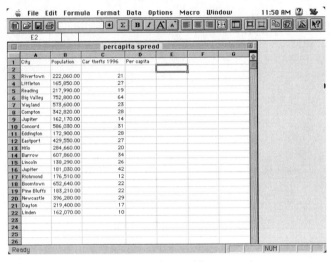

Rates of car thefts for 20 cities, listed in an Excel spreadsheet.

Then you might sort the whole thing by the per capita figures, from highest to lowest.

CHARTING THE COURSE

Spreadsheet programs make it easy to create charts that show graphically what you've discovered with your number-crunching.

The commands for chart-making vary from one program to another, but the basics stay the same: You tell a program which information in a spreadsheet you want charted, what kind of chart you want, with what types of headings, and give the program the OK. It creates that chart for you.

You've got the mayor's budget figures for 1996 and 1997 in a spreadsheet (Figure 11-4). You want a bar graph with one bar for 1996 and another for 1997, for each department. One way to make that chart in Microsoft Excel begins with the spreadsheet up on your screen. Start by selecting all the cells holding information you want in the chart. Usually, when you select cells, you highlight only cells that are adjacent. But there is a way to select cells that are not adjacent, say the column of city departments and the column of 1997 budget figures. First, highlight the city departments column, then hold your control key down and highlight the 1997 column.

For this chart, you want three columns selected: the column listing the city departments, the column listing the 1996 figures, and the column listing the 1997 figures. Now go to the File menu and choose *New*. You'll get a dialogue

CAR in action

Duff Wilson, reporter for the *Seattle Times,* says he often uses a spreadsheet or database management program to create a chronological record.

When four firefighters died in an arson fire on January 5, 1995, Wilson and reporter Eric Nalder used a spreadsheet to record information about the building owners' son, who eventually became a suspect in the case. "I kept information about his activities, any activity I could attach a date or a time to, information from court files, from what he told police, from police reports, from what other people said about him," said Wilson. He could sort this information and track the man's activities. Eventually the suspect went to Brazil, where he was captured. Wilson said the database created with the spreadsheet program would also come in handy when they covered the man's trial.

"Later on," said Wilson, "we extended the same scrutiny to the fire department and how they fought this fire, and the mistakes they made." The two reporters wrote a thorough, specific story, "The Pang Fire: What went wrong," which explored all of the decisions and actions and problems—set out in chronological order—that ended in the death of those firefighters. The details these reporters gathered through investigation and interviewing make the story gripping and complete. The reporters recounted, minute by minute, how events surrounding the fire unfolded: a fire chief sizing up the situation at 7:10 p.m., not realizing the fire had been started in the building's basement; an assistant chief arriving at 7:30 and viewing what he thought was a "manageable" situation because he, too, was unaware of the fire's origin; firefighters trapped in the basement several minutes later when the first floor of the building collapsed; the eight minutes it took for rescue teams to organize outside the building.

box that asks what type of document you want to create; choose Chart and hit your return button. The program will create a column chart like the one in Figure 11-14; this is the type of chart the program is set to create by default. The chart will be small; to expand it to fill your computer screen, click once on the small box in the upper right of the chart.

You can make changes to the chart using the toolbar at the bottom of the screen; many of the icons there represent tools to make different types of charts, including pies and scatter plots. For instance, you could turn the bars into three-dimensional figures, with the bars for one year behind the bars for the other, by clicking on the 11th icon in from the left on the tool bar. The chart in Figure 11-15 would appear.

FIGURE 11-14

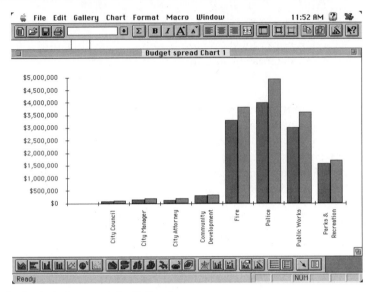

Bar graph of a city budget, created with Excel.

FIGURE 11-15

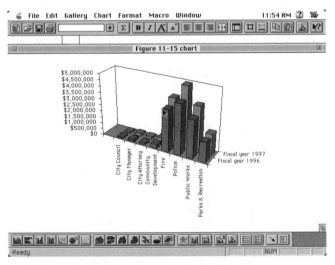

The city budget information presented in a three-dimensional bar chart.

You can also use Microsoft Excel's ChartWizard tool, represented by the next-to-last icon from the right on the top tool bar. All of these tools allow you to create different types of charts, add and change labels and text, and make charts in formats you design.

SPREADING THE NEWS

This chapter shows only a few of the things a computer spreadsheet can do. These software programs are getting more powerful all the time; the more you work with one, the more you'll learn about what it can handle.

But even the simplest spreadsheet techniques give you reporting power. CAR veteran Michael Berens of the *Columbus* (Ohio) *Dispatch* says, "There are hundreds if not thousands of stories that you can do with a spreadsheet. It lets you look at things in a list format. A spreadsheet is just a blank piece of graph paper on your computer screen. You type in the boxes, or you buy the data and put it into the boxes."

When you're learning to use spreadsheets, put some small numbers into the boxes and try simple calculations that you can also check yourself with a calculator. That will help you see if your formulas are correct. Try some basic sorts too.

A Question of Ethics

Remember that with computerized data, just as with other forms of data, you need to consider newsworthiness before using it in a story. Sometimes you can get so excited by the fact that you can get information or figure out something interesting from your database that you may forget to consider newsworthiness, people's right to privacy, or other matters.

Sometimes you are going to find out something nobody knew before because nobody else did the math or the sorting; that's precisely the point of computer-assisted reporting. Do you report it, and how do you report it? Are your calculations and analysis correct? Are there factors you haven't considered? Even government information can be incorrect; you have an ethical obligation to do your absolute best to check the accuracy of the information you include in stories and to attribute that information; it's also the only way to do good journalism.

If the numbers put someone in a negative light, you have an obligation to give that person a chance to address the concerns that your analysis raises. You can't just take the numbers and run.

CAR in action

Melvin Claxton won a Pulitzer Prize in 1995 for a series of stories he wrote and reported for the *Virgin Islands Daily News* showing how the criminal justice system was failing. Claxton used a spreadsheet program to record and analyze more than 5,000 court cases, according to the January 1996 issue of *Uplink,* the newsletter of the National Institute for Computer-Assisted Reporting. The information included a case number, the charges, the offender's sex, whether the case was heard by a judge or a jury, and the outcome. Claxton also used police records, including arrest logs.

Claxton discovered that fewer than 5 of every 100 violent crimes reported to the police resulted in an arrest and that fewer than a third of all convicted criminals went to jail.

Here's the lead to one of Claxton's stories. As you'll see, he doesn't open with a barrage of numbers, though he had plenty of them. He opens with a person:

> He looks like your average 19-year-old, but he isn't.
> A product of the squalid, crime-ridden JFK housing project on St. Croix, he learned about drugs and guns at an early age.
> He learned too well.
> By the time he was 16, police say, he had killed one man and helped murder another—both in cold blood.
> He has never spent a day in jail.
> He has, police complain, literally gotten away with murder.
> His case is far from unique in the Virgin Islands, where crime without punishment is the norm, where careers in crime and violence begin early and where law enforcement and justice systems are so inept and irregular that they perpetuate crime.

When you've put information into a spreadsheet and aren't sure what do do next, think of your readers and the questions they'll want answered. Those questions will lead you to formulas and functions, more questions for interviews, and people who will make your stories rich and compelling.

Chapter 12

SORTING AND MATCHMAKING: USING A DATABASE MANAGEMENT PROGRAM TO FIND MEANING

How many times are snowmobiles crashed by young drivers? Do the local schools unknowingly hire convicted felons? How often do people charged with drunken driving actually get convicted and serve jail time?

Journalists use computer programs called database managers to answer these kinds of questions. Database managers can handle an avalanche of data and pull out from a huge database only the records that meet certain criteria. For example, if you have thousands of records of snowmobile accidents but you want to know how often drivers age 16 and under crash, you can ask the database management program to pull out just the records of accidents involving drivers age 16 and under. If you are trying to learn how many parking tickets are given out on Main Street, you can get only the records for Main Street.

You can also match up separate collections of information with a database manager, revealing new information. For example, suppose you've got a database listing all public school employees and another database listing all people convicted of felonies in your state in the past ten years. The databases both include names, addresses, and dates of birth. With the database management program, you can compare these collections of information and find records that match. Now you've created a database of school employees convicted of felonies.

SORTING AND SERVING UP INFORMATION

The examples you are going to look at in this chapter are all created in Microsoft FoxPro, for the Macintosh; there are many other programs available.

Creating a database from scratch is more complicated than creating a spreadsheet, so you'll need some practice to become skilled at it. First, you'll learn how to do some basic analysis of an existing database with FoxPro. That will help you make sense of the way you create a database in the program.

To turn a database manager into a reporting tool, you need to know how to accomplish these things with the program:

- Choose from a big database just the information you want. If you have a database of state employees, for example, you might want to pull out of it just the names, addresses, and job titles and save those in a file.
- Sort information in a database so you can see it in alphabetical or numerical order. If you have a database of campaign contributors and the amounts they contributed to a particular candidate, you might want them sorted so you see the people who gave the most at the top of your database, and the rest listed in descending order by amount given.
- Sum up these contributions so that if some people on the list made more than one contribution, you can see the total amount each donated.
- Count records so you can see patterns or trends you are interested in. If you had a database of parking ticket records, you could use the database management program to count how many tickets were given in each campus parking lot, for example, and show you how many, grouped by lot, so you'd know that thirty-one tickets were given out in Lot C, fourteen in Lot B, and so on.
- Pull out from a database only certain records that meet criteria you set. For example, you might want to see just the records for contributors who donated more than $5,000. You can do that. You might want to see only parking tickets given out by Officer T. Conway. You can do that too.

Q AND A

Before you begin sorting or searching, though, familiarize yourself with the information in the database so you know what data it includes. If you don't do that at the beginning, you may get confused when it comes time to do your analysis.

Think about what questions you want to ask this information, and how you want your answers presented. Just as you would with records in a spreadsheet, you will interview a database created in a database management program. Getting the answers is more complicated with this type of program than with a spreadsheet, but the thinking is similar. Ask questions, then figure out how to use the program to get your answers.

Finally, just as you would if you were working with a spreadsheet program, double-check your answers and ask others to review your data too. Because you are doing more complicated things with larger collections of information, you want to make sure you are getting correct answers—that the answers you get are really the answers to the questions you ask.

Going to the Dogs—Again

In the last chapter, you looked at a spreadsheet with information gathered from dog licenses. Take a look at the same sort of information put into a database management program, in this case Microsoft FoxPro. Figure 12-1 shows part of the database as you'd see it on your computer screen.

This database looks a little like a spreadsheet, since there's information laid out in columns and rows. At the top of the computer screen you see the names of menus; you'll use pull-down menus and mouse-clicking to analyze the information in this database manager program, as you did when you used the Microsoft Excel spreadsheet program.

There are differences between this database and a spreadsheet, though. In a database manager, the columns are called *fields;* rather than being lettered, the fields are labeled to describe the type of information in each of them. In Figure 12-1, you see fields labeled Firstname, Middlei, Lastname, No for street number, Street for street name, and Area for area of the city. If you had this database on your computer, you could scroll across it and see the other fields: Dogname, Breed, Sex, Color1 for the color of the dog, Color2 for a second color, and Dogage.

These are among the first things you want to know about a database: how many fields there are, how they are labeled, what information is contained in each, and how many records the database holds.

FIGURE 12–1

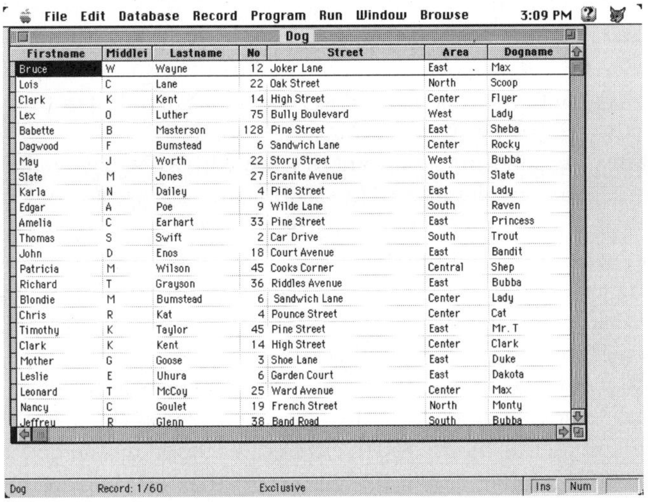

Firstname	Middlei	Lastname	No	Street	Area	Dogname
Bruce	W	Wayne	12	Joker Lane	East	Max
Lois	C	Lane	22	Oak Street	North	Scoop
Clark	K	Kent	14	High Street	Center	Flyer
Lex	O	Luther	75	Bully Boulevard	West	Lady
Babette	B	Masterson	128	Pine Street	East	Sheba
Dagwood	F	Bumstead	6	Sandwich Lane	Center	Rocky
May	J	Worth	22	Story Street	West	Bubba
Slate	M	Jones	27	Granite Avenue	South	Slate
Karla	N	Dailey	4	Pine Street	East	Lady
Edgar	A	Poe	9	Wilde Lane	South	Raven
Amelia	C	Earhart	33	Pine Street	East	Princess
Thomas	S	Swift	2	Car Drive	South	Trout
John	D	Enos	18	Court Avenue	East	Bandit
Patricia	M	Wilson	45	Cooks Corner	Central	Shep
Richard	T	Grayson	36	Riddles Avenue	East	Bubba
Blondie	M	Bumstead	6	Sandwich Lane	Center	Lady
Chris	R	Kat	4	Pounce Street	Center	Cat
Timothy	K	Taylor	45	Pine Street	East	Mr. T
Clark	K	Kent	14	High Street	Center	Clark
Mother	G	Goose	3	Shoe Lane	East	Duke
Leslie	E	Uhura	6	Garden Court	East	Dakota
Leonard	T	McCoy	25	Ward Avenue	Center	Max
Nancy	C	Goulet	19	French Street	North	Monty
Jeffrey	R	Glenn	38	Band Road	South	Bubba

Dog license information stored in a FoxPro document.

ROW BY ROW

The rows in a database like this are not numbered; these pieces of information don't have addresses the way information in a spreadsheet does. And that's because here it's not necessary. In a spreadsheet, the different cells making up each row or record, running across the spreadsheet, must stay together; all the separate pieces must keep their relationship to each other, or the spreadsheet turns into gobbledygook. With a database built in a database management program, that's not true. Don't misunderstand—you're not trying to mix things up so that the database shows Bruce Wayne now owns Blondie Bumstead's dog. You don't want to confuse individual records. But with a database manager, you might pull out only the information in the dog-name field or the owner-name fields, sorting and counting just that information and creating a new database. The relationship across a row isn't what you need to worry about, and the database manager lets you break apart the pieces in a way you can't in a spreadsheet.

Once you know what information you've got to work with, you can start asking questions. You want to interview your data, put your questions into a format the computer program can understand, then get the program to display the answers. When you ask a database management program a question, what you are doing in computer talk is *running a query*. You're asking the program to display only some of the information in the database or to sort the information in a certain way.

GETTING WITH THE PROGRAM

When you start up Microsoft FoxPro, you'll see a window with the name of the program on it and a small command box. FoxPro allows you to type commands into that box, or to use the menus and keyboard commands. For now, you'll see how to use the program using your mouse and menus.

To report your dog story, you want to work with a database called Dog.DBF. The DBF suffix is a convention used by database management programs to name databases created in the programs. Go to the File menu, pull it down and choose *Open*. Find the file you want opened, Dog.DBF, hit OK, and—whoa. With other types of software programs you've used, you start up the program and get a document onscreen. But with FoxPro, you've still got the same title window you started with before. What should you do now?

This is how Microsoft FoxPro works. After you've told it to open a certain database, you've now got to tell it that you want to *browse* (look at) the database. So go to the Edit menu, choose *Browse,* and it will open up the dog data file.

Next, tell the program you want to do more than just look at this database. You want to run a query. Go to the Run menu and choose *New Query.* You'll get a window that looks like the one in Figure 12-2.

FIGURE 12–2

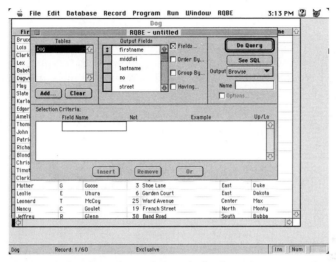

The FoxPro RQBE screen that allows you to choose which information you want the program to pull out of the database and display.

Basically, this window shows your options for asking the database questions. The label at the top of this window, RQBE, stands for Relational Query by Example. RQBE is the way Microsoft FoxPro lets you ask questions of a database.

Look at the left side of the window. There's a small box labeled "Tables." This shows you which databases, or tables, you are working with. In the middle is another box, labeled "Output Fields." This shows all the fields in the database or databases that you've opened. So in the case of Dog.DBF, you see the names you saw atop the columns of the database itself, including Firstname, Middlei, Lastname, and so on.

Next to the Output Fields box are squares labeled "Fields," "Order By," and "Group By." You'll use these to ask the database questions.

To the far right is a button labeled "Do Query." Click on that button when you're ready to get an answer from the database.

Below all of this is a box labeled "Selection Criteria." There you'll designate which pieces of information, out of everything in the database, you want the program to show you.

Each time you begin a new query, you'll start with this window. You'll work with several other windows as well, depending on what you want the program to do. They'll look similar to this, they'll list fields you can work with, and they'll include buttons to click on.

Often, your query will require the program to do more than one thing at a time. For instance, you might want it to display all the records of parking tickets given out on Main Street and sort them according to time of day so you can see if a person is most likely to get a parking ticket in the morning or the afternoon. You have to go through a separate step to set up each part of that query; that's what makes FoxPro and other such programs a little complicated to use.

Don't get tangled up in all of this. Just think through what sorts of results you want from your query; then, one step at a time, tell the program what to do to get your answers. The more familiar you get with the program and with how a query works, the more sense it will all make and the more sophisticated you can get in your querying.

WHAT KIND OF DOG IS THAT?

Let's work through a basic query. Imagine you plan a feature story on dogs in your city, and you want an answer to this question: Which dog breeds are the most popular here?

To get your answer, you'll first want the database management program to pull from the database only the records of dog breeds, without the names of owners, street addresses, or dog ages. After that, you may want to have the program list these in alphabetical order by breed, so you can see which breeds are listed most often in the database. Then you may ask the program to group the records by breed, count how many of each breed there are, and display this list in order from most records (the breed most often listed in the database) to least records.

The program can do all this easily. But for each of the tasks, from choosing records to listing in a certain order, you have to go through different steps with the database management program. It may seem confusing at first, but take it one step at a time.

STEP ONE: WHAT KIND OF DOG IS THAT?

The first thing you need to do when running a query is tell the program which fields (columns of information) you want it to work with and display. You have the RQBE window on your screen. To choose fields, click on the box next to the Fields label.

You'll get a new window to look at, the RQBE Select Fields window shown in Figure 12-3. The box to the left, Table Fields, will list all the fields in the database; the box at the right, Selected Output, is supposed to list all the fields you choose to look at as part of your query. But Microsoft FoxPro assumes at first that you want to look at all of them. FoxPro is wrong, in this case. Click on the button in the center of the box labeled "Remove All" to clear the Selected Output area.

Now you can choose just the fields you want to work with. In this case, that's only the dog breed field. Scroll through the Table Fields box until you find that listing. Click on it once, then click on the "Move" button. The listing for that field should now appear in the Selected Output box. (You can also double-click on a listing to move it from one box to another.)

FIGURE 12–3

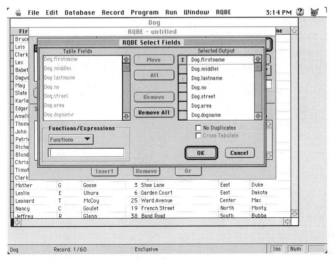

The FoxPro Select Fields screen, where you decide which fields of information you want to work with.

Now click on OK. You'll go back to the first RQBE window. Click on the "Do Query" button, and the program will pull out just the field with the dog breeds in it and display it in a vertical list. There are beagles, Dobermans, Lhasa apsos, collies, and more.

STEP TWO: PUT THEM IN ORDER

If you had only fifty records in your dog database, you could go through this new fifty-item list of breeds and count how many of each breed there were to figure out the most popular breed. But if you had thousands or hundreds of thousands of records, you'd want the program to do the sorting and counting. So you'd need to ask the program to do some more work.

"Order by" will help. You can ask the program to sort the items in the dog breed field alphabetically, starting with *A* and working down, or with *Z* and working back. That will put all the terriers together, all the golden retrievers together. To do this, you need to add something to your query. You need to tell the program to again display only the dog breed field and to order all the pieces of it alphabetically, starting with *A*.

How can you do that? Choose *Run/Query* (Don't choose *New Query*. You don't want to start all over from the beginning. You want the same field selection as before—the dog breed field.) When the RQBE screen comes up, click on the square next Order By. You'll get a new screen display, like the one in Figure 12-4.

FIGURE 12–4

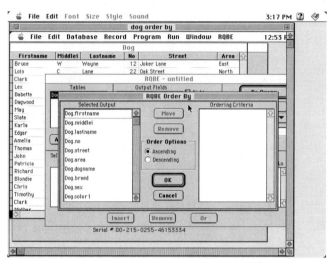

The Order By screen, where you decide in what order you want information presented.

With Order By, you first have to decide if you want the listings in alphabetical order from A to Z, Ascending, or Z to A, Descending. (If you were working with a field that listed numbers, such as amounts of parking fines or campaign contributions, you could list those from highest amount to lowest, or vice versa.) If you want them in ascending order, you do nothing; for descending order, click on the circle next to "Descending."

Then choose from the fields in the Selected Output box the field you want the program to sort by, the dog breed field. Click the Move button so the dog breed listing shows up in the Ordering Criteria box, then click OK. You'll go back to the RQBE screen. Now click on Do Query. You'll see the same field as you did the first time, the dog breed field, but the listings will be sorted alphabetically.

STEP 3: COUNTING DOGS

This is more helpful than the first query result, since the records for each breed are listed together. Still, if you had thousands of records, you'd want the computer to count them and put them into categories, to tell you how many terriers, how many spaniels, and so forth. To get the program to do this, you need to add two more things to your query—Count and Group By.

Choose *Run/Query* again, and when the RQBE window comes up, click on Fields. At the bottom left of the RQBE Select Fields screen is a box labeled "Functions." Remember how with spreadsheets, you could type in a function, such as Sum, along with the cell addresses you wanted worked on, and the program would do the math? These functions work in a similar way, except here you need to tell the program which pieces of information you want counted. Microsoft FoxPro functions include summing and averaging too.

The Functions label has an arrow on it; this means the label is a pull-down menu. Using your mouse, click on the Functions label and hold the mouse button down. The menu of the different functions will open up. Move down to Count, and another menu will pop up next to this one, showing the fields you can use with Count. Choose the listing for the dog breed field. Finally, click on the "Move" button, so that the Count command will be made part of your query. If you forget to click on the "Move" button, the program won't count for you.

(If you were analyzing campaign contributions or other numbers, you could use the Sum function to add up the numbers.)

You want FoxPro to count the breeds, and if you run the query now, it will. But this computer program isn't quite as smart as you might think. It will count these, all right, but unless you tell it to, it won't sort them into categories, to tell you how many terriers and how many golden retrievers there are. You have to tell it to do this, using the Group By command.

STEP 4: GROUPIES

With Group By, just as with Fields and Order By, you need to tell the computer what field or fields to use. Many reporters suggest you think about this by considering how you would present the information in a chart once you got it. With dog breeds, for example, you'd have a column for breed and a column for the count. There would be a listing for beagles, then the number of beagles next to it. So you want to group by breed, so you'd know how many beagles there are and how many of each other dog.

Tell the computer to do this grouping by clicking on Group By on the RQBE screen. You'll get a Group By screen with a list of available fields, like the one in Figure 12-5. Click on the fields you want, in this case, the dog breed field, then click on the Move button, just as you did with Fields and Order By. Then click on OK, go back to the RQBE screen, and click on Do Query.

The table you get would look something like the one in Figure 12-6. The program has pulled out just the information in the dog breed field; it has counted the listings for each breed, grouping the information so you know how many dogs of each are listed in the database. And it's listed the breeds in alphabetical order, from A to Z, or, in this case, from beagle to terrier. You might want to sort (using Order By) by the breed count instead, from largest number to smallest number.

Using queries like this one, you could discover—and tell your readers— which breeds appear to be the most popular and least popular in your city, based on dog license information. You could do the same sorts of counts and sorts for dog names. You could see which areas and streets of the city have the

FIGURE 12–5

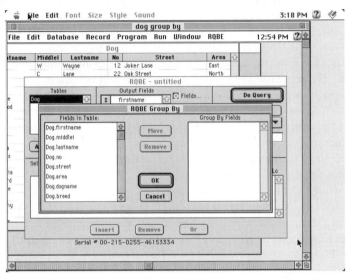

The Group By screen, where you can decide which categories you want information sorted into.

FIGURE 12–6

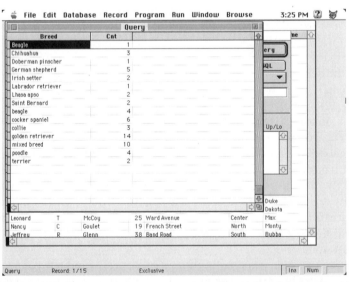

Results of a query asking for a listing of the number of dogs in each breed that are listed in a dog license database.

most dogs, and who owns the most dogs or the least popular breed. You do have to remember, and tell readers, that a database like this one probably doesn't list all the dogs in your city; it lists just the ones whose owners have registered them.

But this sort of database analysis can help you with lots more than shaggy dog stories. You could analyze databases to find out from whom candidates get the most campaign contributions or which areas of your community have the highest crime rates or whether drunken-driving cases in your courts end up in jail sentences for the drivers. Ordering, counting, and grouping information with a query can help you see patterns and discover things that aren't clear from scanning information in a report.

PARTS OF THE WHOLE

You can also use a database manager to grab from a huge database only records that meet certain criteria. Suppose that in skimming the dog license database, you've noticed that the name Mother Goose shows up more than once. You want to ask the database another question: How many dogs does Mother Goose own? To get this answer, you're going to ask the database to pull out records that list "Mother" in the first-name field and "Goose" in the last-name field.

You need to run a new query, so choose *Run/New Query.* Click on Fields, then choose the fields for owner's first name and last name, maybe dog breed, and probably street address. Remember to double-click on the field names or click on the Move button to select them.

You don't need to order the results of this query; you just want to know how many records come up. But you don't want the computer to show you every record; you only want it to do the Mother Goose records. That's where the Selection box on the RQBE window comes in. (Look back at Figure 12-2.)

A SELECT FEW

Here, you set parameters for the query. You tell the computer which fields to work with, and what information, or records, you wanted pulled from the database.

Under the Selection box label, there are four other labels: Field Name, Not, Example, and Up/Lo. If you click in the blank rectangle under Field Name, the look of the box changes. The Field Name label becomes a pull-down menu; a box that you can click on appears under Not and under Up/Lo; and a new pull-down menu with the label Like appears.

With Field Name, you can tell the computer which field or fields you want it to pay attention to. Click on this pull-down menu, which lists all the field names in the dog license database, and choose the Firstname field.

Now move to the Like menu, which lists these other choices too: Exactly Like, Less Than, More Than, Between, and In. You want records that list a first name exactly like "Mother," so choose "Exactly Like" and type in "Mother" under the Example label.

Then go through this same procedure all over again, clicking in the blank rectangle under Field Name, choosing the Lastname field from the pull-down menu, choosing Exactly Like and typing in "Goose." (You might use Less Than, Between, and More Than with fields that hold numbers, such as dollar amounts of campaign contributions.)

You're asking the computer to pull out only the records where the information in the first-name field matches "Mother" and the information in the last-name field matches "Goose."

Run the query, and you'll get a list of all the records in the database for Mother Goose and her dogs, like the one in Figure 12-7.

Always keep backup copies of your data, in case something happens to the copy you're working with. And keep a log of your queries so you will always know how you got your answers, and so you can go back and check those answers again.

MAKING A MATCH

For your feature story, you want to know how many city employees have dogs. You could interview every city employee. But it would make more sense to

FIGURE 12–7

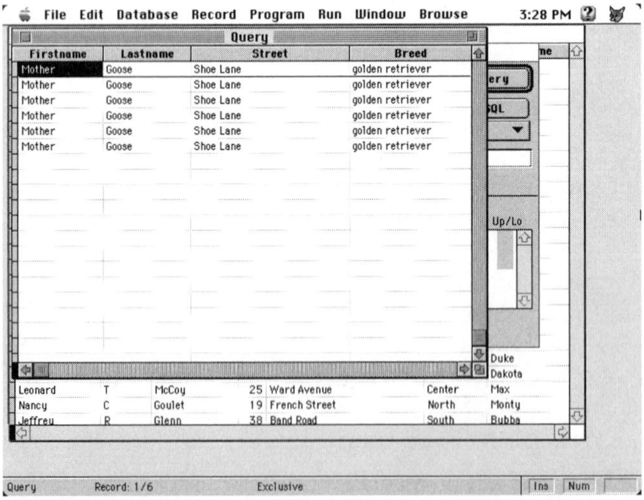

Results of a query asking for all records in a dog license database where the first name of the dog owner is Mother and the last name of the owner is Goose.

FoxPro Tips

What if you're running queries but discover that records aren't always typed into the database in exactly the same way? For example, suppose in your parking ticket database there's a field for location where a ticket was given out. Some of the records list one location as "L-C," while others list it as "Lot C," or as "lot C." FoxPro gives you a couple of options for dealing with such differences.

When you're working with the Selection Criteria box, if you choose Like instead of Exactly Like, you'll get matches that are similar to the example you type in. And if you click on the Up/Lo box, the program will ignore capitalization differences when matching records to that example.

The Not box will come in handy if you want to pull a bunch of records but *not* ones that meet a certain criteria. For instance, if you wanted to know how many dogs in the city were not golden retrievers, you could click on the Not box, asking the program to show you all records in which the dog-breed field is not exactly like "golden retriever."

What should you do if you want to save the results of a query? If you do nothing, the results disappear; your query does not change the original database, but it is not saved anywhere either.

After you've completed the query, click on the small square at the top left of the query window to close it. Do the same thing with the RQBE window. You'll get a dialogue box that asks if you want to save changes. Click on Yes, and you'll be prompted to name the new file you're creating and tell the computer where on your drive to save that file.

use a program such as FoxPro and interview a database of city employees. What you'd need to do is join two databases, one of dog license information and one of city employee information. The program will show you the records that match up in the two databases.

You do this by choosing, in each database, the fields you want the computer to compare. Then you run a query.

You have to have some information in common in order to join databases. If you had a database listing crimes in various neighborhoods and a database showing how many police officers are deployed at various hours of each day, you couldn't join those databases to find out if fewer officers patrol high-crime neighborhoods—unless the databases shared some common information, such as fields listing the neighborhood names or street addresses. For one database, these would be the neighborhoods or addresses where the crimes took place;

for the other, these would be the neighborhoods or streets where officers were assigned to patrol.

For the dog database and the city employee database, you'll have names and addresses as common information you can use to match up the databases. It's usually better not to use only a name to join databases; names aren't unique identifiers. Social security numbers are, but you don't always have those. Even addresses aren't unique identifiers, necessarily; heavyweight boxer George Foreman has five sons named George, so if you had a database with each of their names and addresses, you still wouldn't know which George was which. But using the names and addresses should give you a good match most of the time.

You make the match in Microsoft FoxPro by following these steps. First, open up one of the databases you want to work with, say Dog.DBF. Choose *Run/New Query.* You'll see in the lefthand corner of the RQBE window a button that says Add. Click on that, and you'll choose the database you want to match up with this one. Say in this case it is Cityemp.DBF. Now you'll get a RQBE Join Condition box, like Figure 12-8, similar to the Selection Criteria one you used when you asked how many dogs Mother Goose owned. Use the pull-down menus to choose the first field you want matched, probably the Firstname field in the dog database; to choose "exactly like" or "like" or whatever; to choose the Firstname field in the city-employees database. Then click on OK.

You can add as many criteria as you want to with such a query; go through the same procedure to tell FoxPro you also want to match the last names and addresses in both databases. Click on OK, then run the query.

FIGURE 12–8

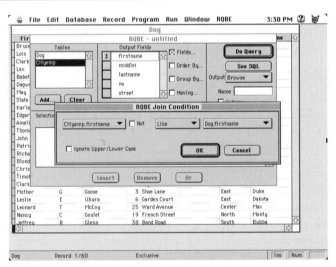

A Join Condition box that allows you to decide which information in one database you want matched with information in another database.

You'll get a list of records where the names and addresses match; this should show you which city employees have licensed dogs with the city. Now you can interview these folks and write about them and their canine buddies. And . . . hmm. You know that the chief of police, Wyatt Earp, has a dog. He brought it to the last city council meeting. But you notice he doesn't show up in your query results. Apparently he hasn't registered the dog, even though a city ordinance says he should. It's time to give him a call, too.

CAR in action

John Archibald of the *Birmingham* (Alabama) *News* used computer-assisted reporting to write a series of stories about school workers who had been convicted of crimes. According to an explanation box that ran with the story on October 9, 1994, the newspaper used information from the Alabama Department of Corrections, the Alabama Administrative Office of Courts, and the Alabama Department of Education. The Department of Education provided two databases containing information on every teacher and school worker in the state, more than 70,000 records.

The newspaper matched those databases with others from the prison system and the probation and parole system—and did this with the help of Department of Corrections workers. The paper also matched the education databases with a database from the Administrative Office of Courts. Reporters then spent months verifying the information they got from the database matching.

The stories Archibald wrote revealed that at least 1 principal and 68 teachers who had taught in the state in the past year had been convicted of crimes and that at least 230 other workers had prior criminal convictions. Archibald found that often background checks were not done on those applying for nonteaching jobs and that checks on teachers were not done in a consistent way.

Ames Alexander and Ted Mellnick of the *Charlotte* (North Carolina) *Observer* did a similar investigation for their paper in 1994. They matched electronic databases from the North Carolina Department of Public Instruction with information from the state Department of Corrections, and, according to Investigative Reporters and Editors' "100 Computer-Assisted Stories," discovered that at least eleven former convicts had taught in the state's public schools in the past year.

(continued)

(continued from previous page)

As with the Birmingham series, for the North Carolina series the reporters carefully verified the information, contacting all the teachers who came up in the match.

After the Birmingham series ran, the state began investigating sixty-five cases and began working with the state Department of Public Safety to develop a bill that would require criminal history checks on anyone who works with children, according to a story that ran in the paper on December 11, 1994. School boards across the state fired or accepted resignations from teachers and school workers with convictions in their pasts.

After the Charlotte stories ran, some teachers named lost their jobs, and state lawmakers introduced legislation enabling school districts to do better background checks on those applying for teaching jobs.

In both cases, the computer analysis was just the beginning. After the CAR, reporters had to check the information they had; go through other background, such as certification and license revocation files maintained by the education departments; and interview many people. Both projects took months to complete.

CREATING A DATABASE

As with spreadsheets, you may sometimes be able to obtain information in an electronic format, on a floppy disk, magnetic tape or compact disk, which is already formatted in a database program or can be imported into your program (more on obtaining databases in Chapter 13.)

If you have to type in information from paper records, you'll find it's not too difficult once you've decided how to set up the database (though it will be time-consuming, depending on how many paper records you've got). But it will pay off in the long run if you spend some time deciding what information you need in your database and in what format, so that when you do your analysis, you have the information you want in the right categories so you can sum it up or sort it out or count it properly.

Imagine you have a bunch of paper records concerning parking tickets given out on campus, and you want to create an electronic database in Microsoft FoxPro. Start by listing questions you may want to ask that database:

- Where on campus are the most parking tickets given out?
- What time of day are the most tickets given out?
- What offenses are tickets most often given out for?
- How much does the university take in in fines?
- Which campus police officer gives out the most tickets?
- Which day of the week are you most likely to get a ticket?

To answer these questions, you will need this information: name of ticketing officer, location of ticket, time of day, day of week, offense, fine, whether the fine was paid, and the amount paid, since the person who got the ticket might have to pay additional fees if he or she is late paying the fine.

You know then that in your database you will want to create at least seven fields. If you want first and last names of the officers, you'll need eight fields.

SETTING UP THE FIELDS

In Microsoft FoxPro, you create a database by asking it to open a document. Go to the File menu and choose *New*. You'll get a table that asks what kind of document you want to create. Choose Table; remember, a database created in a database management program is called a table.

You will be asked to give it a name. If you call this one Parking, the program automatically adds a suffix, in keeping with the conventions of naming databases. (When you go look for the file later, you'll see it's called Parking.DBF and that FoxPro has created a backup file as well.)

After you've done that, you'll see a window (Figure 12-9) where you can type in field names and other information about each field.

When you create a field in a database management program, you also have to decide what kind of field you want it to be and how big it should be. For example, you can create *character* fields, which can hold letters, numbers,

FIGURE 12–9

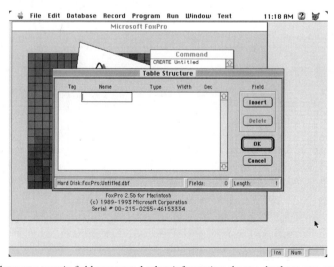

A screen where you type in field names and other information about a database you are creating in FoxPro.

and punctuation. You can also create *numeric* fields, which can hold only numerals. You will want to create a numeric field when you know the information you are putting in is just numbers and you want to do a mathematical calculation such as summing up. Pick the right type of field so you can later carry out the analysis you need to; the program won't let you Sum information in a character field, for example. If a field will hold characters and numerals, create a character field.You make these choices and set up your fields in this Table Structure window. You type in a name for your first field; for example, if you were setting up a database of parking ticket information, you might call that field "Officerl" for the police officer's last name. When you click under Type, that heading turns into a pull-down menu, and "character" shows up as the default setting. You can create numerical fields, date fields, and others.

Under Width, type in the number of spaces you want in the field. You can add or subtract or change this later if you need to.

The Dec column allows you to decide how many decimal points you want in a numerical field.

Once you've completed your setup, click on OK. You'll be asked if you want to add information to this new database right away. If you click on Yes, you'll get something that looks like Figure 12-10. This is a vertical listing, rather than the horizontal one you are used to. The advantage to adding your records this way is that you can see all of one record easily; in horizontal mode, you'll have to scroll across to see the entire record. But if horizontal is what you want,

FIGURE 12–10

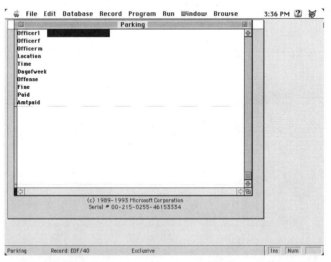

A vertical listing of categories in a parking ticket database, where you can type in first and last name of a police officer, location where a parking ticket was given out, time of day it was issued, day of the week it was issued, offense the ticket was issued for, fine assessed, whether the fine was paid, and how much was paid.

go to the Browse menu and choose *Browse.* To get back to the vertical format, go back to Browse and choose *Append.*

Now all you have to do is start adding your information, one record at a time.

The final setup for the parking ticket database might look like the one in Figure 12-11.

Your completed database would look something like Figure 12-12. Now you could run some queries.

BE CAREFUL, BE CONSISTENT

When you enter information into your database, be consistent in the way you do it and be careful to get the information typed in correctly. Otherwise, you might have trouble pulling out records you want later, and you might not get the right answers to your questions. Don't create "dirty data," which is data with errors and inconsistencies. (More on dirty data in Chapter 13.)

In the January 1996 edition of *Uplink,* the newsletter for the National Institute for Computer-Assisted Reporting, Jennifer LaFleur, database editor for the *San Jose Mercury News,* suggests you have a colleague look at your database after you've typed in some of the data. That person can tell you if the database setup makes sense. LaFleur also suggests that you have someone compare the

FIGURE 12–11

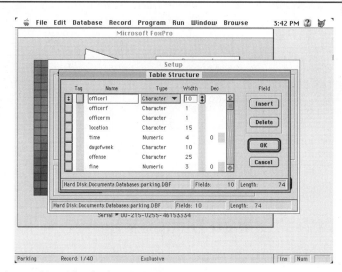

The setup for a parking ticket database in FoxPro.

FIGURE 12–12

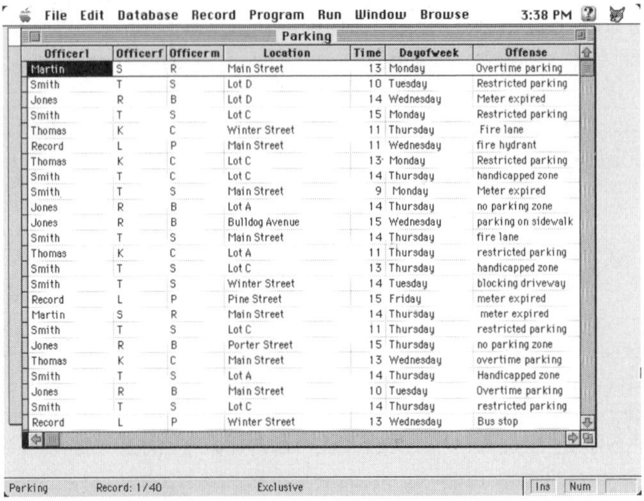

Records in a FoxPro parking ticket database.

Database Tip

When you create a database, it's best to break information into its smallest pieces to make it easy to sort and pull out individual records; this will also make it easier for you to match records in separate databases. With a spreadsheet, you might put the last name, first name, and middle initial of people in one cell, if all you are going to do is sort by last name and count. But with a database program, you may need to match databases by more than one field or sort by more than one. So with name, for example, you might want to create a field for last name, a field for first name, a field for middle initial, even a field for a suffix such as Jr. It may seem like a pain in the neck to do this, but it will make your life easier later.

---

completed database to the original information, to make sure you've got everything right.

WAIT, THERE'S MORE

You've learned the basics a database management program can handle. As you practice queries and try working with different databases, you'll learn about the more complicated tasks such a program can perform. One way to learn is to read stories by professional journalists (if the story states that computer-assisted analysis was performed, or if it's published with several charts, the reporter might have used a database management program) and work backward from the published stories. Figure out what information the reporters might have had in a database, how the database might have been laid out, and what questions the reporters asked of the data.

Start your own analysis with relatively simple databases, such as dog license information or campaign contributions. And when you've finished crunching and sorting, start interviewing people. Always, you need to bring the numbers and facts alive with stories about real people.

Through interviews, you can put your findings in context and figure out which query results are significant. You can also test your findings against what people say is going on. If everything doesn't match up, you have some more reporting still to do to see why the data and people's perceptions don't match.

CHECK AND CHECK AGAIN

News organizations work with outside experts to help them analyze databases; don't be afraid to ask for help from other reporters, editors, and outside consultants (of course, you'll have to get that approved by your editor). Reporter David Armstrong of the *Boston Globe* says that often after he has analyzed databases, he sends his results back to the people who sent him the original information. He tells them how he got his results and asks them if they believe his numbers are accurate, and, if not, why. He has been right so far.

Bill Dedman, former director of computer-assisted reporting for the Associated Press, says AP also sometimes gets help from outside researchers and academics who are experts in their fields. You can probably find experts at your school who can assist you with analyses.

Interviews with experts and people involved in situations or events you are reporting on will also keep you from assuming things that are not true, based on your computer-assisted reporting.

HIGH STANDARDS FOR CAR

Suppose you analyze your database of parking tickets given out on campus and discover that several officers almost never give tickets. Can you assume that this is because they are slacking off on the job, or because the other officers are being overly zealous?

Never assume. The patterns you see raise questions, and you should get answers to the questions. But remember that there can be more than one possible explanation for a pattern like that one. For instance, the officers who give

A Question of Ethics

When the *Birmingham* (Alabama) *News* ran a series of stories about teachers and school workers who had been convicted of crimes, the newspaper staff had to decide whom it would and whom it would not identify in its stories. An explanation box published on October 9, 1994, states that the newspaper staff decided to identify only those people who had been convicted of crimes in the past ten years, except in cases in which a person was convicted of murder or of a sex offense or had been sentenced as a habitual offender. Also, the staff disregarded most property crimes and convictions on misdemeanor charges.

The newspaper staff knew the series would harm some individuals; those named would suffer damage to their reputations and could lose their jobs. But the public had a right to know about the criminal records of people working with their children; the newspaper had a responsibility to report this information.

The staff members took seriously the responsibility they had to be fair and accurate, so all information reporters gathered was verified, and these standards were set to determine who should be named in the stories.

Weighing the public's right to know versus individuals' right to privacy is important. You shouldn't decide not to write a story just because it will harm someone, but you should be clear on why you are writing that story.

It's not a decision you'll have to make on your own. Get your editors to help.

few tickets may work evening hours, when some parking restrictions are no longer in effect.

And do your database queries prove something? Maybe, but be careful. If you analyze speeding tickets and find that certain officers stop black drivers a majority of the time, have you proved that those officers are racist? No. You've proved that those officers stop black drivers a majority of the time. Now you have to interview people to make sure your analysis is right. Don't draw conclusions from scant information.

The two examples (see pages 201–202) of stories done with matching of databases demonstrate important principles you should follow concerning CAR. In both cases, reporters did not simply accept the answers they got from their databases when they matched them up. They verified the information by other means, and they interviewed the teachers and school workers they pulled up with their matches.

Does the airline you fly with have a history of safety problems?

On April 11, 1996, the Cleveland *Plain Dealer* published a story by Elizabeth Marchak that explored problems with ValuJet Airlines. Marchak used computer-assisted reporting techniques to uncover incidents involving "inexperienced pilots, inadequate maintenance and insufficiently trained flight attendants," according to the story. Marchak used several computerized databases, including registration files for airplanes, a list of pilots, and the airline's service difficulty reports about problems with individual planes.

Marchak got the airline's annual report from its World Wide Web site and information about air safety regulations from the Federal Aviation Administration Web page. A CD-ROM directory enabled her to find a pilot she wanted to interview, when she couldn't locate him through telephone directory assistance.

This is only one of many computer-assisted projects Marchak has worked on. She worked on a series of stories concerning the safety of air travel and the FAA, for example. And she used computer databases to report on the most violent cities in America for women, based on Federal Bureau of Investigation information. That story, which she worked on with Joe Hallinan, showed that the most violent cities for women were small and midsized cities, not big cities.

The reporters used computer programs to analyze databases of rape and murder statistics.

That project was "data-intensive," says Marchak, and the ability to analyze that data helped in their interviewing; they had something to base their questions on and weren't just going into interviews cold. She also says the interviewing was important for putting the data they analyzed in perspective and for making sure the data they had was correct.

(continued)

That's simply thorough, fair journalism, and it's extremely important. Because computers make it easy to sift through lots of numbers, they also make it easy to forget the other part of the process—verifying. If the police chief called you and told you the fire chief was a convicted felon, you wouldn't immediately write a story saying that. You'd ask how the chief knew this, see if you could get proof from other sources including court records, and you'd try to interview the fire chief, unless . . .

(continued from previous page)

For the violent-cities story, Marchak also used some commercial online services to see what had been written about specific slayings, after they were able to identify the most violent communities. She searched online to see what communities offered women help and protection, and she posted a query to ProfNet seeking criminal and sociological experts.

The lead to that story included the results of their data analysis, but it also highlighted what they heard from interviews:

> When it comes to the crimes women fear most—murder and rape—the most dangerous places are not America's big cities but some of its small and medium-sized towns.
>
> A computerized analysis by Newhouse News service of 1992 crime data shows that women are more likely to be raped or killed in areas like Rapid City, S.D., Jackson, Mich., and Pine Bluff, Ark., than in New York, Los Angeles or Washington, D.C.
>
> A woman in Pine Bluff is three times more likely to be murdered than a woman in Los Angeles, for instance. Jackson, Mich., women reported being raped four times more often than New York City women.

The results seem to contradict the widely held belief that violent crime—and homicide in particular—is a unique big-city problem.

But the rankings highlight a paradox of crime: Statistics may say one thing, but residents feel another. Many of those who live in dangerous areas say they feel safe and were puzzled by their ranking.

Unless you find out the "hot tip" isn't newsworthy information at all. You have to think about this when you get such a call, and when you run queries with a database. Is what you find out newsworthy? Does the public need to know and have a right to know? Will the good that comes from printing the information outweigh the bad?

If the conviction was five years ago, for arson, you might decide it was newsworthy and that the public's right to know outweighed the chief's right to privacy. But if the conviction was fifteen years old, for writing a bad check, would you do a story? Maybe not. Just because you find something out doesn't always mean you will print it.

The same goes for information you gather through computer-assisted reporting. It isn't better or more important information just because you got it with your computer. Use the same standards to evaluate the importance and validity of that information that you would use to evaluate any other information.

Can you use databases to report breaking news stories as well as major investigative projects?

Yes, and Michael Walsh of the *Muskegon* (Michigan) *Chronicle* has proof. He has added information to many stories on deadline using databases he and others at the paper have obtained or created.

Walsh covers state and federal courtrooms throughout western Michigan and works with colleagues on other beats to produce investigative stories. He began database work in 1990, typing into a laptop computer information from weekly court-issued sentencing sheets.

"This became a habit," says Walsh, "one that took no more than 40 to 60 minutes a week. Today, I have thousands of records, every criminal sentence, from every regional court. Lawyers and even judges call to ask what a typical sentence might be for a crime." (He adds that typing information into the computer is a good way to familiarize yourself with the nuances of the data, such as unusual names.)

In 1992, he got, on paper, all drunken-driving convictions, and the paper hired a typist to put the information into a database. The paper updates this database, which includes drivers' names, dates of birth, addresses, and other information.

Walsh says other databases maintained by the paper include campaign contributions; listings of jail inmates, those making bond, those sent home because of jail overcrowding, and those doing community service work; pet license information; a database of all school employees and expenditure records for each school system; listings of all volunteer firefighters, including names and addresses; the state Department of Corrections master inmate database and sex offender parole list; and records of housing inspections in Muskegon.

Walsh does use such databases for investigative projects; one such story he did showed that almost half of the bench warrants issued by Muskegon County judges were for people who had previously been released from jail as mandated by a court order meant to ease jail overcrowding.

He has compared databases for stories, matching such databases as the firefighters' records and the criminal records. And he has used databases for feature stories such as the one about people with famous names who had gotten in trouble for the law. He found that a man named George Washington was serving time for armed robbery,

(continued)

(continued from previous page)

while another named John Wayne was in jail for larceny, and the
Hardy boys were in jail after weapons and property violations.

But he says the most important use for the databases is in "giving
context to daily news."

"When we write about some traffic fatality involving alcohol
abuse," says Walsh, "we can cite the number of such cases caused by
drunken drivers and what becomes of them.

"When I report that John Doe was ordered to serve three to five
years in prison on a cocaine delivery charge, I can easily find, process, compute and explain how this sentence fits into the big picture,
all on deadline.

"When it comes time for a judge to run for re-election, usually a
sleepy affair, his sentence patterns provide hard evidence, something
meaty to share with readers."

Chapter 13

IT'S COMPUTERIZED, BUT IT'S NOT ONLINE, PART II: INFORMATION ON FLOPPY DISK OR TAPE

The information you need for stories can't always be delivered online or by compact disk. Sometimes you're going to have to accept paper records and type the numbers and names from these into your computer.

Or . . . you might still be able to get your data in a computer format, on floppy disk or on a reel of magnetic tape. With these, you'll be able to get information into your computer more quickly and start finding meaning in it.

DISK OR TAPE

You've probably used floppy disks to store your own work on computers. If you can get government officials to put information on a disk, and you've got compatible software programs on your computer, you'll be able to pop the disk in, open the database, and go to work.

Government officials may also hand over data stored on big reels of magnetic tape called nine-track tape. This format, used with big mainframe computers, is not as convenient or easy to work with as a floppy disk. You'll need a nine-track tape drive or a tape reader and a special software program to get the information into your computer and translate the information to data a PC can use. Tape readers and drives are expensive, but you might find an office on your campus has one. Nine-track may eventually disappear, but in the near future you'll find many government agencies still use it.

WHERE DOES THE INFORMATION COME FROM?

Whether you work with a database you obtained online, on tape, or on disk, or whether you create one from paper records, you have to do a kind of reporting some journalists aren't yet used to, says Bill Dedman, former director of computer-assisted reporting for the Associated Press. Dedman, at an AP computer-assisted reporting conference in May 1996, reminded reporters that they have to pay attention not just to the information they get, but also to how that information is gathered and stored. Knowing this will help you figure out if the information you have is accurate, if it's stored consistently, how old or new it is, if information is missing, and if some information is incomplete because only part of it is kept, or only one question is asked instead of two.

There are several questions you should ask about information you get on disk or tape (or about a database you download from the Internet or get on CD.) First, you need to know how big the database is, how much space it will take up on your computer. Your PC's hard drive has only a certain amount of storage space; if a database requires more space than you have available, you can't work with it. You may have to work with parts of the database instead of the whole thing, analyze the data on a different computer, or get rid of some of the other stuff saved on your hard drive. Find out how many megabytes (millions of bytes) a database will take up and if your computer can handle it.

WHICH SOFTWARE?

Second, if you're getting information on a floppy disk, you need to know what format the information comes in. A database is created using some type of software. Will that software be compatible with what you have, or can you import the information you are getting from that outside source into a software program you have? The answer these days is that you probably can import it, because many programs can translate information from other programs. For example, if your city clerk is going to give you information in a Lotus 1-2-3 spreadsheet, and you have Microsoft Excel, your program probably will be able to read the spreadsheet anyway; the programs are created so you can do this. If you have a newer version of the software used to create the database, you should still be able to work with it.

If you get information in PC format and you work on a Macintosh, that's trickier, but there are programs that translate documents from one format into another.

HOW DO THEY KNOW WHAT THEY SAY THEY KNOW?

Third, with any data in any format, you need to ask what information is actually in the database and how the information was gathered.

These probably sound like basic questions. After all, you've asked for certain information, so that's what you should be getting, right? Sometimes a database will hold information you don't need; sometimes what you wanted isn't there or isn't clearly recognizable. Many reporters who've worked with CAR suggest you talk with the people who created the database about how they obtained and stored their information, so you'll know that the data you want are really in the database you're getting.

If the information is gathered through a survey, questionnaire, or form people have to fill out, get a copy of that item. You'll want to know how questions are phrased, how easy it might be for people to make mistakes in filling out the questionnaire or form, and how often people neglect to answer certain questions or fill in certain blanks. All of this may have some bearing on the accuracy and significance of the data.

MAKING TRACKS

If you are getting a nine-track tape, there are other things you need to know. This book isn't going to take you through all the nitty-gritty of dealing with this format; if you're given a tape, find a computer guru to help you out. (Making friends with a computer guru is always a good idea.)

You may want to learn some of the nine-track computer lingo, though. If you have to accept a nine-track tape, you'll know what questions to ask about it so you and your computer guru can get the information on tape into your computer. And if some government official balks at giving you information on tape, you can dazzle him or her with your knowledge of nine-track. This may make it harder for someone to get away with telling you the information you want just isn't available in a format you can use. Questions you'll need answers to include these:

- ASCII or EBCDIC? There are two common codes used to store information on nine-track tape. ASCII is a universal computer language, the standard for PCs. EBCDIC is an older programming language. If the information you get is in EBCDIC, you'll need to convert it to ASCII. You have to know which one you are dealing with so you can translate the information properly. There are many programs that translate from one to the other.
- What format does it come in? Ask for information in a "fixed format," which will make it relatively easy for you to import the information into a database manager.
- How big are the blocks? On nine-track tape, information is stored in blocks of a certain size. You need to know what size so you can translate the information into something your PC can read. Block sizes can be fixed—all the same—or variable.
- What's the tape density? The density of a tape tells how much information is stored on a set amount of tape. It's measured in bits per inch. Most tapes use 6,250 bits per inch (bpi).

■ Is the information labeled? This has to do with the way infomation on the tape is organized. You need to tell your computer if the tape is labeled or not.

RECORDS AND FIELDS

You also want to get the record layout, a codebook if there is one, and a print-out of some of the records.

Remember how you looked at the record layout, showing the different fields in a database, in Chapter 12? When you get a database from an agency, know how many fields there are, how they are labeled, what order they are in, what the labels mean (what information is stored in each field), what types of fields they are, and how many records you are getting. You need these answers to find and analyze specific information in the database. But these answers can also help you figure out if the data are complete and accurate. If you are told, for example, that there will be twenty-three fields, and you get twenty-five, some-thing's not right. If you are told you have 10,023 records, and you have 8,945, something's not right again. If a field is supposed to be numeric, but there are no numbers in it, you might not even have the database you asked for or the record layout information may be wrong.

Sometimes fields will have information in them that is really a code. For example, if a database has a field for recording a person's race, instead of a word or letter in that field, you might see a number. The agency might have assigned a number to each race category, so 1 might be white, 2 black, 3 Hispanic, and so on. If there are codes, you need the key, or codebook, to decipher them.

If you get a printout of some of the records, you'll be able to see if the record layout and the codebook really match up with the data you are getting.

You don't have to become a nine-track expert. There are outside agencies, including the National Institute for Computer-Assisted Reporting, that will trans-late information on nine-track tapes for you, for a fee. You may also be able to find someone on campus who can do this for you.

The computer analysis showed that in South Florida, more than two-thirds of coronary artery bypass graft surgeries on people at least 70 years old were done on men, even though women made up 60 percent of the population 70 or older.

SAME DATA, DIFFERENT PROGRAMS

When you have a database in a PC-readable format, you can usually copy the infor-mation into a computer program on your computer, whether that be a spread-sheet program or a database manager. With spreadsheets, you may be able to simply save a copy of the information in the proper format. And you can usually import between spreadsheets and database managers. With Microsoft FoxPro, for

It was all on the tapes.

Reporters at the *Sun-Sentinel* in Fort Lauderdale, Florida, used data from nine-track tapes to review 1.44 million traffic tickets given to 973,000 drivers; to build a database of information about Broward County school employees; and to determine whether doctors in South Florida were failing to diagnose heart disease in women.

Scott Anderson, newsroom computer resources editor, aided in the computer analyses for all three stories. The paper used a nine-track tape reader, and database mangement, spreadsheet, and statistical software to analyze the database.

Buddy Nevins, the *Sun-Sentinel's* Miami bureau chief, told readers:

> Last year in Broward and Palm Beach counties, black drivers were far more likely to be convicted of a traffic offense than whites, a *Sun-Sentinel* computer analysis has found. And they were convicted of more charges per person than whites.

After reviewing personnel data, including information about the highest paid employees and those with the most sick leave saved up, staff writers Bill Hirschman and Fred Schulte wrote:

> Broward's public school system has spent millions of dollars hiring relatives of employees, paying substantial overtime to certain employees and making large payments to retirees for unused sick leave.

After the paper analyzed data on hospital stays and information from the 1990 U.S. Census, staff writer Glenn Singer reported:

> Women in South Florida and across the country are dying needlessly of coronary heart disease, many the victims of discrimination by doctors who fail to consider that diagnosis, experts say.
>
> Moreover, women sometimes become their own worst enemy, tending to find excuses to delay treatment after heart disease has been diagnosed, physicians and researchers say.

example, you can use the Import command to create a FoxPro table with information from a database created with a different program.

AIRING OUT DIRTY DATA

Once you have the data in the right format on your computer, you're ready to go—right? Whoa. Before you start analyzing the information with your spreadsheet or database program, you need to check for dirty data. *This is true whether you got a database on tape or disk or downloaded it from the Internet.* Often databases are missing information, or information isn't stored in a consistent way, or the information doesn't match up with the information in the record layout. Even databases you create yourself can have dirty data, because people make mistakes typing. Dirty data can also happen because a computer glitch damages a file or because signals being transmitted online got messed up. If you get dirty data from an agency, don't assume there's a conspiracy against you. But do try to get the problems straightened out.

How do you determine if you've got dirty data? Well, you're not always going to know, but there are some basic things to check. First, see if you have the number of records and the number of fields you are supposed to have.

Look for inconsistencies in the way information was typed into the database. Is the name of a hospital, for example, typed in as "South County General," "S. County General," and "S. County Gen"?

Compare labels of fields and types of fields in the database against the record layout and see if everything jibes.

Add up numbers and see if your totals match the totals you've been given. Look for gibberish in any fields, or numbers where there should be letters, or letters where there should be numbers.

If you find things that don't make sense, discuss them with the people who gave you the data. They may not be aware there are problems, or they may have a simple explanation—for example, the record layout you got is old, and new fields were added recently.

OBSTACLES TO OVERCOME

Government officials and heads of organizations don't always jump for joy when journalists ask them for computerized databases. Of course, they don't often jump for joy when journalists ask them for anything. You may have to fight for what you want:

You may be told that you can have the information but that it's not possible to provide it in computerized format. Ask why. If you can get a printout of data, it's probably kept in a computer. Carry blank disks with you and ask for copies of data; contact the computer gurus who know how the data is stored and find out if it's really true that you can't get a copy. Talk the nine-track talk. Don't accept this answer at face value.

Sometimes you'll be told the data you want is not public record, so you are not entitled to have it. You should negotiate with the people in charge, citing the law in your state or federal law, and try to change the minds of those who are denying you the information.

When the *Boston Herald* sought its city's parking ticket database on nine-track tapes, city officials said they could decide in what form to provide public records and offered to give the records to the *Herald* only on paper, at a high cost. *Boston Globe* reporter David Armstrong was working for the *Herald* at the time, trying to report on the parking ticket situation. He says in the January 1995 issue of *Uplink,* the newsletter for the National Institute for Computer-Assisted Reporting, that the officials complied with the *Herald's* request for the tapes only after the state attorney general threatened the city with legal action. The fight for that data took three years.

As more journalists become involved in computer-assisted reporting, more journalists fight to get governments to give them records in electronic form. Some open-records laws do not yet mention records in electronic format.

The Freedom of Information Act, approved in 1966, allows people, including journalists, to request records from all deparments and agencies of the federal government, including regulatory commissions and government-owned corporations. It does not include Congress or the federal courts. Documents, papers, reports, and letters are considered "records" under the FOIA; the *Associated Press Stylebook and Libel Manual* also notes that in court rulings the term "record" has been deemed to include films, photographs, sound recordings, and computer tapes.

There are loopholes in the act, and it can take a lot of time to get information under a Freedom of Information Act request. So file one as a last resort.

Under the FOIA, you must submit a formal request, in writing, to the agency from which you're seeking the information. The agency must respond by giving you that data or stating which exemption—there are nine in the act—allows it to keep the information from you. You can appeal the decision to the head of the agency, and if that appeal is denied, you can sue the agency in U.S. District Court.

The FOIA doesn't cover state and local governments, and laws concerning electronic records vary. According to "Access to Electronic Records—A Guide to Reporting on State and Local Government in the Computer Age," published by the Reporters Committee for Freedom of the Press and updated in 1996, the statutes of forty-four states specifically state that electronic records are subject to the same public records law as paper records, while federal judges have agreed that the FOIA extends to records in electronic form. You may still have to fight to get the computerized database, but the law will give you some ammunition.

An official may agree to provide the data in computerized form, for an exorbitant amount of money. Fight this, too (talk to your editor and figure out how the paper will fight it). Get the official or agency to provide you detailed information showing exactly how the copy will be made and how much time and money it will cost. Charging huge fees is one way some people try to keep the public from getting data.

Chapter 14

AFTER CAR: INTERVIEWING, OBSERVING, AND TELLING READERS WHAT IT ALL MEANS

> *The nearly 14,000 doctors in metropolitan Washington inhabit a lopsided world of medical care.*
>
> *It is a world with excesses of specialists but shortages of family doctors, clusters of patients hospitalized for avoidable medical problems, and scarcities of doctors in many communities that need them most, according to a yearlong study by* The Washington Post.
>
> *In the affluent, largely white neighborhoods along the border of Northwest Washington and Bethesda, there is one pediatrician for every 400 children. But in the poor, mostly black neighborhoods to the southeast—neighborhoods where many toddlers are not immunized and infants often die needlessly—there is one pediatrician for every 3,700 children.*
>
> SOURCE: ©1994 *The Washington Post.* Reprinted with permission.

The numbers in this lead, crafted by *Washington Post* staff writer Amy Goldstein, were mined using computer-assisted reporting. But the strengths of all the stories in Goldstein's series, "Worlds Apart—Health Care in Washington," are the strengths of any great stories reported using computer-assisted techniques. The data gathered through CAR anchors the stories. But they work because the reporter tells readers what the numbers and trends mean and why they matter, and she shows how people are affected by what's being documented.

You may begin your research with a computer, going online and browsing the Web, downloading information from a BBS, or contacting experts via ProfNet. You may import numbers into a database management program, sort and add and pull out significant data.

But you won't be ready to tell tales yet. You have to do more reporting, the old-fashioned kind; you have to gather quotes and anecdotes and listen to people describe their joys and fears and desires and problems. You can't get readers involved in a story unless you reveal people in that story. To do that, you're often going to have to talk to someone in person. There may be some stories you can do mostly through online interviews, but remember all you'll miss in those interviews: tone of voice, mannerisms, setting, and the chance to look your interviewees in the eyes.

CHECK, PLEASE

Interviews can also help you determine if the information you discovered using your computer is accurate and significant. You might have dirty data; the person putting information online might have a hidden agenda; you might not have the whole story yet.

Suppose a mysterious package appeared on your desk, stuffed with pages of budget numbers that seemed to show that city officials are fudging things, or you got a great anonymous tip by telephone or interviewed someone who had a charge to make against some organization. You'd check and double-check what you'd learned by talking to people, the people with the power to change things, the people with the expertise in a certain area, and the people affected by what you are writing about. Check out the information you gather with your computer too.

WHAT IT ALL MEANS

One way to check out online information is through interviews, which Michael Walsh of the *Muskegon* (Michigan) *Chronicle* says are absolutely essential to making sense of computer-gathered data, to figuring out the whys and hows and putting information in a context.

"Reporters have to realize that what a computer produces is only the start," he says. "It's not the end process. For example, you crunch the numbers and find out that most homicides in your town were committed by teen-agers. So what? Armed with that factoid, the next call or visit is to *people*—police, prosecutors, social workers, clerics, teen killers, etc. It is people who give meaning to the numbers. Numbers alone are numbing, at least in the copy."

A STRONG START WITH CAR

So why use CAR at all? By now you shouldn't have to ask that question. But here is the answer, again: Your computer can enable you to get more information, often more complete information, quickly. Online, you can locate experts and other sources you wouldn't even have known were out there, never mind having the time and money to do it. The computer can analyze huge amounts of numbers and other facts, sort things out so they make sense, quickly and accurately.

At the end of your computer-assisted reporting, you ought to have better information to work with. *That* ought to mean you have better questions to ask in your interviews. That ought to mean you get a more interesting, more in-depth story. It ought to mean you can't be snowballed as often. It ought to give you confidence and power and knowledge. You know how it feels to go out to an interview unprepared. Everybody has done it sometime, if only when a news event happened on deadline and somebody had to get to the scene immediately. The adrenaline rush lasts only so long. Then you have to come up with good questions. Chances are when you get back to the office and start to write, you suddenly have lots of other questions you didn't think to ask. Or you have some conflicting information to deal with, but you only just realized it.

CAR won't eliminate that. But CAR can help you ask smart questions; it can help you get the people side of your story and tell the whole story.

Once Upon a Time ...

After your reporting is done, you have to put to work all your skills as a writer. CAR won't do the writing for you. But look at what it has given you—lots of information. And that's the best place to be when you start to write, standing on top of a heap of data, rather than holding ten or twenty scraps and hoping they will be enough.

It is easy to be overwhelmed by all that data or to forget that the data alone won't make your stories sing. Every story must deliver information clearly, concisely, and in a way that grabs readers' attention. Good writing is good writing is good writing, no matter how you gathered the information you are writing about.

Here are five reminders of ways, after CAR, to report and write great stories.

1. Show people and include telling details.

Reporter Amy Goldstein and William Casey, director of computer-assisted reporting at the *Washington Post,* used computers to analyze heaps of data for its health care series. Goldstein, for example, got computerized information from the American Medical Association that Casey used to create a database of doctors in the Washington area with jobs outside the federal government. The CAR for the series included combining information from that database with information about the area's residents; figuring out ratios of doctors to residents in various communities; and analyzing hospital discharge records looking for patterns of hospital stays.

Armed with that data, Goldstein also interviewed many physicians, patients, health care authorities, and medical school officials, and her stories revealed people as well as numbers. The people make the numbers matter. In one story, she profiles a doctor who works in a poor community:

On the roof of a shopping center—a shabby strip along Benning Road NE where drunks gather and a murder occurred last year—are two signs for the doctors' offices that fill the second floor.

One sign reads, "Family Dentistry—children and adults." The other announces the presence of a general surgeon and a foot doctor.

But the podiatrist retired in 1992. Both the surgeon and the dentist are dead.

These days, Robert W. Yancey is the only doctor using the cavernous space. He arrives late in the afternoon, after his full-time job at a nursing home has ended for the day.

Four evenings a week, the internist unbolts the heavy locks, carries his medical supplies up the steep flight of stairs and treats patients into the night.

Many of them elderly and most of them poor, the patients require elementary kinds of care. They weigh too much, have high blood pressure or arthiritis or have been taking expired medicine.

The work is not glamorous. It is not lucrative. Yancey skirts rats in the basement when the boiler balks.

But he is keeping a promise to the surgeon, his late friend and mentor Robert E. Lee, that he would treat his patients as long as he could. And the truth is, even if he is tired when he arrives, he enjoys talking with them and knowing that he helps many people feel better.

SOURCE: ©1994 *The Washington Post.* Reprinted with permission.

Goldstein couldn't get this information out of a computer. She had to talk to the doctor and see the building. This and stories of other people, including a poor asthma patient, bring the computer-assisted research to life.

When Ray Robinson and Michael Diamond investigated the safety of charter buses for the *Press of Atlantic City*, they analyzed more than a million records of truck and bus inspections conducted by states. Using online databases, they retrieved stories from other newspapers about bus companies. They found that of the 1,000 charter buses that came through their area every day, about 10 percent were not safe enough to be on the road.

But Robinson says the details they gathered through observation and the interviews they conducted made the story complete.

"I don't know how many days we spent at inspection sites where state inspectors were pulling the buses off (the road), and we were crawling around with the mechanics looking in the wheel wells," he says. "We saw a lot of great stuff out there that we wouldn't have gotten just from the computer database. One bus pulled in with its bumper dragging on the pavement behind it."

Another bus came in leaking something that inspectors first thought was water, says Robinson. They were wrong.

"This bus was leaking diesel fuel all over the highway," says Robinson, "and we got to talk to some of the passengers about what they thought about the inspections." The interviews gave the reporters a good sense of who was being affected by lax inspection and poor conditions of the buses, "mostly elderly, retirees who wouldn't do too well crawling out of a bus after an accident," he adds.

Another important story the *Press* ran involved people having trouble getting mortgages because of their race.

"These tend to be people who haven't been in the country very long, they're poor, they're kind of frightened by people like newspaper reporters, and it's very difficult to go to these people and get them to talk," says Robinson. "Getting the data and analyzing it was easier."

But it was important to the story to show how this situation was affecting real people, he says.

"If we hadn't been able to point to actual human examples of this and have pictures of real people who had trouble getting a mortgage, this thing would have read like some sort of report from a state agency."

CAR paired with interviews and observations creates a potent mix. Use the data you've gathered to prepare for interviews. Then get out there and talk to people and see what's going on for yourself.

2. **Choose carefully which numbers you use in a story. Lead with numbers only when they are compelling.**

Some CAR projects, especially major investigative ones, result in lots of numbers. Having put a lot of time into the analysis, reporters sometimes feel they must tell readers every bit they've learned.

Michael Berens of the *Columbus Dispatch* says, "The best computer-assisted stories are the ones that you can't really tell are computer-assisted reporting.... [T]he best story is the one where the numbers are invisible."

You have to think hard about readers and why they should care about these pieces of information and this story. Piling up a lot of statistics usually won't do the job. Pick the most important and compelling numbers, then tell readers *what they mean* and tie them to the people in your story. Think about the whys; think about what is being done or not being done to change a situation you're reporting.

If the numbers and other facts are important to include for readers but don't really fit in a story, put them in a chart or graphic. And when you have to use numbers, make them understandable. How many is four percent? Is that enough to be alarmed about? How many is a million? What is a byte?

> Hundreds of sick and extremely premature babies are born each year in Ohio hospitals that medical experts say may not be equipped to care for them. And many are dying.

That's the lead to a story from the *Plain Dealer* about Ohio's system for ensuring that at-risk babies get proper medical care. Reporters Joan Mazzolini and Dave Davis used computers to gather and analyze data and came up with plenty of statistics and patterns. But they didn't load their stories with numbers; they began by telling readers how large a problem there was and what the human cost was.

The paper also ran graphs showing the number of infant deaths at various Ohio hospitals and a map graphic showing the number of premature births in different parts of the state.

In one of the *Boston Globe*'s stories in a series on elevator and escalator safety, "Risky Ride," reporters Shelley Murphy and David Armstrong told readers this:

> Nearly 40 percent of the state's 28,289 passenger and freight elevators have not been inspected during the past year, despite a state law requiring annual tests by inspectors assigned to the state Department of Public Safety, according to a computerized analysis of state elevator-inspection records.
>
> In some areas of the state, the problem is even more alarming. In Worcester, nearly three out of four of the city's elevators have not been inspected in the past year.

The reporters also noted that when inspections are done, recommendations for safety repairs are not always followed. But this information didn't lead the story. Instead, the reporters opened with a scene, showing what happened when a family entered an elevator in a Boston building and a 3-year-old was trapped between the elevator car and a door and seriously injured. The reporters demonstrated the effects of a problem on real people.

That series included graphics concerning the numbers of elevators and escalators not inspected across Massachusetts, the numbers of escalator accidents reported at each subway station in Boston, and about how to get off escalators safely.

3. Explain, when necessary and relevant, how you gathered your information. But don't go overboard.

Walsh of the *Muskegon Chronicle* says "chest-thumping" about computer skills turns readers off. Attribute information you get via computer just as you would any other information. If it's important that readers know where a database comes from, or that two databases were matched up to create a new database, tell them as simply as possible.

Don't try to dazzle readers with your computing skill. Some of them may be interested in what type of PC you used; most want to know how the story you have been computing matters to them. Usually, you and your methods are not the story. Think of a reader, any reader. Why will she or should she read the story? What will he or she need to know first? What are your best quotes, your most telling facts, your most interesting information? What do you want your reader to be thinking about by the end of the story? (Not, "Wow, that reporter sure knows a lot about computers.") Let the answers to those questions guide your writing and explanations about your computer work.

"If the mayor called to say he's quitting, would we herald the news with 'According to a telephone transmission, the mayor today said he was resigning'? Computers, like telephones, are tools. Nothing more. That's not to say we should not attribute information; that's certainly appropriate. But I hesitate to make the attribution the news," says Walsh.

Sometimes, CAR stories include a sentence explaining that the paper used computer analysis. Sometimes newspapers explain where information was obtained. If a reporter uses online resources, he or she will explain that if it is pertinent to the story.

The *Plain Dealer* included with its stories on at-risk infants a box listing some of the reporters' findings and an explanation that they used computers to analyze information from more than 250,000 Ohio birth and death certificates for 1992.

When Stephen Buttry, staff writer for the *Omaha World-Herald,* wrote about Nebraskans using the World Wide Web, he explained that he conducted more than fifty interviews, many of them through e-mail, so readers would know how he reached people for the story and how he learned about what and why they were all doing online. Telling them that he conducted interviews online helped demonstrate the reach of the Internet.

The *St. Petersburg Times* ran a series of stories, "A Dangerous Age," showing that many elderly people in Florida were being committed to mental institutions against their will. In an explanation box that ran along with the stories, the paper's staff noted that court files on psychiatric files usually are sealed and not available to the public. They told readers that the paper got court orders to get access to the sealed records, reviewed more than 4,000 cases, and used a computer to analyze a database of cases. Readers were also told that reporters interviewed psychiatrists, psychologists, nurses, nursing home and hospital administrators, mental health advocates, lawyers, patients, and family members and reviewed various public records.

Do readers need to know how or where you got information so they can evaluate what your story says or understand the evidence you've gathered? Then tell them what they need to know, but don't show off.

4. After you've done all your reporting, computer and otherwise, plan your story.

Traditionally, many reporters have been weak in the area of planning the story. This may not be as much of a problem when you are writing a four-paragraph brief, but if you've been working on an investigative project or any story that called for some extra research, planning makes sense. You may want to work with an editor to figure out what information to feature in a story, what numbers, what information should be pulled out in a chart, and what should stay in a story—or shouldn't be used at all.

Try writing a lead and ending and then listing four or five points you want to make in the story. Go through your notes, circling the best quotes and information. Look at the data you've analyzed and figure out what you need and want to include. What are the main points you want to demonstrate? Which pieces of information best demonstrate the main points? And is there anything you need to check into further before you write?

5. If there is no story, don't write one.

Sometimes writers fall in love with certain information and find it hard to give up. That can happen with CAR projects, especially after a reporter has spent many hours or even weeks going after and analyzing certain information, then finds it isn't really central to the story.

This happened to Michael Berens of the *Columbus Dispatch* when he was working on his series, "Cash Register Justice," about how some people are jailed for minor offenses because they can't pay their fines, while others who commit serious crimes are set free because they can pay. One part of the series was a story about campaign contributions to judges. Berens says he originally thought this would be a big part of the series, because he expected to find out that lawyers gave lots of money to judges. But he didn't find that, so that part of his series ended up being less significant and much shorter.

"This was painful to me," he says. But he also says reducing the length of that story improved the story and the series.

All the computer analysis in the world won't make someone read a story if the story doesn't matter or doesn't say something new. If yours doesn't, take what you've learned about CAR and move on.

Chapter 15

LEGAL AND ETHICAL QUESTIONS AND CAR

Computers can't break laws or invade privacy. They can't tell marvelous stories, reveal heroes, or bring to light policies and actions that are hurting people or communities.

Journalists using computers can do all these things. With that power comes responsibility to create accurate, newsworthy, significant journalism. There are ethical guidelines that help journalists decide how and what to report; there is law that protects journalists' freedom to do their job and law that requires journalists to do it responsibly.

Computer-assisted reporting requires at least the same attention to ethics that you give to other kinds of reporting; the ease with which you can retrieve information electronically may demand even more vigilance on your part. As for the legal issues, the laws are in flux concerning electronic information and access to records. What you need to do is apply to computer-assisted reporting what you already know about libel and privacy law, and pay attention to new cases that show up in courts and the news concerning journalism and cyberspace and electronic data.

ETHICS AND COMPUTER-ASSISTED REPORTING

Ethics has to do with how journalists go about doing their jobs. Many news organizations have guidelines to help journalists decide what is ethical, such as the Society of Professional Journalists Code of Ethics (see Apendix C). Generally those guidelines suggest that journalists have a responsibility to act for the public in gathering and reporting information that readers have a need and a right to know. The SPJ code's preamble says, "Members of the Society of Professional Journalists believe that public enlightenment is the forerunner of justice and the foundation of democracy. The duty of the journalist is to further those ends by seeking truth and providing a fair and comprehensive account of events and issues."

Often, reporters think about ethics only in terms of what guidelines might suggest they *not* do. But many codes of ethics created by journalism organizations, like the SPJ code, suggest that ethical behavior also includes what journalists *should do:* that they should seek the truth, writing stories that are as accurate and complete as possible; that they should strive always to be fair in their reporting and writing; and that they should minimize harm to others.

Computer-assisted reporting doesn't require a whole new set of ethical guidelines. But it requires journalists to pay more attention than ever to *how* they seek and report the truth and *how* they treat news sources and readers. This extra care is necessary because the Internet and other online resources make so much information, even personal information, easy to retrieve; because it is easier to get people to trust you online in ways they might not during a face-to-face interview, and therefore reveal more of themselves; because database management programs allow journalists to create records that didn't exist before, marrying two databases and revealing something new about a person or persons, agencies or governnment groups; and because the computer can give journalists answers in seconds, rather than the hours or days traditional reporting techniques might require.

With electronic reporting, the ethical questions "come to us quickly, and they may come to us more subtly," says Robert Steele, director of ethics programs at the Poynter Institute for Media Studies. "I'm not sure the ethical issues leap out at you quite as quickly."

If you have to spend four days in the county clerk's office going through paper records, you will have time to think as you are working about the ethical questions. But if you can get your information in three minutes on the World Wide Web or on Lexis/Nexis, you don't have as much time to mull over the ramifications of gathering and using the information.

This ease in getting information or creating new profiles of people and groups should make journalists more careful than ever to make sure they are acting out of a true desire to get at the truth and serve readers, not out of some self-serving goal—getting back at someone, showing how much power they have, or simply showing off computer skills. You should be asking yourself all the time: Why am I doing this? Is this really newsworthy? Will this do more harm than good?

Ethical behavior always involves weighing harm versus good and, for journalists, the needs and desires of readers against the rights of an individual to privacy. In previous chapters of this book, you've read material that raises ethical concerns about computer-assisted techniques. For some of these concerns, there are no hard-and-fast answers. You must decide, interview by interview and story by story, what is ethical.

Consider the answers to some of these questions:

- What is the purpose of this research or story? Am I truly reporting something that readers need or have a right to know?
- What are all the ways I can gather the information I need?

- What good will this reporting do? What harm will it do? Does the good outweigh the harm? Is there another way to gather the information?
- Who will be affected by this research or story?
- How can I make sure my information is accurate?

MAKING THE ETHICAL CALL

If you can, consider the ethical dilemmas before and during the reporting, not after.

The Poynter Institute's Steele advocates "front-end ethics," talking about issues early, setting up protocols before problems arise, and having reporters and editors and photojournalists discuss potential problems from the beginning of a project to its end.

"Be proactive," he advises journalists. "Don't wait until your editor comes after you." And don't feel you have to make ethical decisions alone. Let your editor know what you are working on and the ethical concerns it raises.

Together, you can discuss the newsworthiness of a story, the best ways to report it, and the ways to minimize harm while maximizing accuracy and fairness.

AND SPEAKING OF ACCURACY AND FAIRNESS ...

Learning to use the computer as a reporting tool is one way to fulfill the ethical mandate that journalists seek the truth, since computer-assisted reporting is one more way to gather information for interviews and stories.

But you also have a mandate to be accurate and thorough. So remember that information you find online, or even in a database given to you by a government agency, may not be correct or complete. You've read it before in this book: Whatever the information you gather with your computer, check it out. As the SPJ code cautions, journalists must "test the accuracy of information from all sources and exercise care to avoid inadvertent error."

SOME OTHER REMINDERS

The sources you reach online may not tell the whole story. If you interview online, you are reaching only people who own computers and are computer-literate enough to make contact with you. And you may be getting people who have a particular interest in your subject; that's not necessarily a cross-section of the general public. Make sure you are getting every angle of a story, not just the computer-reported side.

If you are online, do your best to figure out where your information originated. The source may have an agenda that you're not aware of. If you get a hot tip by e-mail, find out if the sender is who he or she says he or she is and verify the information just as you would verify any tip you got. Always give people a chance to answer charges made against them.

If you are using conversations you had via e-mail or newsgroups or other online resource, make sure you don't take quotes out of context. You have to be careful about this when you do face-to-face interviews; remember to be just as careful with online ones. Remember that the reader wasn't there to read the whole conversation.

If you find something significant in a database, check it out. Make sure your numbers are right. Then talk to people. Never assume, and never write a story based only on your analysis. Talk to the people who gave you the data and to anyone else affected by what you believe you have discovered.

Accuracy and fairness also have to do with attribution. Make sure you tell readers who and where your information comes from, so they have some framework in which to evaluate the information themselves.

DECEPTION

You may have heard the joke about how on the Internet, nobody knows you're a dog. In other words, when they go online, people can pretend to be whoever they want. And that includes you, the journalist.

Deceiving sources is never a good way to get information for a story. Reporters do resort to this when they believe it is the only way to get an important story. If you are trying to document mistreatment at a local youth detention center, the only way to really see what is going on might be to get a job there as a janitor. Deception comes with a high price. Your credibility is on the line, and you may harm others who come to trust you.

Online, it may be tempting to enter a conversation on a newsgroup or in a chat room without identifying yourself and gather quotes for a story. But is that ethical behavior? No. People have a right to know that they are talking to a journalist who is going to use what they say in a story. If you are thinking about concealing your identity in cyberspace, ask yourself what your motives are and if there isn't a better way to get the information you want. Maybe people online shouldn't be so trusting, so sure that what they say goes just to people who have interests common to them. Nonetheless, it's wrong to deceive them about who you are and why you are "listening in."

You should also be careful about promising sources that you'll conceal their identities. It can be easy while you're "conversing" online to just say "yes." But anonymous sources should be used sparingly; most of the time, readers have a right to know who you are quoting. You should also ask your editor about your newspaper's policy regarding the use of anonymous sources.

The ethical bottom line is this: Treat all information, whether you got it through an in-person interview or online, the same. Verify it, attribute it. Do your best to make your stories accurate and fair, no matter what kind of reporting you use. And remember that you have great power to do good and harm; consider the newsworthiness of what you report and write. Take responsibility for your work.

CAR and the Law

In Chapter 13, you read about fighting for access to computerized databases under the federal Freedom of Information Act and state access laws.

Because computer-assisted reporting and electronic publishing are still fairly new, there have not been many legal decisions showing how the law of libel or other matters applies to CAR. The law will continue to evolve, and journalists working with online resources or electronic databases must take the same care with those resources—and the stories they write using the information they've gathered—that they take with any others.

Libel in Cyberspace

The *Associated Press Stylebook and Libel Manual* defines libel this way: "Libel is injury to reputation. Words, pictures or cartoons that expose a person to public hatred, shame, disgrace or ridicule or induce an ill opinion of a person are libelous."

The freedom journalists have to do their job comes partly from libel law rulings, especially the famous *New York Times* v. *Sullivan* decision. In that case, the Supreme Court ruled that public officials can't recover damages for a statement published regarding their official duties unless they can prove that the person publishing acted maliciously or with reckless disregard for the truth. This means the journalist knew, or had good reason to suspect, that what he or she was about to publish was false and did it anyway.

Other rulings set guidelines for public figures and private individuals. Public figures, who have put themselves in the public eye, also fall under the malice standard.

That standard has been extended to limited public figures, who would be considered public figures only in regard to a certain issue. If your next-door neighbor led a protest against a proposed prison, the neighbor probably would be considered a limited public figure in stories about that one issue.

But private individuals fall under a different standard. Private individuals have to prove only that a reporter was negligent by failing to do his or her best to make sure a story was accurate.

Obviously, the best thing is not to libel anyone at all. The next best thing is to be sure that you have a good reason for publishing something harmful and that what you are publishing is provably true.

If you do run into a problem, cyberspace is going to raise an important issue. Is a person speaking on a newsgroup or mailing list a private individual or a public figure? Certainly there are people who show up often on these electronic discussion groups; if you monitor them for a while, you'll see the same names come up again and again. But does that necessarily mean they are public figures? Or are they limited public figures?

This is a question the courts will decide eventually. For now, you should treat these people as private individuals.

WHO DOES YOUR MESSAGE REACH?

If you post to a newsgroup or on a bulletin board a statement such as "I'm trying to get information about a jerk named Joe Smith," you are publishing something defamatory. Make your queries straightforward, because any such posting raises questions—about Joe Smith and about you—in the minds of readers.

Remember that postings to newsgroups and mailing lists and forums are often archived for some period of time. That means that a message you send can be pulled up by anyone who knows how to search for it. Some World Wide Web search engines, for example, can use a writer's name as a keyword to pull up archived messages. If you don't want something you've written to be available that way, you'd best send it as a private e-mail message.

And even that may not be private. The administrators of computer systems often have access to everything on a system, including your account.

GIVE US THE RECORDS

The lack of privacy brings up another thing journalists have to consider in the computer age—what should and should not be kept on a computer's hard drive.

Again, it's not entirely clear yet how all of this is going to shake down, but if a law enforcement agency subpoenas information you've gathered for a story, that subpoena might include everything on the hard drive of the computer you've worked on. Even if you erase information from a hard drive, it often can be retrieved with special software. The best rule may be not to save any sensitive information on your hard drive.

PRIVACY

As cyberspace expands, the courts and those creating and using new technology will govern how much information journalists can get about individuals. In your search for truth, you should use whatever tools you have at your disposal to get information vital to readers.

But if you invade someone's privacy without good cause, you'll be in trouble, and you can do a lot of harm. Courts consider whether the information you went after was newsworthy enough to justify such invasion.

COPYRIGHT AND PLAGIARISM

CAR also raises concerns about copyright and about a related ethical issue, plagiarism.

Plagiarism, the use of someone else's words without crediting that person, is deemed by journalists' ethics codes as unacceptable.

Copyright law is meant to protect the right of authors to control the reproduction of their creative work and to be compensated fairly for it. Federal law generally prevents the use of someone's creative work without his or her permission.

The law, however, does allow for "fair use." This means brief portions of a copyrighted work can be copied and used, say, in a classroom. News reporting also is generally considered fair use.

Because information passes back and forth so freely in cyberspace, and because it can be difficult to figure out where online information comes from, journalists must be especially vigilant in avoiding plagiarism or copyright enfringement.

Keith Woods, an associate in ethics at the Poynter Institute for Media Studies, urges reporters to take special care.

"On the Internet, information has fewer anchors. Information has been pulled from its roots and thrown into cyberspace, " says Woods. "There's an assumption that once I post it you can have it. But everyone doesn't feel that way," he says.

When someone posts something on a newsgroup, for example, can you use that posting without the person's permission, or does he or she own the copyright to that statement? This area of law hasn't been explored much yet. So it's best to err on the side of safety, as well as ethical behavior, which would require you to ask permission. When you report a story, you are generally not going to use too many canned comments anyway; you are going to interview a person yourself and get information.

When you quote from information online, it's important to be clear about the sources so readers can judge the information. It's also important to give people credit for their ideas.

It can be hard to tell where information comes from when you're looking at a Gopher document or World Wide Web site. But if you can't find out, you should not simply incorporate the work into your own and treat it as yours. This is unethical, might cause copyright problems, and is unwise. How can you be sure the information you pull off an online site is reliable if you don't know where it came from?

Do all you can to find out. Many Web sites include links to information about the creators of the site and e-mail addresses of people you can address questions to. Gophers and other Internet resources often include files of information about the sites and sources of the information stores on them. Use this data when you need to attribute information.

The advent of the Internet and other online services, and the recognition that computers can help journalists tell stories they couldn't tell otherwise, makes this an exciting time to be a journalist. So do the issues involving cyberspace's evolving ethics and law. You have the right and responsibility to make ethical decisions about your work, to understand how the laws apply to what you do, and to advocate law that keeps free the flow of information to the public.

Chapter 16

THE LEARNING GOES ON

"Now! Now!" cried the Queen. "Faster! Faster!" And they went so fast that at last they seemed to skim through the air, hardly touching the ground with their feet, till suddenly, just as Alice was getting quite exhausted, they stopped, and she found herself sitting on the ground, breathless and giddy.

The Queen propped her up against a tree, and said kindly, "You may rest a little, now."

Alice looked round her in great surprise. "Why, I do believe we've been under this tree the whole time! Everything's just as it was."

"Of course it is," said the Queen. "What would you have it?"

"Well, in our country," said Alice, still panting a little, "you'd generally get to somewhere else—if you ran very fast for a long time as we've been doing."

"A slow sort of country!" said the Queen. "Now, here, you see, it takes all the running you can do, to keep in the same place. If you want to get somewhere else, you must run at least twice as fast as that!"

—Through the Looking Glass, by Lewis Carroll

The Queen could have been talking about cyberspace and the world of computers. Both change constantly; new software, hardware, and online resources keep popping up. You can't ever learn everything there is to know.

Don't despair about that. You've already learned the basics of computer-assisted reporting. Now you can build on what you know, figuring out what you need for one story, then learning a little more with the next story, and a little more with the one after that.

You understand what computers can do and what online resources offer; you're willing to try new reporting techniques; you question information you gather, doing all you can to make sure it's accurate, including conducting interviews and making observations; you love to tell great stories and know you can only do that if you have plenty of data to work with.

News organizations are looking for reporters with just those attributes and skills. They'll expect you and your fellow journalists to keep building on them too. As more news organizations begin publishing online, journalists will need to consider the best ways to tell stories on the World Wide Web and the best ways to interact with readers in cyberspace. There's a lot of uncharted territory for you to explore.

According to an article, "The New Journalist," in the April 1996 *American Journalism Review,* some editors say they now look for job applicants who are comfortable with computers and the online world. They want journalists who can work with hypermedia and who appreciate what new technology offers journalists. All of this means that you need to keep learning computer skills, as well as more traditional reporting techniques and storytelling skills.

So plunge into computer-assisted reporting, starting with a fairly simple database or a story that requires some online research. How far you go, how much you learn, is up to you.

LEARN THE POWER OF SOFTWARE

But don't get overwhelmed at the beginning. Take on new things a little bit at a time. Once you've mastered the basics of a spreadsheet or database management program, don't abandon the program. Try to figure out, off deadline, one more thing it can do. And then another. Manuals for the programs are often hard to understand, but there are hundreds of books you can buy that make these programs easier to understand and use.

If you know you want to ask your database a question but can't figure out how to get the answer, turn to one of those books. Or find another journalist (or a computer guru) who can help. Don't worry about your questions being elementary or foolish. Explain what you're trying to do, then listen and learn.

READ EVERYTHING

Read. Everything. Read journalism publications and great stories in newspapers and magazines, online and off. You can explore reporting techniques, legal and ethical issues, and great writing by reading. You can get story ideas, too.

If you study newspapers online you'll get some sense of how storytelling is changing to fit this new technology. You'll see how publications reach out to readers in cyberspace.

Read computer magazines; they keep up on the latest Internet developments and great sites on the Web (also the wild and weird sites).

STUDY AT THE ONLINE SCHOOLS OF JOURNALISM

Subscribe to journalism mailing lists, then sit back and read the messages posted. In them, journalists discuss ways to search the Internet, databases that reporters can get and ways to analyze them, terrific stories and stories that didn't work out.

And check out the Web sites for journalism organizations, where you'll find reporting and writing tips, information on all sorts of journalism issues, and links to useful online databases and publications.

TELL TALES

Pursue the stories that grab you, using *all* your reporting tools, including the computer ones. Then tell those stories as well as you can. That's what all the searching and sorting, all the computing, is for.

Go wherever your computer and questions take you. Be curious, hungry for answers, persistent, and willing to put up with a few false starts and potholes. It will be an interesting journey.

APPENDIX A:
WORLD WIDE WEB SITES

Below are Universal Resource Locators for World Wide Web sites mentioned in this book. By the time this book is published, some of these URLs may have changed; the Web does not stay the same day to day or even hour to hour.

If you try a URL that's no longer correct, a page may come up on your computer screen showing what the new URL is. If not, you may need to use a search tool to find what you are looking for.

Happy surfing!

NEWSPAPERS AND MAGAZINES

Atlantic Monthly
http://www.theAtlantic.com/atlantic

Boston Globe
http://www.boston.com

Hartford Courant
http://www.courant.com

HotWired
http://www.hotwired.com

New York Times
http://www.nytimes.com

People
http://pathfinder.com/people

Philadelphia Inquirer and *Daily News*
http://www.phillynews.com

San Jose Mercury News/Mercury Center
http://www.sjmercury.com

Time Online
http://pathfinder.com/time

Wall Street Journal
http://www.wsj.com

SITES FOR JOURNALISTS

Beat Page
http://www.reporter.org/beat

"Computer Assisted Research: A Guide to Tapping Online Information" by
Nora Paul, library director at the Poynter Institute for Media Studies
http://www4.nando.net/prof/poynter/chome.html.

Investigative Reporters and Editors
http://www.ire.org

National Association of Black Journalists
http://www.nabj.org

National Press Photographers Association
http://sunsite.unc.edu/nppa/index.html

National Institute for Computer-Assisted Reporting
http://www.nicar.org

Poynter Institute for Media Studies
http://www.poynter. org

ProfNet—the online Professors Network
http://time.vyne.com/profnet

ProfNet's Experts Database
http://time.vyne.com/profnet/ped/eg.acgi

Reporters Network
http://www.reporters.net

Society of Professional Journalists
http://www.spj.org

GOVERNMENT

Federal Aviation Administration
http://www.faa.gov

FedWorld
http://www.fedworld.gov

Library of Congress
http://marvel.loc.gov

THOMAS: Legislative Information on the Internet
http://thomas.loc.gov

U.S. Census Bureau
http://www.census.gov

U.S. Department of Housing and Urban Development
http://www.hud.gov

U.S. Patent Office
http://www.uspto.gov

White House
http://www.whitehouse.gov

DIRECTORIES AND SEARCH TOOLS

AltaVista
http://www.altavista.digital.com

Deja News
http://www.dejanews.com

Excite
http://www.excite.com

Galaxy, a directory of Internet resources
http://galaxy.einet.net

HotBot
http://www.hotbot.com

Infoseek
http://www.infoseek.com

Liszt site (to search for mailing lists and Usenet newsgroups)
http://www.liszt.com

Lycos
http://www.lycos.com

Opentext Index
http://index.opentext.net

tile.net (to search for mailing lists, Usenet newsgroups, FTP sites)
http://www.tile.net

WebCrawler
http://www.webcrawler.com

Yahoo!
http://www.yahoo.com

MISCELLANEOUS

American Kennel Club
http://www.akc.org

American Red Cross
http://www.crossnet.org

Bureau of Missing Socks
http://www.jagat.com/joel/socks.html

EarthStation 1: The 1938 "War of the Worlds" radio broadcast, including
Orson Welles' opening monologue
http://www.attention.net/wandarer/wotw.html

Elvis Spotter's Page
http://ace.cs.ohiou.edu/personal/smccormi/elvis.html

Greenpeace
http://www.greenpeace.org

Internet Society
http://www.isoc.org

National Rifle Association of America
http://www.nra.org

Public Broadcasting System
http://www.pbs.org

Yuckiest Site on the Internet
http://www.nj.com/yucky/index.html

APPENDIX B:
EXERCISES

THE INTERNET

1. Using a newsreader program or a World Wide Web search tool, find newsgroups and listservs that pertain to a beat you cover or stories you're working on or ones that just grab your interest. Subscribe to one or two of these and follow the messages for two weeks. While you're monitoring the messages (and reading the FAQs, or course, if any exist) do the following:

    a. Come up with five story ideas based on messages you read. Explain how you got each idea, what sort of story you'd write (news or feature), what the focus of the story would be, what sources you might use, and why a reader would want to read the story.

    b. Describe in a few paragraphs how useful you found the information posted to the newsgroups and listservs you monitored. Why was it useful—or not useful?

2. Using keywords—perhaps ones from your beat or stories you are working on—search for newsgroups and listservs. Then try a Veronica search of Gopherspace, an Archie search of FTP servers and a search of the World Wide Web with a search engine, using the same key words for each search. Compare what you found with each resource:

    a. List any newsgroups and listservs you found.

    b. List the top five results you received from each of your other searches. Check out the top one in each list and answer the following questions:

        1. Which search yielded the most results?

        2. What is the online address or file name for each of the top five items you found using the various search tools?

        3. Describe the information each offered. How up to date is the information?

        4. Which would be most useful to a reporter? Why?

        5. Did your search yield data that wasn't really related to the topic you had in mind? How could you narrow your search or change your key words to solve that problem?

(If you have access to bulletin board systems, online commercial databases such as DIALOG, or online services such as America Online, you could do similar searches using these resources.)

3. Working with classmates and searching with Veronica and a World Wide Web search tool, find government sites for the state you attend school in.

Based on the information you find at some of these sites, come up with a list of stories you could do that use some of the online information. List people you would have to interview and other sources you would have to consult, besides the online ones.

4.   Using Deja News or another tool that searches the archives of Usenet newsgroups, search for messages sent by a certain person. See how much you can learn about one person by reading his or her newsgroup postings. What questions would you ask this person if you were writing a profile of him or her?

5.   Go to the ProfNet Experts Database Web site (http://time.vyne.com/ profnet/ped/eg.acgi) and search, using key words, for experts on a certain subject. Then go to a WWW search engine and see what other information you can find about those experts on the Web.

6.   You believe the U.S. Senate is discussing a bill with little-known riders that will affect your city and state. Go to the Thomas page (http://thomas.loc.gov) and search for all information relating to your city or state. List your findings and explain what stories could be done jumping off from this information. Why are these stories important to readers?

7.   Go to The Beat Page (http://www.reporter.org/beat) or FedWorld (http://www.fedworld.gov) on the World Wide Web. Follow links to sites that grab your attention or to sites related to your beat or a story you are working on. Find three sites that you think are useful. Where does the information from each site come from? How do you know that for sure? Is the information attributed? Is there a mailing address or person to contact to ask questions? Explain what you think is useful about each site. What other reporting would you need to do to do a story based on information you found at one of these sites?

8.   Try a WWW search with one search tool using a very broad key word, such as health or crime. Write down the URLs of the first three results, and go to those sites. What's at each site? Is the information relevant to your search, considering the key word(s) you used? Is it a site that would be useful for a journalist? Why or why not? Can you tell where the information at each site comes from?

Next, try the same search with a different search tool. Are your results the same? If not, how are they different?

Now, using one of these two search tools, narrow your search using more specific terms and Boolean operators or other methods suggested in online instructions for using that search engine. Write down the key words you use, and again, write down the first three results. Are they different from those of your first search? If so, explain how. Check out each of these sites. Would they be useful to journalists? Why or why not?

Try a search one last time with one of the search tools, changing the key words or search parameters again. How are your results different this time?

Which search was most successful? How and why?

SPREADSHEETS AND DATABASE MANAGEMENT PROGRAMS

(The databases used as examples in Chapters 11 and 12 are available for downloading from the Harcourt Brace Web site at http://www.hbcollege.com.)

1.   Work with the budget figures described in Chapter 11, or obtain two years' worth of budget figures (perhaps the current budget and the budget proposed for next year) from the city you live in; from your university or college; or from a department at your university or college. Create a spreadsheet using the figures you've obtained.

Then do the following:

a. Calculate the increase from one budget to the next for each line item in the budget, including expenditures and revenues.

b. Calculate percentage differences for each line item.

c. Using the most recent budget, figure out what percentage of the total budget each individual item gets.

d. Using the spreadsheet program's Sum function, check the totals for budget categories you've been given. Are they all correct?

e. After reviewing your results, figure out what questions you would need to ask to write a story about the budgets. What doesn't make sense? What do you need to know more about? What gets the most money? Why? What do the percentage difference figures tell you about budgeting priorities? What has changed the most since last year's budget was passed?

List the people you would like to talk to and the questions you would like to ask. Explain why each question is important, in light of the budget information you analyzed.

2.   Using the proposed budget for a city or state, complete the calculations listed above. Then, if possible, compare your calculations with a city or state official's written statement or speech about the proposed budget and funding priorities. Do your calculations reflect the priorities and spending plans the official said were part of the budget preparation?

3.   Using the dog license spreadsheet described in Chapter 11, answer the following questions by sorting the information in different ways:

a. What's the most popular dog name?

b. Who has the most dogs registered?

c. What type of dog is the most popular?

d. Is one street more heavily populated with dogs than another?

e. What color of dog is most popular?

4.   Using the parking fine spreadsheet, calculate the following:

a. the average parking fine.

b. the median.

c. the mode.

Why would it make sense to use one or the other of these numbers in a story to explain to readers what is up with parking fines? Explain.

5.   Working with classmates, profile your class on a database you create, using a spreadsheet or database management program. Create categories of information you can compare and contrast, such as number of years each person studied a foreign language, and which language, home states, states each person has visited, favorite movie, favorite TV show, favorite book, number of years each person studied math, favorite subject, and the car each drives. Have each person type in his or her own information. Then use the spreadsheet program or database management program to answer questions about your class. For instance, how many different states have members of the class, as a whole, visited? What's the average number of years classmates have studied foreign languages? Look for trends in car ownership, movie choice, and other categories. You might also be able to calculate the average, median, and mode of states visited, parking fines paid, years studying a foreign language, or of other information in the database.

6.   Using the dog license database described in Chapter 12, figure out what the most popular dog breed is. To do this, you'll want your database management program to show you only the dog breed records, group them by breed and count them, and to sort them so they are listed from most popular breed to least popular.
   Using the same database, look through the categories of information and list other questions you'd need answered before you could write a story about this information. For example:

- How often do dog owners name their dogs after themselves?
- What area of this city has the most dogs? What street?

7.   Look at the parking database mentioned in Chapter 12, and list all the questions you could get answers to by using your database management program. What patterns or trends would you look for? What information would you want to pull out of the database? For example, what time of day is someone most likely to get a ticket? On what day of the week? Which offenses are cited most in ticketing? Use the techniques outlined in Chapter 12 to answer your questions.

8.   A database of bicycle accidents is available on the Harcourt Brace Web site, at http://www.hbcollege.com. Look at the database, noting the categories of information included. Then list questions you would need answered if you were writing a story about this subject. What trends or patterns might you look for?

9.   Imagine you have the following databases. For each, list categories you would use as different fields in a database you created with a database management program. In the dog license database, for example, you had fields for owner's last name, first name, middle initial, street, street number, dog name, and so on. What fields would you create to hold information from these databases? What sorts of stories might you be able to do using the information in each database?

  a. traffic accident records
  b. patient treatment records from local hospitals
  c. fire department records of all emergency calls
  d. property tax records
  e. city or state or university salaries
  f. inspection records for area restaurants or nursing homes
  g. gun homicides in the state
  h. fire safety inspections of on-campus buildings (or inspections of food service areas or elevators)
  i. speeding tickets
  j. contributions to state legislators' campaigns
  k. toxic chemical spills data including information about emergency response to the spills
  l. pet licenses
  m. recycling rates for communities
  n. marriage licenses
  o. salaries for state, county, or local workers

10. Working with classmates, contact officials at various university departments or government agencies and find out what databases are kept in computerized form. Do the departments or agencies consider these databases public information? Do they provide this data to members of the public or journalists in computerized form? What does your state law mandate regarding such computerized information? Interview professional journalists in your area to see whether they've been able to get such data in computerized format and whether they've had difficulty obtaining information they believed should be available to the public under state law.

11. Using a database management program, match the dog database and the city employees database described in Chapter 12. How many matches did you get? Do your results spark any questions you might want to ask one of these city employees?

12. Imagine you can match the pairs of databases mentioned below. For each pair, list stories you might do based on the matches:

  a. city voter registration list/death certificate list or city voter registration list/addresses of vacant lots in city
  b. convicted felons/foster parents or school employees
  c. people charged with motor vehicle violations/school bus drivers or driving-school teachers
  d. gun permit applications/dates of major crimes

   e. people in prison/people receiving welfare benefits

   f. home mortgage data/census data on neighborhood and racial demographics

   g. school spending records/data on student achievement at various schools

   h. arrest records/court records of convictions

   i. contributions to state candidates' campaigns/list of state contractors or of lawyers and law firms in state

APPENDIX C:
SOCIETY OF PROFESSIONAL JOURNALISTS CODE OF ETHICS

Adopted by the Society of Professional Journalists September 21, 1996.

PREAMBLE

Members of the Society of Professional Journalists believe that public enlightenment is the forerunner of justice and the foundation of democracy. The duty of the journalist is to further those ends by seeking truth and providing a fair and comprehensive account of events and issues. Conscientious journalists from all media and specialties strive to serve the public with thoroughness and honesty. Professional integrity is the cornerstone of a journalist's credibility. Members of the Society share a dedication to ethical behavior and adopt this code to declare the Society's principles and standards of practice.

SEEK TRUTH AND REPORT IT

Journalists should be honest, fair and courageous in gathering, reporting and interpreting information. Journalists should:

- Test the accuracy of information from all sources and exercise care to avoid inadvertent error. Deliberate distortion is never permissible.
- Diligently seek out subjects of news stories to give them the opportunity to respond to allegations of wrongdoing.
- Identify sources whenever feasible. The public is entitled to as much information as possible on sources' reliability.
- Always question sources' motives before promising anonymity. Clarify conditions attached to any promise made in exchange for information. Keep promises.
- Make certain that headlines, news teases and promotional material, photos, video, audio, graphics, sound bites and quotations do not misrepresent. They should not oversimplify or highlight incidents out of context.
- Never distort the content of news photos or video. Image enhancement for technical clarity is always permissible. Label montages and photo illustrations.

- Avoid misleading re-enactments or staged news events. If re-enactment is necessary to tell a story, label it.
- Avoid undercover or other surreptitious methods of gathering information except when traditional open methods will not yield information vital to the public. Use of such methods should be explained as part of the story.
- Never plagiarize.
- Tell the story of the diversity and magnitude of the human experience boldly, even when it is unpopular to do so.
- Examine their own cultural values and avoid imposing those values on others.
- Avoid stereotyping by race, gender, age, religion, ethnicity, geography, sexual orientation, disability, physical appearance or social status.
- Support the open exchange of views, even views they find repugnant.
- Give voice to the voiceless; official and unofficial sources of information can be equally valid.
- Distinguish between advocacy and news reporting. Analysis and commentary should be labeled and not misrepresent fact or content.
- Distinguish news from advertising and shun hybrids that blur the lines between the two.
- Recognize a special obligation to ensure that the public's business is conducted in the open and that government records are open to inspection.

Minimize Harm

Ethical journalists treat sources, subjects and colleagues as human beings deserving of respect. Journalists should:

- Show compassion for those who may be affected adversely by news coverage. Use special sensitivity when dealing with children and inexperienced sources or subjects.
- Be sensitive when seeking or using interviews or photographs of those affected by tragedy or grief.
- Recognize that gathering and reporting information may cause harm or discomfort.
- Pursuit of the news is not a license for arrogance.
- Recognize that private people have a greater right to control information about themselves than do public officials and others who seek power, influence or attention. Only an overriding public need can justify intrusion into anyone's privacy.
- Show good taste. Avoid pandering to lurid curiosity.
- Be cautious about identifying juvenile suspects or victims of sex crimes.
- Be judicious about naming criminal suspects before the formal filing of charges.

- Balance a criminal suspect's fair trial rights with the public's right to be informed.

Act Independently

Journalists should be free of obligation to any interest other than the public's right to know. Journalists should:

- Avoid conflicts of interest, real or perceived.
- Remain free of associations and activities that may compromise integrity or damage credibility.
- Refuse gifts, favors, fees, free travel and special treatment, and shun secondary employment, political involvement, public office and service in community organizations if they compromise journalistic integrity.
- Disclose unavoidable conflicts.
- Be vigilant and courageous about holding those with power accountable.
- Deny favored treatment to advertisers and special interests and resist their pressure to influence news coverage.
- Be wary of sources offering information for favors or money; avoid bidding for news.

Be Accountable

Journalists are accountable to their readers, viewers and each other. Journalists should:

- Clarify and explain news coverage and invite dialogue with the public over journalistic conduct.
- Encourage the public to voice grievances against the news media.
- Admit mistakes and correct them promptly.
- Expose unethical practices of journalists and the news media.
- Abide by the same high standards to which they hold others.

FOR FURTHER READING

ANALYZING INFORMATION

Victor Cohn. *News & Numbers, A Guide to Reporting Statistical Claims and Controversies in Health and Other Fields.* Ames: Iowa State University Press, 1996.

Phillip Meyer. *The New Precision Journalism.* Bloomington: Indiana University Press, 1991.

BULLETIN BOARD SERVICES

John Hedtke. *Using Computer Bulletin Boards,* 3rd ed. New York: MIS Press, 1995.

Bruce Maxwell. *How to Access the Federal Government's Electronic Bulletin Boards.* Washington, D.C.: Congressional Quarterly, 1996.

COMPUTER-ASSISTED REPORTING

Heidi Anderson. "Cyberspace as a Journalism Tool." *Editor & Publisher,* Interactive Newspaper section, Feb. 17, 1996, pp. 14I, 16I, 34I-35I.

David Armstrong. "Cyberhoax!" *Columbia Journalism Review,* September/October 1995, pp. 12, 15.

Rose Ciotta. "Baby, You Should Drive This Car." *American Journalism Review,* March 1996, pp. 34-39.

Bruce Garrison. *Computer-Assisted Reporting.* Hillsdale: Lawrence Erlbaum Associates, 1995.

Brant Houston. *Computer-Assisted Reporting, A Practical Guide,* New York: St. Martin's Press, 1996.

Investigative Reporters and Editors and the National Institute for Computer-Assisted Reporting. *100 Computer-Assisted Stories.* Columbia: IRE, 1995.

National Institute for Computer-Assisted Reporting. *Uplink,* NICAR's monthly newsletter. Columbia, Mo.

Nora Paul. *Computer Assisted Research: A Guide to Tapping Online Information,* 3rd ed. Poynter Online. http://www4.nando.net/prof/poynter/chome.html

Randy Reddick and Eliot King. *The Online Journalist: Using the Internet and Other Electronic Resources,* 2nd ed. Fort Worth: Harcourt Brace College Publishers, 1997.

Neil H. Reisner. "On the Beat: Computer-assisted reporting isn't just for projects anymore." *American Journalism Review,* March 1995, pp. 44-47.

John Ullman. *Investigative Reporting: Advanced Methods and Techniques.* New York: St. Martin's Press, 1995.

Steve Weinberg. *The Reporter's Handbook: An Investigator's Guide to Documents and Techniques,* 3rd ed. New York: St. Martin's Press, 1996.

COMPUTERS

Charles Rubin. *The Little Book of Computer Wisdom: How to Make Friends With Your PC or Mac.* New York: Houghton Mifflin, 1995

ETHICS

Jay Black, Bob Steele, and Ralph Barney. *Doing Ethics in Journalism: A Handbook with Case Studies.* Boston: Allyn and Bacon, 1995.

GATHERING INFORMATION

Bruce Maxwell. *How to Access the Federal Government on the Internet.* Washington, D.C.: Congressional Quarterly, 1997.

The Reporters Committee for Freedom of the Press. "Access to Electronic Records, A Guide to Reporting on State and Local Government in the Computer Age." Fall 1994 and Spring 1996 Update, Arlington, Va.

THE INTERNET

Paul Glister. *The New Internet Navigator.* New York: John Wiley & Sons, 1995.

Harley Hahn and Rick Stout. *The Internet Complete Reference.* Berkeley: Osborne McGraw-Hill, 1994.

John R. Levine, Carol Baroudi, and Margaret Levine Young. *The Internet for Dummies,* 4th ed. San Mateo: IDG Books Worldwide, 1997.

GLOSSARY

Archie—A program that searches for files stored at FTP sites.

ASCII—American Standard Code for Information Interchange: a universal computer language, the standard for PCs, used to store information on nine-track tape.

anonymous FTP—See FTP.

Boolean logic—A way of searching for information using key words and the Boolean operators **and, or,** and **not** to define how narrow a search should be.

browser—A software program used to navigate the World Wide Web.

bulletin board system or BBS—An online resource you can use to send and receive e-mail, participate in discussion groups, and gather information from online databases.

byte—A unit of measurement used to describe the amount of space that information takes up on a computer hard drive or on a floppy disk. Each byte is made of of eight bits; it takes eight bits to describe one character or space on a computer.

cell—The name for the rectangles on a spreadsheet document that can hold information.

commercial information service—An online service, such as America Online or CompuServe, that offers e-mail, files you can download, access to the Internet, conferences organized around various subjects, and other resources.

database—A collection of related information, usually put into some uniform format.

database management program—A software program used to pull out certain pieces of information from a database, to sort information to reveal patterns or trends, and to match separate databases to yield new information.

download—To transfer information from a remote computer to yours using a special software program

EBCDIC—A computer programming language used to store information on nine-track tape.

FAQ—A document providing answers to frequently asked questions about a subject or Internet resource.

field—A column in a database created with a database management program.

FTP or file transfer protocol—A program that allows you to log into another computer and download or copy files from that computer to your own. With many FTP sites, you don't need to know a different login for each site; you can use a login of **anonymous** to get to all the information available to the public.

Gopher—An Internet resource that organizes information into menus.

home page—A starting point for a World Wide Web site. This may be the place where someone puts the main and most important information, or it may be just a table of contents, listing other pages you can get to from that page. It may also include links to pages or files of information on other sites.

hypertext—Information stored on the World Wide Web using a programming language called Hypertext Markup Language or HTML. With HTML, information is set out in documents called pages, with links, or hyperlinks, to other pages embedded in it. With video and sound links, it's called hypermedia.

IRC or Internet relay chat—An Internet resource that allows you to correspond in real time with others who are on the Internet at the same time as you.

Jughead—A resource that searches for key words that occur in the menu titles of files stored on a particular Gopher server.

listserv—An online discussion group, usually centering on a particular topic. It's also called a mailing list. You subscribe to such groups using an e-mail program.

newsgroup—See Usenet newsgroups.

nine-track tape—Magnetic tape used to store information.

search engine—A tool that allows you to search the World Wide Web and other Internet resources using key words.

spreadsheet—A software program that allows you to record information in an orderly way, analyze numbers, perform calculations, and sort numbers and text to look for trends, patterns, and changes.

Telnet—A resource that allows you to log onto a remote computer and gain access to information stored on that computer.

URL—Universal Resource Locator: the address of an Internet site.

Usenet newsgroups—Online discussion groups centered on various topics.

Veronica—A tool that searches for key words in the menu titles of files stored throughout Gopherspace.

WAIS—Wide Area Information Servers: resources that allow you to search particular online databases using keywords.

World Wide Web—A part of the Internet where information is stored as hypertext, with links embedded in each document.

PERMISSIONS

LITERARY CREDITS

Page 1 Reprinted with permission from the *Columbus* (Ohio) *Dispatch*

Page 7 ©*Chicago Sun-Times* 1997 by Tom Brune and Deborah Nelson

Page 7 *The Buffalo News*, 1995

Page 35 *The Standard-Times*, New Bedford, MA

Page 80 Reprinted with permission of the *Star Tribune*, Minneapolis-St. Paul

Page 186 *The Virgin Islands Daily News*

Page 217 Reprinted with permission from the *Sun-Sentinel*, Fort Lauderdale, Florida.

Page 217 Reprinted with permission from the *Sun-Sentinel*, Fort Lauderdale, Florida.

Page 217 Reprinted with permission from the *Sun-Sentinel*, Fort Lauderdale, Florida.

Page 224 Reprinted with permission from *The Plain Dealer*

Page 225 Reprinted courtesy of *The Boston Globe*

Pages 249–51 Sigma Delta Chi's first code of ethics was borrowed from the American Society of Newspaper Editors in 1926. In 1973, Sigma Delta Chi wrote its own code, which was revised in 1984 and 1987. The present version of the Society of Professional Journalists' Code of Ethics was adopted in September 1996.

ILLUSTRATION CREDITS

Figure 3–5 CapAccess screen reprinted by permission of WETA-TV, Washington, D.C.

Figure 6–2 Columbia Law School Library—may also have line from Innovative Interfaces, Inc.

Figures 11–2, 11–5, 11–8, 11–9, 11–11, 11–14, 11–15, 12–1, 12–2, 12–3, 12–4, 12–5, 12–6, 12–7, 12–8, 12–9, 12–10, 12–11, 12–12
Screen shots reprinted by permission from Microsoft Corporation.

INDEX